LOS PROFETAS

THE PROPHETIC ROLE OF HISPANIC CHURCHES IN AMERICA

Daniel F. Flores
General Editor

Foreword by
Bishop Joel N. Martinez

WIPF & STOCK · Eugene, Oregon

Wipf and Stock Publishers
199 W 8th Ave, Suite 3
Eugene, OR 97401

Los Profetas
The Prophetic Role of Hispanic Churches in America
By Flores, Daniel F.

Softcover ISBN-13: 979-8-3852-7676-9
Hardcover ISBN-13: 979-8-3852-7677-6
eBook ISBN-13: 979-8-3852-7678-3
Publication date 2/17/2026
Previously published by Wesley's Foundery Books, 2022

This edition is a scanned facsimile of the original edition published in 2022.

To our beloved *abuelitas*, faithful witnesses of *Jesús* who taught us to live, pray, write, and speak with the Galilean accent.

CONTENTS

DIACRITICS

The following diacritics and non-English letters are used throughout this book.

Acute accent: Á, á, É, é, Í, í, Ó, ó, Ú, ú
Ash: Æ, æ
Cedilla: Ç, ç
Circumflex accent: Â, â, Ê, ê
Umlaut: Ö, ö, Ü, ü
Grave accent: À, à, È, è
Tilde: Ñ, ñ
Til: Ã, ã, Õ, õ
Macron: ā, ē, ī, ō, ū

The following Greek letters are used throughout this book.

Α, Β, Γ, Δ, Ε, Ζ, Η, Θ, Ι, Κ, Λ, Μ, Ν, Ξ, Ο, Π, Ρ, Σ, Τ, Υ, Φ, Χ, Ψ, Ω

α, β, γ, δ, ε, ζ, η, θ, ι, κ, λ, μ, ν, ξ, ο, π, ρ, ς, σ, τ, υ, φ, χ, ψ, ω

ά, έ, ή, ί, ό, ύ, ώ

FOREWORD

DR. DANIEL F. FLORES has provided a timely and insightful collection of contributions from Hispanic/Latino practitioners and scholars that merits careful reading and serious attention from anyone who seeks to be in mission and ministry with the peoples of the diverse and growing Hispanic/Latino communities throughout the United States.

The title of the book, *Los Profetas: The Prophetic Role of Hispanic Churches in America*, is both an affirmation of Hispanic/Latino leadership in the US context and a critique of the tendency in both the academy and the church to overlook, underestimate, and marginalize the gifted voices and wisdom of this leadership.

In the preface, Dr. Flores clarifies his use of the term *prophetic* in the title. He notes that the book "is not about self-proclaimed prophets, nor do any of the contributors claim this title. Rather it is about Spirit-inspired people who speak from the margins about God's work in church and society." In these essays, it becomes clear that the writers are credentialed first by their deeply rooted engagement in the soil of historically marginalized communities and secondarily by their academic preparation and ecclesial authorization. As one reads, one cannot but be challenged by the sense that the pushed out, pushed down, and pushed around are now pushing back.

It is also important to note the diversity of the historical, cultural, and socioeconomic contexts from which these gifted leaders emerged to serve as faithful witnesses to God's continuing work of transformation in and through all the faith traditions including Pentecostals, evangelicals, and mainline Protestants. Dr. Flores, in inviting a diversity of contributors, has both affirmed and recognized that the calling and ministry of prophetic work are evident in all our religious traditions and that we have much to learn from each other.

Another important theme of the collection is its emphasis on the historical and present challenge of language usage that can either promote acceptance and community or lead to exclusion and a threat to the community. Spanish is the dominant language in this hemisphere and the second most common language in the United States. Several of the essays speak clearly to the need for a future in which a language difference is valued as a gift to be shared and celebrated, not ignored or denigrated.

Dr. Flores and his spouse, Rev. Thelma Flores (one of the contributors to this volume), have been good stewards of the legacy and contributions of the Wesleyan movement in the church universal. "O for a Thousand Tongues to Sing" by Charles Wesley, a much-beloved hymn from the Wesleyan tradition, is a reminder that all the tongues and all the accents of all the peoples are needed in singing praises to the Triune God. This also should be a minimum expectation in all our prophetic work. Why? So that we make sure we don't miss anyone!

Again, I commend Dr. Daniel Flores for this thoughtful and provocative collection of essays. May it become part of a wider effort by the General Board of Higher Education and Ministry to welcome all the gifts, listen to all the voices, and include all the accents of our increasingly diverse prophetic leaders until the day there is but one Shepherd and one flock.

Bishop Joel N. Martinez, United Methodist Church (retired)

PREFACE

"WHO ARE YOU?" That indignant retort from a fellow clergyperson set us back on our heels. Thelma and I had invited clergy from a local United Methodist Church congregation to have an informal discussion on the opportunities for outreach to the thousands of predominantly Hispanic migrant agricultural workers who made their annual treks to the blueberry fields of west Michigan. Of course, we were not the first persons of color to be treated with suspicion or have our authority questioned. This is too frequently an unhappy shared experience of Black, Indigenous, and people of color (BIPOC) leaders in religious and secular institutions. Bible students will recall that St. Paul, a bilingual Jew from Asia Minor, was accused of being a notorious Egyptian agitator (Acts 21:38). What was it that set them off on Paul? Was it his accent? Skin tone? Hair? Facial features? Clothing? I wonder.

Hispanic and Latino people are often stereotyped as inferior when they speak their Spanish-accented English. The truth is that everyone has an accent. Accents function to emphasize or identify a person's place of regional or national origin. Immigrants with thick accents are unfairly perceived as lacking intelligence, having a substandard education, possessing naïveté, and harboring unpatriotic sympathies. In the Broadway musical *West Side Story*, the Stephen Sondheim song "America" sets the tone for the immigrant experience of marginalization. In this clever, Latin rhythm-fueled dialogue, the Puerto Rican characters gather on the rooftop of their New York City tenement apartment building to dance and sing about the pros and cons of living in mainland America. Bernardo delivers the cynical punchline about the pressure to assimilate: "Better get rid of your accent."[1] Interestingly, novelist Julia Alvarez chose this theme to tell the story of the Dominican immigrant experience in *How the Garcia Girls Lost Their Accents*.[2] Postcolonial theorist Gloria Anzaldúa reflected on the effects of Pan American University's requirement that all Chicano students take two speech classes with the intent to get rid of their accents: "Attacks on one's form of expression with the intent to censor are a violation of the First Amendment. *El Anglo con cara de inocente nos arrancó la lengua.* Wild tongues can't be tamed, they can only be cut out."[3]

In the Gospels, the Galilean accent surely drew unwanted attention to the denying disciple Peter. While Jesus was being arrested and processed, Peter warmed himself by a fire. Something he said or did might have triggered observers to associate him as a follower of Jesus (John 18:15–27). In his classic book, *Galilean Journey: The Mexican-American Promise*, the late Roman Catholic theologian Father Virgilio Elizondo related the Galilean accent to his experience as a Mexican American in South Texas.

> Galilee was the home of the simple people—that is, of the people of the land, a hardworking people, marginalized and oppressed regardless of who was in power or what system of power was in effect. They were the ones who were left out and exploited by everyone else. They shared the fate of other peoples living on the margins of "better civilizations." Nobody looks for leadership from or has high expectations of those who live in the sticks, the *barrios*, the *ranchitos*, or inner-city slums.[4]

---

1 Stephen Sondheim, "America," *West Side Story*, accessed February 3, 2022, www.westsidestory.com/America.

2 Julia Alvarez, *How the Garcia Girls Lost Their Accents* (Chapel Hill, NC: Algonquin Books of Chapel Hill, 1991, 2010).

3 Gloria Anzaldúa, *Borderlands / La Frontera: The New Mestiza* (San Francisco: Aunt Lute Books, 1987), 54.

4 Virgilio P. Elizondo, *Galilean Journey: The Mexican-American Promise*, rev. and expanded edition (Maryknoll, NY: Orbis, 2000), 52.

Father Elizondo's assessment is still valid in the twenty-first century across a broad section of the church universal. While many commendable efforts have been made at diversifying leadership in the secular society, much work remains to be done regarding advancing the diversity of leadership in the church. Few are the tall steeple churches where the lead pastor is of Hispanic or Latino origins. It is more common to limit the appointment of bilingual leaders, whether they are Hispanic or not, to specialized or Spanish-speaking ministries.[5] To add insult to injury, this ecclesial form of systemic racism fails to recognize the prophetic power these leaders demonstrate as they fulfill many leadership roles while advancing the kingdom of God.

This book is a testament to the many contemporary prophetic leaders in the Hispanic/Latino Protestant and evangelical communities of America. It is not about self-proclaimed prophets, nor do any of the contributors claim this title. Rather, it is about Spirit-inspired people who speak from the margins about God's work in church and society. Forty years ago, educator and historian Antonio M. Stevens-Arroyo published an ambitious book *Prophets Denied Honor: An Anthology on the Hispanic Church in the United States.* His stated purpose of the book was to "allow people to speak for themselves and to offer to the patient reader a profile of the powerful forces summoning the Latin American people of the United States to a new articulation of their Catholicism."[6] While Stevens-Arroyo succeeded in his task, he also missed a significant segment of the Hispanic church, the mainline Protestants, evangelicals, and Pentecostals. This book is offered as an informal friendly amendment. Like Stevens-Arroyo, it modestly seeks to amplify the voices of Hispanic/Latino believers who continue to be excluded, silenced, or ignored not just by our Roman Catholic family, but by the majority-white Protestant, evangelical, and Pentecostal

---

5 The Reformed Church in America stands apart for their courage in appointing Rev. Eddy Alemán, a Nicaraguan refugee who came to the United States by way of Canada, as the general secretary of their predominantly white denomination. See "Synod Approves Eddy Alemán as General Secretary," Reformed Church in America, June 9, 2018, www.rca.org/synod-approves-eddy-aleman-as-general-secretary/.

6 Anthony M. Stevens-Arroyo, *Prophets Denied Honor: An Anthology on the Hispanic Church in the United States* (Maryknoll, NY: Orbis, 1980), xv.

churches. It is also a prophetic response to the unbridled xenophobia and anti-immigrant public discourse of our times. What makes points in the political theater simultaneously inflicts immeasurable harm on millions of people. Although Hispanics and Latinos represent many races and speak many languages, they share related cultural heritages rooted in Mexico, Puerto Rico, Dominican Republic, Cuba, Central America, and Latin America. Amazingly, these highly diverse people recognize that their own accented prophets have been called to testify to the injustices of their marginalization and the more powerful reality that they are fully and generously loved by God.

When we use the term *prophet* we are acknowledging the person's role in building the kingdom of God. We are less concerned with self-appointed prophets who are seekers of fame, fortune, and power. This is not intended to be another diatribe against such false prophets; we leave that unhappy task to someone else. The prophets we are concerned with do not claim to be prophets in the biblical or mystical sense. On the contrary, they consider themselves *compañeros*, or co-laborers, with the everyday people of God. However, I would argue they are prophets in at least two senses. First, they share some historical traits with the French Calvinist Huguenots and their protocharismatic cousins, the Camisards. The Camisards' egalitarian exercise of spiritual gifts earned them the nicknames "prophètes" and "prophètesses." They were commonly known in England as "the French Prophets."[7] These French-accented refugees and immigrants must have seemed strange to their eighteenth-century British hosts. Like many Hispanic and Latino people, they were able to integrate but never fully assimilate. Second, these contemporary Spanish and Portuguese heritage prophets share in the poverty and marginality of Jesus, the prophet par excellence. When they speak, write, and pray they do it consciously and unconsciously

7 For a detailed study on the Huguenot immigrant experience in England see Bernard Cottret, *The Huguenot in England: Immigration and Settlement c. 1550–1770* (Cambridge: Maison des Sciences de l'Homme and Cambridge University Press, 1991), originally published as *Terre d'exil* (Paris: Aubier, 1985). For more on Huguenot thought, see Hillel Schwartz, *The French Prophets: The History of a Millenarian Group in Eighteenth-Century England* (Berkeley: University of California Press, 1980).

with their Galilean accents. This collection of writings amplifies their stories and ideas in the first-person prophetic voice. It is because of their distinctive Galilean accented voices that we refer to them as *profetas*.

Profetas are often overlooked for leadership roles, perhaps due to perceptions of their accents, demure carriages, social statuses, skin tones, hair textures, and somatotypes. Some represented in this book are practitioners on the front lines of parish ministry. Others are professionals in administration and higher education. All are deeply committed to their callings. The theological, political, and social perspectives represented by these contributors are diverse. Their voices reflect their rich Argentinian, Brazilian, Mexican, Puerto Rican, and Tejano heritages. Their contextualized conceptualizations of the kingdom of God are meant to awaken and challenge the church. We invite our readers to interact with the contributors with honesty and with civility. Together, we will commit to practicing the dictum attributed to Father John Wesley: "But as to all opinions which do not strike at the root of Christianity, we think and let think."[8]

Three years ago, at the kind invitation of Dr. Gus Reyes, former CEO of the National Hispanic Christian Leadership Conference (NHCLC), I accepted the honorific title of Director of the NHCLC Scholars. This honor was previously held by Dr. Samuel Pagán, the eminent Old Testament scholar. A few years ago, Dr. Reyes asked me to edit several short articles for an NHCLC-sponsored series published in *Christianity Today*. I believed that we needed to craft a learned response to the growing anti-immigrant, anti-Latino, and Christian nationalism rhetoric that had infected American Christianity and spread into the national public discourse. Dr. Reyes agreed. I assembled a small group of contributors and assigned each one to discuss their understanding of prophetic ministry from the vantagepoint of their tradition and experience. Our goal was to change the narrative to present a positive view of the Hispanic/Latino people of the Protestant, evangelical, and Pentecostal churches and the people under the care of their ministries. We realized from the onset that the task was insurmountable because of

8 John Wesley, "The Character of a Methodist," §1 in *The Methodist Societies: History, Nature, and Design*, ed. Rupert E. Davies, vol. 9 of *The Bicentennial Edition of the Works of John Wesley* (Nashville: Abingdon Press, 1989), 34.

the tremendous racial, ethnic, and religious diversity of Hispanic and Latino people. We wondered if our voices would be heard above the din of xenophobic rhetoric. However, we reasoned that not attempting to speak would be the greatest failure of all. From the start, veteran publisher Kathy Armistead agreed to champion our cause to the GBHEM team. As she prepared to retire, Jennifer Manley Rogers took up the challenge as editor to guide our manuscript to press. On behalf of the contributors, we wish to acknowledge the talents of GBHEM Publishing and Catchphrase that helped make this book possible. Special thanks are due to our copyeditor, Marissa Wold Uhrina. This book is a far better read because of her expert copyediting skills and keen eye for detail. The COVID-19 pandemic slowed down our writing considerably. More troubling to us was the disproportionate mortality rate among Hispanics and other people of color. We lament the unspeakable loss of their precious lives. We hope that our combined voices will honor their legacies and preserve their blessed memories.

Prophets with the Galilean Accent

The Galilean Jesus commissioned his disciples, who, bearing his marks of marginalization, were empowered by the Holy Spirit to be living witnesses of the presence of God in the world. These Hispanic and Latino prophets with the Galilean accent operate under the same covenant of grace as the majority-world prophets. They strive to imitate Christ in his acts of healing and compassion in their appointed places of service. Drawing from their unique cultural and linguistic heritages, they deliver God's counsel to communities of faith, higher education, and local and national political leaders. In these and other contexts, they demonstrate what Walter Brueggemann described as possessing "passion and pathos, the power to care, the capacity to weep, the energy to grieve and then to rejoice."[9] The reality of their marginalization does not negate or diminish their message as they are empowered by the Holy Spirit. They rise to what Luke Timothy Johnson calls their "prophetic profession" expressed by "'speaking truth to power' and through

9 Walter Brueggemann, *The Prophetic Imagination* (Philadelphia: Fortress, 1978), 42.

bearing the suffering that follows inevitably from a clash of fundamentally divergent visions."[10]

The following chapters offer a glimpse into their shared ethos as a diverse people of faith who follow in the prophetic tradition of Jesus and speak with the Galilean accent. Their diverse viewpoints will inform, surprise, and challenge readers to bend the arc of recognizing prophetic ministries in their midst while encouraging them to do likewise.

Daniel F. Flores, PhD
General Editor
César Chávez Day 2022

---

10 Luke Timothy Johnson, *Prophetic Jesus, Prophetic Church: The Challenge of Luke-Acts to Contemporary Christians* (Grand Rapids, MI: Eerdmans, 2011), 181–82.

Profetas in the Fields

THELMA HERRERA FLORES

THIS CHAPTER IS BASED in part on my ministry experiences with migrant agricultural laborers at Misión Holland in Holland, Michigan. I will present *La Mesa Campesina* (The Peasant Farmworker's Table) as an integrated model of historical and theological resources designed to address the poverty of Hispanic/Latino migrant agricultural workers in the United States. The poor economic condition of this population is undisputed. However, lack of money is only a symptom of a substantially larger reality. The poverty I refer to extends well beyond economic deprivation. More fundamental is the poverty of opportunities to engage in fruitful conversation about spiritual matters of faith, salvation, and liberation. This creates spiritual isolation that affects and impoverishes all of us. Resources such as William Langland's "Piers Plowman" and the writings and sayings of Tomás Rivera, César Chávez, and Óscar Romero offer helpful insights while embodying indispensable spiritual gifts. When they are brought together, they create a synthesis model for evangelical ministry to *Campesinos*. These four exemplars offer their gifts to the poorest of the poor who live off the land as disinherited peasants. What unites these individuals is that they each arose from within their communities with a full understanding of the culture and struggle of their people. These four persons used their unique gifts to reach out to, interact with, and serve their community. Each of them contributes their unique gifts to the banquet table: pilgrimage, mortality, community, and the Holy Sacraments. The popular

Salvadoreña hymn "Vamos Todos al Banquete" speaks clearly to the validity of everyone's worth:

Vamos todos al banquete,
A la mesa de la creación,
Cada cual con su taburete,
Tiene un puesto y una misión.[1]

This hymn welcomes all people to God's banquet table. Not long ago I hosted a luncheon for some friends in my townhouse. The table was crowded, and it seemed like there was not enough room for one more person. As I sat away from the table one of my guests insisted that we all squeeze in like family. And we did. This is how it is with God's banquet table. I brought my *taburete* (my own chair/stool) and joined in the festivities. God has called each of us to his banquet table. Moreover, God has given each of us a position and a mission. The *Mesa Campesina* model seeks to alleviate spiritual poverty by bringing together the best gifts that are sensitive to the cultural needs, struggles, and spiritual yearnings of *Los Campesinos.*

Demographics

Farmworkers

There are two types of nonresident farmworkers in the United States: seasonal and migrant. The term *seasonal farmworkers* refers to foreign guest farmworkers who enter the country only to work in the harvest season. The term *migrants*, on the other hand, refers to persons who reside in the United States but must travel away from home for agricultural work. In many cities, such as Crystal City, Texas, people live in permanent residences during the off-season. They move to temporary quarters, to labor camps, in the various locations of the harvest. In the Spanish-speaking community, such migrants are often referred to as *campesinos.*

While many migrants are US citizens, some foreign nationals travel across international borders to find work. The federal government issues

---

1 Guillermo Cuéllar, "Vamos todos al banquete / Let Us Go Now to the Banquet," *Santo Santo Santo* (Chicago: GIA, 2019), 412.

H2A visas to foreign workers, which restricts them to agricultural work. Their nonfarmworker family members may accompany them with a valid H4 visa, which forbids them from seeking work. H2A and H4 visa holders must return to their country of origin after the season is over or at least every three years. They do not share the same benefits that other migrants and seasonal workers enjoy as US citizens.

Migrants or Immigrants?

The terms *migrant* and *immigrant* are often conflated. Immigrants are those individuals who cross an international border to become permanent residents in another country. If they come to the United States legally, they may fall under the protection of US Citizenship and Immigration Services or international asylum laws. While some new immigrants might not aspire to become farmworkers, their lack of employable skills might force them to become migrant or seasonal workers too. Undocumented immigrants are subject to arrest and deportation. Farmers might avoid hiring them for fear of prosecution and penalties. Therefore, it is less likely to find undocumented immigrants in the farming community. In this chapter, I use the terms *migrants* and *campesinos* interchangeably to refer to all farmworkers who migrate for the purpose of work. This is not to diminish the sacred worth of people who enter the country without legal documentation or seek refugee status. It is only meant to focus on the special needs of *campesinos*.

Population

It is unknown exactly how many farmworkers come to Michigan annually. The Migrant and Seasonal Farm Worker (MSFW) Enumeration Profiles Estimate 2013, though over seven years old, provides the most recent available data on the total number of farmworkers. Drawing on the data from that report provides a useful snapshot of the migrant population in Ottawa County as compared to the total in the state of Michigan. According to these estimates, as many as 9,084 migrant workers and their families come to Ottawa County annually.[2]

---

2 "Migrant and Seasonal Farmworkers Enumeration Profiles Study," Michigan Department of Civil Rights, June 2013, http://michigan.gov/documents/dhs/FarmworkerReport_430130_7.pdf.

West Michigan

During the early 1960s, the demand for labor in the food processing industry put pressure on the local farming communities. The Heinz Company began to recruit migrants from local farms to work in the pickle plant in Holland. Following this practice, Bil Mar Foods also recruited migrants from the farms. The astronomical growth of the company's turkey business drove up the demand for cheap labor. It made several unsuccessful attempts to recruit Mexican workers from the border near El Paso, Texas. At last, the company found a way to supply its labor needs from Puerto Rico. After consulting with Puerto Ricans who had settled in the area, Bil Mar Foods devised a migrant labor pipeline between Ottawa County and Puerto Rico.

> Bil Mar initially hired more than 100 temporary workers from that country [Puerto Rico] by sending them plane tickets. The DeWitts would pick them up in Detroit and then transport them with an old school bus to Borculo. After the busiest part of the processing season ended, they would go back to their homeland [Puerto Rico].[3]

In my face-to-face exchanges with some of the migrant workers of Ottawa County, I have noted most of them are Latino males somewhere between twenty and forty years of age. These migrants come from Mexico, Guatemala, and other parts of Latin America. A great number of them also travel from homes in Florida, Georgia, Tennessee, and Texas to pick seasonal fruit and vegetables such as blueberries, peaches, apples, and asparagus. I have also ministered to a group of Haitians in the blueberry fields of Ottawa County. (On one occasion, my octogenarian mother eagerly ran into the blueberry bushes to hand-deliver Walmart gift cards, Haitian Creole New Testaments, and care packages to these Haitian field hands.)

Although most of these laborers are single men, there are some women and a few families with school-aged or younger children. I have encountered a few middle-aged couples and seniors that were older

3 Michael Lozon, *Mr. Turkey: A Biography of Bil Mar Foods Co-Founder Marvin DeWitt* (Zeeland, MI: DeWitt Foundation, 1999), 79.

than the typical age group. The low numbers in this group probably can be attributed to the strain of the long hours of back-breaking work.

Socioeconomic Challenges

The level of education of these laborers is below that of a high school diploma. Therefore, agricultural work is one of the few types of employment accessible to these laborers. Their life is such that they journey from their home in search of a way to provide for their basic physical needs of food and shelter. These are the working poor. Working in the *piscas* is not a one-off scenario. It is a tradition within these families to continue this work generation after generation. This lifestyle affects all members of their household, and it becomes cyclical. The school-aged children are pulled out of school in March to travel to the *piscas* to help their parents pick crops in the fields. They often return to their schools in the fall after the school year has already begun. All of the travel back and forth from home to the farms in various states results in many missed months of valuable education. The reality of this subsistence offers very little opportunity for educational and financial success and stability. This seasonal work is their primary annual income. Therefore, it is almost impossible to break from this cyclical existence.

Spiritual Resources

These migrant agricultural workers typically work six days per week from before sunrise to late in the day after sunset. Their day off is at the discretion of the farmer, the nature of the weather, and the abundance of the harvest. This is the only day the workers have for rest, relaxation, grocery shopping, laundry, and so on. After visiting with some of the workers I learned that attending church is not an easy possibility. Many of them do not have a means of transportation that would enable their presence in a worship service. It would be inaccurate to state that they lack an interest in spiritual matters. On the contrary, the majority of those I visited with were open to being prayed for, to receiving and reading biblical literature, and to hearing a word of hope and exhortation. For the most part, these migrant workers simply have extenuating circumstances that prevent them from attending any type of worship service outside of their campgrounds. Consequently, I cannot classify them with any certainty of being "religious nones." A new religious movement must be explored to provide access for these individuals.

The challenge for the church is to be able to have a pastoral presence with this community of migrant workers. An outside-the-box type of worship service would have to be brought to them at a feasible time in their schedule. This *conjunto* approach is grounded in the scriptures and with the imaginative leading of the Holy Spirit. The resources I plan to use include William Langland's poem "Piers Plowman," Tomás Rivera's novel . . . *y no se lo tragó la tierra*, Óscar Romero's spiritual writings, and César Chávez's work with the United Farm Workers. Together, they embody *La Mesa Campesina*, a model for a new religious movement for the migrant worker community.

"Piers Plowman"

"Piers Plowman" is a medieval English poem with a religious focus. It instructs on proper service and adoration of God as expressed through obedience to his divine commands. This, however, does not suffice in describing "Piers Plowman." This poem lends itself to many and various interpretations. This fourteenth-century work attributed to William Langland enlivens our eyes and ears to a presentation of Christian history through the medium of several dream visions.

Along the way, the reader is introduced to different characters, some of which are literal and others allegorical. Presenting the characters in such a manner is what makes "Piers Plowman" so intriguing. This method allows one to step back in time and experience the thoughts, lives, interests, cares, and concerns of the audience. According to C. S. Lewis, allegory is not limited to medieval thought:

> Allegory, in some sense, belongs not to medieval man but to man, or even to mind, in general. It is of the very nature of thought and language to represent what is immaterial in picturable terms. What is good or happy has always been high like the heavens and bright like the sun. Evil and misery were deep and dark from the first.[4]

4 C. S. Lewis, *The Allegory of Love: A Study in Medieval Traditions* (London: Cambridge University Press, 1936, 2013), 55.

"Piers Plowman" is only one example of a Christian allegory. According to Philip Schaff, *The Shepherd of Hermas* is "the oldest Christian allegory . . . and it has been compared with Bunyan's *Pilgrim's Progress* and Dante's *Divina Commedia*."[5] In *The Shepherd of Hermas*, Hermas also receives instruction through visions. His visions are from an angel who is dressed like a shepherd. The purpose of the angel's message is "to call Hermas and through him the church to repentance."[6]

In *The Shepherd of Hermas*, the genre of religious romance is employed as a teaching device. Despite the fact "Irenaeus quotes it as divine Scripture and the Alexandrian fathers . . . regard it as divinely inspired," both Ambrose and Augustine ignored it.[7]

The Shepherd of Hermas, like "Piers Plowman," was very popular in the ancient church. These stories were popular because they spoke the language of the populace. This is a lesson that must be mastered. Lamin Sanneh, a former professor of mine, often said, "The message must be translated."[8] In other words, we must speak to be understood. Hans-Georg Gadamer, in his book *Truth and Method*, agrees as evidenced in the following: "No text and no book speaks if it does not speak a language that reaches the other person."[9] However, I am convinced that it is the third person of the Trinity, the Holy Spirit, who illumines our mind so that we might understand the love of God as expressed through his words. The proclamation of the gospel requires the quickening of the Word by the Holy Spirit in human hearts.

Agricultural Symbolism

In "Piers Plowman," the main character, William, is dressed as a sheep. This would, of course, suggest that he is a lost sheep. His

---

5 Philip Schaff, *History of the Christian Church*, vol. II (Grand Rapids, MI: Eerdmans, 1910), 680.

6 Schaff, *History*, 680.

7 Schaff, *History*, 690–91.

8 Lamin Sanneh, "World Christianity: Religious and Cultural Issues" (classroom lecture, Yale University Divinity School, New Haven, CT, 1998).

9 Hans-Georg Gadamer, *Truth and Method* (London and New York: Continuum, 2006), 398.

outerwear visibly portrays William's inner struggles, a pilgrim on a quest for Truth.

> There I dreamed a dream that was indeed wonderful:
> I was in a wilderness, but where I knew not.
> I set my face eastward, where, high against the sun,
> I saw a tower, trim-built on the top of a hill;
> And a deep dale beneath it, and a dungeon in it,
> With deep dark dykes that were dreadful to see.
> A pleasant plain full of people lay between these places,
> With every manner of man, poor, middling, and rich,
> Toiling or travelling as the world's way took them.
> Some spent their lives at the plough, and were seldom idle,
> Seeding and sowing and strongly laboring
> To gather what the gluttony of wastrels would again scatter.
> Some spent their lives in pride, and were dressed in apt style,
> Coming all tricked-out in conspicuous clothing.[10]

According to this poem, the whole gamut of society is present and busy doing what they would normally do to occupy their time. They carry on with their daily tasks of plowing, buying and selling, begging, making a pilgrimage, preaching, and so on. For Langland, they are oblivious of their proximity to hell. Is this dream merely a vision, or is it particularly telling of his inner struggle?

The Gift of Pilgrimage

The leader and guide of this pilgrimage is none other than Piers the Plowman. The plowman discloses the way to Truth. Unfortunately, it is quite a complicated journey, not one that is achieved easily or instantaneously. It is a progression: the soul's progression from being self-serving to loving the Lord, God, with single-minded devotion, the kind of devotion that causes one to yield one's life completely to God and yearn for him with every fiber of one's being. "As a deer longs for flowing streams, so my soul longs for you, O God. My soul thirsts for God, for the living God. When shall I come and behold the face of

10 William Langland, *Piers Plowman* (Hertfordshire, UK: Wordsworth Editions, Limited, 1999), 3.

God?" (Ps 42:1–2, NRSV). Langland believes that hard work, honest living, and charity are what will lead the pilgrims to their encounter with Truth. Piers the Plowman equates plowing with pilgrimage as evidenced by the following from Passus 6, lines 59–66.

> Said Piers, 'I shall put on, then, a pilgrim's dress,
> And take you all with me until we find Truth.
> I shall put on my poor clothes, all ragged and patched,
> My gaiters, and my gloves to get warmth in my fingers,
> Sling my seed-bag round my neck instead of a scrip,
> And bring along in it a bushel of bread-corn.
> This I myself will sow, and then soon after
> Will pilgrim-it like a palmer, in search of pardon.[11]

The Plowman's sowing is indeed his pilgrimage. According to this quotation, once he has completed his task of plowing, he will be dressed with palm leaves, for this is how pilgrims who have visited the sacred places of the Holy Land attired themselves.

William's quest for Truth begins with a realization of good and evil, of heaven and hell. It is at this point that his spiritual eyes are opened. He is forced to examine his life. The church assists by teaching him about Truth and Falsehood. Thus, equipped with the basics, he begins his pilgrimage. His journey is not a simple one or, for that matter, a speedy one. A single encounter is not the ultimate goal. We are to renew that relationship daily. One must, by necessity, work out one's salvation by loving God with our entire being. Only then, through the merits of God's grace, might we be able to love our neighbor as much as ourselves.

Tomás Rivera's *. . . y no se lo tragó la tierra*

Crystal City

My familiarity with migrant workers stems from the fact that I was born in Crystal City, Texas, a migrant-worker town in south Texas. This is a place where poverty and food insecurity is a way of life. One

---

11 Langland, *Piers Plowman*, 61.

of the sons of that community was Tomás Rivera. He was one of my father's lifelong friends. Tomás wrote a semi-autobiographical novel, *. . . y no se lo tragó la tierra* (*And the Earth Did Not Devour Him*), about the migrant life of the 1940s and '50s.[12] He tells his story through the eyes of a young boy from Crystal City. This book resonated with me because my grandparents, parents, and mother-in-law were all migrant workers. They understood the harshness of picking cotton in the hot Texas sun. They also knew what it was like to travel from south Texas to Michigan riding on top of a truck laden with onions.

As a young boy, Tomás and his family also would travel far and wide to the *piscas* to pick crops in the fields. Despite his difficult upbringing, Tomás was the first Mexican American in Crystal City to earn and receive his PhD. This was quite an accomplishment considering the limited literacy, high poverty, and outright racism Mexican Americans faced in those days.

The Gift of Mortality

In this book one of the topics Tomás Rivera talks about is death. Death is almost always a topic we shy away from. Perhaps witnessing past experiences of death has caused us to harbor angry feelings. This is exactly what happened to him. The novel's young, nameless Chicano witnessed the grave illness and death of his aunt and uncle. And if that were not enough, he saw how it affected his mother. As the primary caregiver, her days were awash in tears. The young boy could do nothing to alleviate her pain, so he became angry. Over the years he had suppressed those feelings of anger. It was not until his father suffered a heat stroke while working in the fields that those feelings that had been tucked deep into the crevices of his being came rushing back into his heart, into his mind, and into his very soul.

Let me share a portion of a conversation between the boy and his mother on the occasion of his father's illness.

---

12 Although the book is not autobiographical, Rivera added his "artistic insight" to incidents he witnessed as a young boy. See Oscar Urquídez-Samoza, "Tomás Rivera," in *Chicano Literature: A Reference Guide*, ed. Julio A. Martínez and Francisco A. Lomelí (Westport, CT: Greenwood Press, 1985), 335.

Se hubieron venido luego, luego, m'ijo.
No veian que su tata estaba enfermo?
Ustedes saben muy bien que estaba picado del sol.
Porque no se vinieron?

You should have come right away, my son.
Did you not see that your father was sick?
You knew very well that he was suffering from a heat stroke.
Why didn't you come home?

Pues no se . . . yo como quiera si le dije que se sentara debajo del árbol
Que está a lo orilla de los surcos, pero el no quiso.
Fue cuando empezó a vomitar.

Well, I don't know . . . anyway, at least I told him to sit down in the shade of the tree
located at the end of the furrow.
But he didn't want to, that's when he began to vomit.[13]

Seeing his father sick like that affected the boy, and so he blurted,

Siempre alguna enfermedad.
Siempre rogandole a Dios.

Always some kind of sickness.
Always pleading with God.

Porque nosotros enterrados en la tierra como animales sin ninguna esperanza de nada?

Why are we always forgotten in the dirt like animals without any hope of anything?[14]

The young boy blamed God for their troubles. He cursed God for his father's illness. Even when he learned that his father was on the road to recovery and would not be swallowed up by the earth, he did not repent.

---

13 Tomás Rivera, . . . *y no se lo tragó la tierra* (*And the Earth Did Not Devour Him*) (Houston: Arte Público Press, 1992), 32, 108.

14 Rivera, . . . *y no se lo tragó la tierra*, 33, 109.

> *Vio hacia la tierra y le dio una patada bien fuerte y le dijo, 'todavia no . . . todavía no me puedes tragar.'*
>
> Instead, he looked down at the ground and kicked it with a great force and yelled, 'Not yet! You shall not devour me yet.'[15]

This echoes the words found in 1 Chronicles 29:15: "To be sure, we are like all our ancestors, immigrants without permanent homes. Our days are like a shadow on the ground, and there's no hope" (CEB).

What Tomás Rivera's character of a nameless young Chicano demonstrates for us, from a migrant worker's perspective, is the harsh and painful realities of life. A life without hope, a life filled with anger, fear, and insecurity. I believe it is our responsibility to offer them hope, to offer God's grace. Hope is born of our human experience and the inspiration of God's presence in our lives: "This hope doesn't put us to shame, because the love of God has been poured out in our hearts through the Holy Spirit, who has been given to us" (Rom 5:5, CEB).

Dust to Dust

Ash Wednesday was a significant time when I was overwhelmed by my ministry experience in *el barrio*. Receiving ashes is not a sacrament. However, this visible symbol of penance ranks as a quasisacrament for many Hispanic people of Roman Catholic or other liturgical church backgrounds. For them, Ash Wednesday is more than a day of penitential prayer and fasting. It is a time to reckon themselves as mortals under the merciful care of an immortal God.

The outreach center I directed was located across the street from Diamond Hill Elementary, a predominantly Hispanic Title I school in Fort Worth, Texas. I wondered how we were going to reach all these wonderful brothers and sisters. Parents, grandparents, and guardians were all sitting in their parked cars waiting for their children to be dismissed from school. My husband, Daniel, and I put on our clerical robes and stoles and walked outside to the steps of the center. Taking our bowls filled with ashes we approached the people in their vehicles. Every one of them willingly, graciously, and respectfully accepted the ashes from these United Methodist hands. After we finished with the

---

15 Rivera, *. . . y no se lo tragó la tierra*, 36, 112.

fifty or so cars we turned and saw a very long line that had formed near our tent. We stood underneath our makeshift chapel to serve the people. Daniel and I each ministered to at least one hundred people. There were children, parents, grandparents, aunts, and uncles. Some elderly folks were brought to us in wheelchairs. All of them were waiting patiently to receive the imposition of the ashes. When we finished Daniel and I went into our educational building just behind the sanctuary building for a rest and a drink of water before we headed to our church campus to lead the evening Ash Wednesday worship service. Just as we started to sit, one of our laity came in and informed us that others wanted to receive the ashes. So, there we stood in the breezeway between the chapel and the educational building amid garbage cans and recycling bins, receiving God's people, praying for them, and placing a cross of ashes on their foreheads. I thank God for the opportunity afforded to us. Our meeting with them was unconventional, but I believe as we stood there praying together, we were standing on holy ground.

César Chávez

Mexican Catholicism

Roman Catholicism is the leading faith tradition of many Mexicans, and it is culturally extensive. Many Mexicans understand Catholicism as part of their identity. It is not just their religion; it is who they are. This identity is passed on with great pride through families as a legacy. This is exactly how César Chávez was nurtured: "His spirituality was shaped by his family and grounded in what Latina/o theologians have termed 'Abuelita Theology.'"[16]

Chávez's family lived away from the city because of segregated housing. There were no catechism classes, so his grandmother taught him the tenets of his Roman Catholic faith.

> Mama Tella [grandmother] gave us our formal religious training. . . . She was always praying, just praying. Every evening she would sit in bed, and we would gather in front of her. . . . After

16 Robert Chao Romero, *Brown Church: Five Centuries of Latina/o Social Justice, Theology, and Identity* (Downers Grove, IL: InterVarsity Press, 2020), 124.

> the Rosary she would tell us about a particular saint and drill us on our Catechism.[17]

After Mama Tella finished tutoring Chávez in the Catholic faith, the family traveled to the Catholic Church to request that he and Rita be allowed to participate in and fulfill his first communion.

> The Anglo priest refused saying . . . they have not had any religious training. They can't take communion . . . they must attend class here in Yuma first. To this, Juana [mother] retorted, "They can't because we live out in the valley twenty miles away. We can't travel that far every week." She firmly insisted, "Well, ask them something." . . . The priest proceeded to drill the Chávez children with questions from the Catholic catechism, and because of their thorough training in "abuelita theology," César and Rita passed with flying colors. The children received their first communion the following day.[18]

Chávez and his family, like Tomás Rivera's family, were also migrant farmworkers. Working in the *piscas* allowed Chávez to wholly experience the appalling working conditions and the mistreatment of the migrant agricultural workers. The familiarity with this kind of suffering led Chávez "together with Dolores Huerta, Fred Ross, and his cousin, Manuel Chávez, to launch the National Farm Workers Association."[19]

Chávez's organization was unique in that it was rooted in his Christian faith: "His movement of farmworkers was first and foremost a faith-based movement because César understood the power of faith."[20] He did his work in the name of Jesús. He fused Mexican Catholicism with the social justice teachings of Catholicism.

---

17 Mario T. Garcia, *Gospel of César Chávez* (Lanham, MD: Sheed & Ward, 2007), 26–27.

18 Romero, *Brown Church*, 125.

19 Frederick John Dalton, *The Moral Vision of César Chávez* (Maryknoll, NY: Orbis, 2003), 8.

20 Garcia, *Gospel of César Chávez*, 31.

Virgen de Guadalupe

La Virgen de Guadalupe has "become the 'Mother' of the Brown Church."[21] She is the patron saint of Mexico, and many shrines honoring her can easily be found throughout the United States, Mexico, and Latin America.

> La Virgen points us to Christ, and she has been a powerful symbol of the fact that God loves the indigenous people of Mexico and is their protector. . . . Many Latinas and Latinos in the United States look to La Virgen as a symbol of faith, identity, hope, female empowerment, and cultural liberation.[22]

La Virgen was the central religious symbol for the National Farm Workers Association. And fellow activist Dolores Huerta honored her as well.

> She is a symbol of the impossible, of doing the impossible to win a victory, in humility, of being able to win with the faith. I mean that's the important thing that she symbolizes to the union: that with faith you can win. You know with faith you can overcome.[23]

In his march to Sacramento, Chávez challenged the injustices against farmworkers. He did this by using his Christian faith to unify the farmworkers under the banner of the Virgin of Guadalupe: "Chávez fashioned this famous march from the Central Valley to Sacramento as a penitential pilgrimage, or '*peregrinación*.' Drawing from popular Mexican religious tradition, he called the march, 'Penitence, Pilgrimage, and Revolution.'"[24] While Protestants would not promote the veneration of La Virgen, it is important to recognize the potency of this symbol for Mexican Catholics.

---

21 Romero, *Brown Church*, 69.

22 Ondina E. González and Justo L. González, *Christianity in Latin America: A History* (Cambridge: Cambridge University Press, 2008), 56, 58.

23 Dolores Huerta quoted in Romero, *Brown Church*, 71.

24 Garcia, *Gospel of César Chávez*, 12, 16.

The Gifts of Fasting and Prayer

The inclusion of such terms as *penitence* and *pilgrimage* in the name of the march reveals just how much Chávez was influenced by his Mexican Catholic faith. The Sacramento march used a spiritual practice that was part of the Mexican Catholic tradition.

> The penitential procession is also in the blood of the Mexican American, and the Delano march [1966] will therefore be one of penance—public penance for the sins of the strikers, their own personal sins as well as their yielding perhaps to feelings of hatred and revenge in the strike itself. They hope by the march to set themselves at peace with the Lord, so that the justice of their cause will be purified of all lesser motivation.[25]

Along with penitence and pilgrimage, fasting and prayer were fundamental to Chavez's faith and played a key role in his leadership. The purpose of joining together prayer with fasting is to connect us to God. Fasting is biblical, and examples can be found within the Old and New Testaments. In Nehemiah 9 the Israelites fasted and lifted prayers of praise and confession after sinning against God. In Esther 4:16, Queen Esther fasts with Israel and prays for the strength and courage to approach the king and ask that Israel might be spared from Haman's plot. Daniel 9 tells about Daniel fasting and praying for the people because of their disobedience. He asked God to have mercy on the chosen people. In Matthew 4:1–11 Jesus fasts for forty days and forty nights.

Prayer, when combined with fasting, is brilliant because instead of relying on personal power, we can connect to God and draw on Divine power. This is exactly what Chávez did. His implementation of these two disciplines allowed him to see staggering results. Chávez was convinced that God had heard the cries of the farmworkers.

> The only justice is Christ—God's justice. We're the victims of a lot of shenanigans by the courts but ultimately, down the line, real justice comes. It does not come from the courts, but it comes from

25 Garcia, *Gospel of César Chávez*, 96, 97.

> a set of circumstances and I think God's hand is in it. God tends to write very straight with crooked lines.[26]

The Gift of *Familia*

Chávez, steeped in abuelita theology, understood the importance of popular icons, like la Virgen de Guadalupe, and of prayer, fasting, and pilgrimage. The Mexican Catholics held these beliefs in high esteem, and Chávez recognized and appreciated the cultural values that bound his people together. While not all migrants are Mexican, Latinos share this gift of appreciation and desire for close family ties, or *familia.*

Óscar Romero

Central American Catholicism

Óscar Romero's background is a rather conventional one. He was born into a poor and humble family with no special privileges. At the age of fourteen, he entered the seminary and was ordained in 1943 at the age of twenty-five. During his ministry, El Salvador was in the midst of a violent civil war.

> Over and over, he challenged those in power to care for their countrymen; he encouraged the campesinos to pray, to live more truly by the vision of the New Testament; and he reminded his entire audience of how Jesus came to earth in poverty, enduring the pain and humiliation of the cross before the triumph of his resurrection. Because Christ knows all the suffering on earth . . . we can believe in and work for his kingdom on earth.[27]

In 1977 Romero was appointed archbishop of San Salvador. With this new position, his basic message did not change. He still believed and preached that the good news of the gospel was for the poor and the oppressed. Romero's conviction was based on Matthew 25.

---

26 Garcia, *Gospel of César Chávez*, 31, 32.

27 Óscar Romero, *The Scandal of Redemption*, ed. Carolyn Kurtz (Walden, NY: Plough, 2018), 1, 2.

> Calling upon the scriptural authority of Matthew 25 and the biblical truth that all people are created in the image of God, Romero declared that Christ was present in the face of the rural poor of El Salvador. When they were tortured and abused, so was Christ; when children died of hunger, so did Christ; when they cried out to God and the church for liberation, so was Christ.[28]

Romero firmly maintained that the true church of Christ must be on the side of the poor, as further evidenced in the following.

> The face of Christ is among the sacks and baskets of the farmworkers; the face of Christ is among those who are tortured and mistreated in the prisons; the face of Christ is dying of hunger in the children who have nothing to eat; the face of Christ is in the poor who ask the church for their voice to be heard. How can the church deny this request when it is Christ who is telling us to speak for him?[29]

Romero's Central American Catholicism was very much an institutional one. His ministry used the Catholic belief and traditions as practiced within the Church itself. As an archbishop he emphasized *la misa* (the Eucharist) and baptism. This was the common ground between him and his people.

The Gifts of the Sacraments

Sacramental spirituality is the spirituality that is expressed through the sacraments. The sacraments can be understood as conduits of God's grace. They give us the strength to live a holy life and mature in our faith. Within the Roman Catholic Church, there are seven sacraments: Baptism, Eucharist, Confirmation, Reconciliation/Confession, Anointing of the Sick, Holy Orders or Ordination, and Marriage. Most Protestants recognize only baptism and the Eucharist as sacraments or ordinances. A few holiness and Pentecostal traditions include

---

28 Romero, *Brown Church*, 168.

29 Marie Dennis, Renny Goldman, and Scott Wright, *Oscar Romero: Reflections on His Life and Writings* (Maryknoll, NY: Orbis, 2000), 35.

foot washing as an ordinance. The Salvation Army does not celebrate any sacrament or ordinance.

Liturgy professor James F. White referred to baptism as "the sacrament of equality."[30] When I was a pastor in Fort Worth, Texas, I had the experience of reaching out to Hispanic Catholics. As a United Methodist minister, I found it intriguing that it was very difficult to get people from the *barrio* into the church and sitting in the pews. As mentioned earlier, I was the director of a faith-based outreach center located across the street from Diamond Hill Elementary School, a predominantly Hispanic Title I school. Every afternoon my staff, community volunteers, and I provided snacks for the children of the school. We developed a relationship with this community. They knew that my husband and I were pastors, yet they would not enter the church—that is, until one day a young mother, a recent immigrant from Mexico, visited our Wednesday-morning service at the outreach center. Afterward, she asked if we would be willing to baptize her baby girl. Her daughter was scheduled to have surgery, and she was desperate for her to be baptized before the procedure. We had a conversation, and we set the day and time for the baptism. To our surprise, when they returned the whole family, including the extended family, was present. This family had high regard and belief in the sacraments, the grandmother having been baptized a Presbyterian in Mexico. They understood that in baptism their daughter not only received the blessing of the church, but she was received equally into the family of God.

Sacrifice

Óscar Romero was assassinated on March 24, 1980, while leading *la misa* (the Eucharist) in the chapel of the Divina Providencia hospital. The Gospel reading for that day was John 12:23–26, which speaks of a grain of wheat falling to the earth and dying.

> Archbishop Romero's last words beckoned his listeners to present their own lives as a sacrifice for others in the model of Christ. From the spiritual nourishment of the Eucharist, and Christian lives poured out in service, justice and peace would flow to the

30 James White, *Sacraments as God's Self Giving* (Nashville: Abingdon, 1983), 96.

> people of El Salvador. . . . Whoever offers their life out of love for Christ . . . will live like the seed that dies.[31]

What Henri J. M. Nouwen said of Romero in the following quotation is something that pastors and leaders should strive for:

> Romero does not speak from a distance. He does not hide his fears, his brokenness, his hesitations. It is as if he puts his arm around my shoulder and slowly walks with me. He shares my struggles. There is a warmth in his words that opens my heart to listen.[32]

The church should be incarnate among the poor. We should not set ourselves apart from them or deem ourselves above them.

> Let whoever desires this world's privileges and not the persecutions that come from this commitment listen to the awesome paradox in the gospel: "Blessed are you when people hate you and reject you and insult you and say you are evil, because of the Son of Man. Rejoice on that day and leap for joy, because your reward will be great in heaven" (Luke 6:22–23).[33]

Theology *en Conjunto* as Renewal

The Rural Prophets

All too often society has a negative perspective on migrant agricultural workers. Yes, they are poor and oppressed, but they are still people of God and loved by God. They have dreams, ambitions, and talents to share with their community and beyond. The prophet Amos is an example of an agricultural worker used and elevated by God. According to the biblical book that carries his name, Amos was from Tekoa, and he earned his living as a livestock breeder and a tender of sycamore trees (Amos 1:1; 7:14). Amos, however, was much more than an agricultural worker, much more than a simple man from a small village. He

31 Romero, *Brown Church*, 172.

32 Óscar Romero, *The Violence of Love*, trans. James R. Brockman, SJ (Maryknoll, NY: Orbis, 2004), ix.

33 Romero, *The Violence of Love*, 192.

was able to manage his familiar, if not mundane, rural life to connect with God and leave a long-lasting legacy.

> This prophet is nowadays above all known as an advocate of justice, as someone who had the courage to speak out against the maltreatment of the poor. In that capacity Amos from Tekoa has served (and still serves) as a source of inspiration for protest and reform movements in various parts of the world.[34]

Amos, like the Shepherd of Hermas and Piers Plowman, received visions from God. More than that, Amos was akin to César Chávez and Óscar Romero in that he was passionately moved by what he witnessed. This "prophet's moral outrage was provoked by the suffering and hardship he saw around him."[35]

Another biblical example is Jesus. It is from him whom we receive the mandate on and the example of how to care for the poor and the oppressed in our communities. God loves the poor and wants his people to demonstrate a compassionate and sympathetic heart toward them. In Leviticus 19:9–10, we read that God demanded of the Israelites that the harvest be left unpicked at the edges of their fields. This was done so that the poor and the foreigner also could have food. Later, in verse 15, we read about God's impartiality: "Do not pervert justice; do not show partiality to the poor or favoritism to the great, but judge your neighbor fairly" (NIV).

Luke 4:18–19 says that Jesus came to set the oppressed free: "The Spirit of the LORD is upon me, because he has anointed me to bring good news to the poor. He has sent me to proclaim release to the captives and recovery of sight to the blind, to let the oppressed go free, to proclaim the year of the Lord's favor" (NRSV). And then in verse 21 Jesus informs his audience that "today this scripture has been fulfilled in your hearing" (NRSV). What does this statement mean? It signifies that Jesus was claiming that mission as his own. Jesus was reaching out to all people.

---

34 Goran Eidevall, *Amos* (New Haven, CT: Yale University Press, 2017), 3.

35 Eidevall, *Amos*, 6.

Sacred Space

The characters of Piers Plowman, Tomás Rivera, César Chávez, and Óscar Romero all share something very intimate with *campesinos*. It is their strong connection with the land and the disinherited people of the land. This imagery brings us back to the book of Genesis and the story of Cain and Abel. Abel had the risky task of negotiating with his brother who had the upper hand, sometimes with deadly consequences. This is still true with the migrant agricultural workers, who must negotiate their existence in a strange land, conduct business in a foreign language, live on meager accommodations until the season of seed and harvest is over. In this ever-moving pilgrimage, they may discover that Christ is walking next to them in the crop rows and drinking with them in the irrigation ditches. They have the unique vantagepoint from which to experience what Jewish philosopher Martin Buber called the "I–Thou" relationship with God.

In his classic book *I and Thou* (originally published as *Ich und Du* 1923, then translated to English in 1937), Buber posited that something divine occurs in the space of dialogue between sentient beings. The biblical patriarch Jacob called the place Bethel. This space is what the Hebrew sages referred to as *macom*. It is the secret place where *Ha-Elyon* (the most-high God) dwells and the place where our divine inheritance resides. The Celtic tradition refers to the phenomena where the divine and the mortal connect as the "thin places." Anyone who has dared to dream about their church will have reason to affirm that there are many "thin places" yet to be discovered. In his hymn "Wrestling Jacob," Charles Wesley imagined this as the place for holy conversations.

My prayer has power with God;
The grace unspeakable I now receive;
Through faith I see thee face to face.
I see thee face to face, and live!
In vain I have not wept and strove—
Thy nature, and thy name is Love.[36]

---

36 Charles Wesley, "Wrestling Jacob," hymn 136, in *A Collection of Hymns for the Use of the People Called Methodists*, ed. Franz Hildebrandt and Oliver Beckerlegge,

My friend Tom Locke, president of the Texas Methodist Foundation, loves to talk about what he has come to identify as "the world that God imagines." This phrase expresses Locke's understanding of God's vision for the world. Furthermore, it reflects his deep commitment to dialogic orthopraxy as a way of being. This is perhaps the most intriguing aspect of Locke's philosophy of service to the church. The notion of "the world that God imagines" encourages all those who enter these dialogues to be energized by the Holy Spirit. These dialogues are, by nature, about the mission of the church. Those of us who are practitioners recognize that because of holy conversations, many works of grace and mercy exist that otherwise would not have been initiated or sustained by the local church. This dialogic approach has provided the dynamism to birth new ministries on the edge of growth. Many unseen perspectives enable the church to cultivate excellence in ministry. It is this commitment to a dialogue that provides for perpetual creativity within the church. The intimate "I–Thou" relationship we experience in fervent prayer is a divine charism. It inspires hope that our church, with all its bumps and bruises, has depths of beauty yet to be revealed.

Conclusion

Justo L. González pioneered the concept of reading the Bible through Hispanic eyes. According to González, this contextual hermeneutic focuses on salvation and liberation: "What we mean by 'Hispanic eyes' is the perspective of those who claim their Hispanic identity as part of their hermeneutical baggage, and who also read the Scriptures within the context of a commitment to the Latino struggle to become all that God wants us and all the world to be—in other words, the struggle for salvation/liberation."[37] The church universal could be challenged to go one step further and read Holy Scripture as *campesinos*. The stories, struggles, and position of the agricultural laborers are uniquely theirs and not necessarily part of the general Latina/o experience.

---

with James Dale, vol. 7 of *The Bicentennial Edition of the Works of John Wesley* (Nashville: Abingdon, 1983), 252.

37 Justo L. González, *Santa Biblia: The Bible through Hispanic Eyes* (Nashville: Abingdon, 1996), 28–29.

This is not to segregate them; rather, it is to highlight the fact that Latina/o migrants have a myriad of historically distinct experiences. We must acknowledge the strength of character and determination of these migrant workers. They are not just people working in the fields; they are our brothers and sisters. Using the analogy of *La Mesa Campesina*, we can invite them to bring their *taburetes* and dine with their *compañeros*—Piers Plowman, Tomás Rivera, César Chávez, and Óscar Romero. In other words, they will be in a faith community that recognizes and celebrates the cultural values and spiritual resources that nurture them. They will find at *La Mesa Campesina* a rich feast that celebrates their life experiences of pilgrimage, mortality, family, prayer, and the sacraments.

Profetas in the Community

GRETCHEN L. AVILA-TORRES

MANY HISPANIC CHRISTIANS IN my circle come from a Pentecostal background. This tradition is especially prominent in Puerto Rico, where I was raised and taught to love God in the Pentecostal Church of God. There are many wonderful things about Pentecostalism. However, my experience and theological learnings led me to be closed, rather than open, to other faith traditions and the wider world. When my husband, Rev. Javier Torres, and I were called to be pastors of Templo Jerusalén Church in Holland, Michigan, we encountered a significant biblical and theological challenge. We felt something was missing in the church. The church was self-contained inside its building, doing church services but barely with a relationship with the community and other churches around it. The church mirrored my own narrow outlook.

As I entered the world of theological education, the walls around me crumbled. My view of Christ and the church widened. I wanted the congregation of Templo Jerusalén to experience this broader sense of Jesus as well. After years of theological study, Javier and I spent several months sharing a wider view of Jesus with our congregation, focusing primarily on the incarnation. Traditionally, Pentecostal churches like ours lean into the divine aspect of Jesus's nature and tend to overlook Christ's humanity. By emphasizing his humanity and developing a richer Christology, Templo Jerusalén's self-image changed. They began to see the incarnation as more than a one-time event and to see they have a role today as the body of Christ. Our congregation has become more open, moves more easily beyond its walls, and partners more readily with other congregations and ministries in developing the kingdom of God.

To better understand the paradigm of incarnational ministry, we begin by reviewing who God is and how the Triune God engages with the world. The one Triune God is eternal and exists in three persons, the Father, the Son, and the Holy Spirit. Humanity knows God through the Scripture that shows the Father, Son, and Holy Spirit working in creation and human history, specifically through Israel's story and the Son's advent in the world. The Triune God is one essence and three persons. God's being is in one another, experiencing a mutual indwelling and communion. The Triune God's Oneness is relational, and none of the persons can be who they are without the other two.

This understanding of the Trinity avoids idolatry and the Trinitarian heresies flowing out of the third and fourth centuries. The Father, Son, and Holy Spirit do not act as independent centers of will and action, and neither does God transition from one person to another to make possible God's action and work in the world. Every person of the One God is involved in every act of God. The Trinity's work in the world is undivided: "God's unity is such that any work that God does is the work of all three persons of the Trinity. Father, Son, and Spirit all, for instance, do the work of creation and redemption."[1] To understand God's work for the sake of human beings and the rest of creation, it is scripturally appropriate sometimes to emphasize the particular role of one person for a specific action because everything comes to us from the Father through the Son and by the Spirit.

The Incarnated Son came into the world showing his ideal relationship with the Father in the Spirit. Also, he portrayed his perfect love to the Father and the Father to the whole of humanity. Jesus is God. He is not an ordinary human being who needed to be adopted by God;

1 Beth Felker-Jones, *Practicing Christian Doctrine: An Introduction to Thinking and Living Theologically* (Grand Rapids, MI: Baker, 2014), 71.

instead, he is the only begotten Son who came to show God's love and redeem all creation. Jesus's divinity is attested to in John 10:30, "The Father and I are one," and John 20:28, when Thomas cries out to the risen Jesus, "My Lord and my God!"[2] The baptismal formula presented in Matthew 28:19 shows equality and no distinction between the Father, the Son, and the Holy Spirit. Christian baptism is administered "in the name of" not three Gods, not two creatures plus one God, not three parts of God, and not three stages of God, but one God who is eternally Father, Son, and Spirit.[3]

I intend to demonstrate how one Pentecostal tradition's position toward discerning Jesus's dual natures has implications for its practice of discipleship. The Pentecostal tradition emphasizes his divine essence more than his humanity, even though we theologically believe that he bears both natures. I will explore how giving less importance to Jesus's human nature negatively affects the church's identity, life, and work. When the church recognizes Jesus's integral being in both essences, it understands Christ's work more deeply as it participates in the Triune God's redeeming plan for all of creation. Ignoring Jesus's incarnation and its consequences for practical theology in the church will bring confusion, an identity crisis, and a tarnished image of God in ministry. Also, a thin Christology might hurt the Church's mission's progress and cause disunity in the body of Christ. I will argue that some deeply rooted traditional convictions regarding the person of Christ can be barriers to the execution of the church's calling.

To help understand this, I invited Bishop Rev. David Vargas, president of the Iglesia de Dios Pentecostal M.I., Region Mediano Oeste[4] in the United States, to discuss the Pentecostal view of the incarnation as it pertains to practical theology. I will present the questions and answers, as well as my perspectives. I am very grateful to Bishop Rev. David Vargas for accepting my invitation and graciously participating in my project.

---

2 Felker-Jones, *Practicing Christian Doctrine*, 63.

3 Thomas C. Oden, *Classic Christianity: A Systematic Theology* (New York: HarperOne, 2009), 115.

4 Pentecostal Church of God International Movement, Midwest Region, English translation.

Q & A with Bishop David Vargas

I began by asking Bishop Vargas this question: What is the Pentecostal Church of God's view concerning the incarnation in terms of practical theology? What is the Pentecostal Church of God, M.I.'s perspective, related to paying closer attention to the incarnation? Bishop Vargas explained that the Church has to understand the purpose of the incarnation. We have to see Jesus's initiative to become human, like you and I, to identify with us for reconciliation with the Father and provide us restoration, hope, and salvation.

I then asked, What is the image of God in the man and woman? Vargas presented his perspective of *imago Dei* in humankind as God's essence of love in them. Jesus came to reveal the Father, a Father of love and peace. I addressed Vargas regarding the creation story in the book of Genesis, trying to analyze his concept of the significance of *imago Dei*. He responded by citing chapter one of Genesis. We appreciate the creation, the beginning of all things. Humans have to realize that a Creator creates them. And to understand what God intended humans to be, they have to know what it means to be humans, so, in Vargas's perspective, they must understand what it means to be created in the image of God. In Genesis 1 and 2, we observe that God created humankind to have a unique and conscious relationship with the Triune God.

When we read Genesis 1 and 2, we find that God created human beings to relate with God, one another, and the rest of the creation. When humankind sinned in Genesis 3, the image of God in humanity was distorted and broken. Sin tarnished the image of God in humans as well as the inherent goodness of nature. The first human creatures' unfaithfulness, listening to the serpent, led them away from God's Word, taking them to disobedience. Still, the first promise of redemption from sin and death was made by God toward humanity. Understanding the *imago Dei* and sin is essential because it leads humans to see that God took humanity seriously (because God's essence is in them). All this is why Jesus, the Son, was sent to become human with the purpose of giving salvation and reconciling the God–human relationship, one another, and the creation. In other words, Jesus restored that image of God in humans through him. Humanity finds its basis in the one real human, Jesus of Nazareth. All this is essential to understanding Jesus's humanity.

Bishop Vargas continued our conversation, saying that it is vital to follow Jesus's praxis of love and divine unconditional initiative toward humanity. Jesus let us know that it is crucial to do everything by love, unconditionally, denying ourselves in favor of others to have a fruitful ministry. We must be that bridge to connect and bring others to have communion with the Father through Christ. Humanly, Christ wanted humanity to retake the position God granted them at the beginning. The only way humanity could retake its former stance from the creation is by Jesus's incarnation.

How Does Vargas Critique the Pentecostal Position on Incarnational Ministry?

I committed myself to this research to understand the missing pieces and some theological and biblical disconnections that the Pentecostal tradition is experiencing as an essential organization. We do not have a clear incarnational stance on practical theology. My eagerness is to see that Jesus's humanity is still in place through his body, the church. Besides the redemption plan accomplished through Jesus, the incarnational church, the church projects that salvation plan to the world. The church is continuing Jesus's ministry on earth. To perform Jesus's roles in ministry in a practical way, the church has to pay closer attention to both of Jesus's natures.

I asked Vargas what the Pentecostal tradition does not understand about the incarnational stance on practical theology. What is the base on which we are standing? What are the influences or inclinations that are making us rely more on a thin Christology? I perceived that Bishop Vargas recognizes the importance of observing the incarnation to have an active ministry, but in practice, in general, I still see a thin Christology in church. Vargas recognizes that some ministers do not understand incarnation well enough to define it. I was not surprised by this statement. I thanked Bishop Vargas very much for his time in the interview, but I was not satisfied with my questions about the position of Christ's humanity in our organization. I think it is necessary to begin discipling through catechism by analyzing different biblical and theological perspectives. It is vital to know God as the Triune God and how he operates in unity in his distinctive persons. Then, we can concentrate on Christ's work and his purpose, not leaving theological anthropology out. In addition to continuing to educate ourselves in the other theological loci to have a broad knowledge of God, creation, Christ, redemption, humanity, and end times, they will lead us to know our real identity in Christ as a church and what is our purpose and mission.

Martin William Mittelstadt observes that Pentecostal Christology, formerly derived primarily from experience, also allows for serious reflection and scholarship.

> Early Pentecostalism was primarily oral because for the first half-century and more, Pentecostals, untrained in academic environments, did not generally engage formal Christology or even the life of Jesus. And when they did, what was written down in tract form, evangelistic booklets, or sermons was almost always—except for denominational statements of faith—appropriated through personal and altar-like responses. However, this non-academic development does not necessarily preclude Pentecostals from conducting sound exegetical discipline and reflection; Pentecostals delight in advancing their pragmatic views of Jesus. Further, while the creeds are not generally taught in order to facilitate proper interpretation of Jesus, Pentecostals tend to rely on the Holy Spirit to reveal the Christ of the Scriptures.[5]

Is this deficiency of understanding the incarnation the reason for the infrequent celebration of the Eucharist? Vargas recognizes that we have been taught not to take the Lord's Supper unworthily because *juicio come para si*, "judgment eats for it." Do we understand the benefits of sitting at the table and the true meaning of the cup and bread? Some traditions talk a lot about judgment but not about benefits. The latter is why some Christians back off in participating in the celebration of the Eucharist, thinking, *I don't take it, and I don't want judgment.* The Lord's Supper projects Jesus's vision for the evangelistic plan for the world. It is crucial to teach Eucharist by the hand of baptism in

---

5 Martin William Mittelstadt, "Christology," in *Encyclopedia of Pentecostal and Charismatic Christianity*, ed. Stanley M. Burgess (London: Routledge, 2006), 98.

discipleship. Doing this way, I believe the people of God will value and come with joy to the Lord's Table.

Why Celebrate the Eucharist?

I asked Vargas why it is important to celebrate the Eucharist. He responded, saying that besides the evangelistic aspect, the Eucharist celebration is a thanksgiving celebration for God's Word and providence and makes us part of the creation. It is the Lord's presence through the power of the Holy Spirit. It is also an invitation to be in community and service. These aspects are vital for our Church to celebrate the Eucharist, leading us to practical theology regularly. We do not want to be merely religious but followers of the footsteps of divine Jesus. Emphasizing the humanity of Jesus will lead us to understand that real spiritual life can be carried along with the biblical paradigm.

Why Is It Essential to Take into Account Jesus's Incarnation in Ministry?

According to Vargas, if we want to have an effective ministry, we must do so out of love, taking into account divine initiative. Jesus became a man and ministered wholeheartedly and unconditionally to teach his disciples and the future church that everything we do in ministry must be out of love and be for others' sakes. We must be bridges to connect people to Christ through the Holy Spirit and bring them to have fellowship with the Father through Christ.

How Does a Thin Christology Have Implications for the Practice of Ministry, Discipleship, and Mission?

I love the way Dr. J. Todd Billings presents the importance of taking into account our participation in Christ. It is vital to observe and follow Jesus's human nature for the practice of ministry, discipleship, and mission. The human Jesus was the One who took around three years to train twelve disciples (I can say more than twelve disciples because he had so many followers) to build his church in mission. According to Billings, we are united to Christ, the Servant; "our participation in

Jesus Christ entails nothing less than entering into an ethic of humble service that reflects the obedient servanthood of Christ."[6]

It is essential to realize that as Christians, we live into our adopted identities as children of God.[7] We did not earn it by our own inherently redemptive action, but through Jesus's humanity-redemptive work. The church cannot ignore or give less importance to Jesus's human essence. Christena Cleveland helps us see what happens when we do not understand and follow what Jesus did in the incarnation and the cross's meaning. First, let's understand that the church is the place where human beings encounter the promise of reconciliation, justice, and the grace of salvation. God provides these things through the Word, the action of Christ on the cross, and the fulfillment of God's promise of human *imago Dei* restoration in his resurrection, which will be fulfilled in the eschaton. Scripture mentions in Revelation 7:9 that people from all nations, tribes, and languages will be united in worshiping the Lord at the end of the times. All of this sounds beautiful as expressed in theory, but what happens when this unity is challenged, when hostility and divisions enter the church? All of this seems simple enough to preach every Sunday, but I have always felt that something is missing.

Cleveland says that categorizing people in the body of Christ according to our perspective of who is a "right" or "wrong" Christian prevents the church from operating at a higher level of integration. Learning from one another will lead us to grow more like Christ. Labels cause an environment of division and hostility that keeps Christians defensively in their individual perspectives, analyzing "them" or "us," right Christians or wrong Christians. These hostilities and divisions create a situation where the Great Commission ceases, restraining our growth in Christ and our ability to reach others. Cleveland says, "I think that our differences enable us to speak richly and directly to the hearts of all types of people."[8] According to Cleveland, in order to follow God, the

6 J. Todd Billings, *Union with Christ: Reframing Theology and Ministry for the Church* (Grand Rapids, MI: Baker, 2011), 148.

7 Billings, *Union with Christ*, 150.

8 Christena Cleveland, *Disunity in Christ* (Downers Grove, IL: InterVarsity Press, 2013), 21.

culturally alike churches must cross into other cultures because that is what Jesus did in the incarnation and the cross.[9]

Suggestions for Challenging Pentecostal Assumptions

I (Torres) have some recommendations that perhaps will challenge the Pentecostal Church of God tradition. I eagerly encourage our organization to require all brothers and sisters called to ministry to pursue vital academic training before engaging in ministry. The organization must have unobstructed and established theological views and liturgical order. I know that we are known to do our worship spontaneously, led by the Holy Spirit, but we must follow the scriptural paradigm. I strongly encourage us to include discipleship in the study of creeds in order to facilitate the proper interpretation of Jesus's life, work, and ministry that we could model as the apostles were able to do. Analyzing and following those creed models, we could end with our own credo from biblical and theological doctrines. Having our credo will help us firmly walk even though we have to accept some biblical concepts by faith because they are still a mystery.

I want to see the Eucharist celebration more integrated and better portrayed in sermons to experience and cultivate our life in communion. The world can experience Jesus through his body. The Eucharist celebration is more than celebrating the human's deliverance from sin or just remembering Jesus's sacrifice on the cross, and having the fear that we might be eating judgment because of our uncertainties of how to follow Jesus.

Knowing Incarnation

The "Image of God in Humans"

How are humans distinct from the rest of creation? Humankind is a creature with whom God has established a unique relationship, and such creatures are called to respond to God. To know what it means to be human, we must know what it means to be created in the *image of God*.[10]

9 Cleveland, *Disunity in Christ*, 21.

10 Felker-Jones, *Practicing Christian Doctrine*, 98.

Humans' uniqueness is that they are created in God's image to have a self-conscious relationship with God. This *imago Dei* in human beings makes it possible to interact with the Triune God and the rest of creation (Psalm 8). To better understand theological anthropology, it is vital to see the human as a creature, a sinner, and a new creation in Christ.

God breaks the creation pattern when God distinctively creates human beings from the rest of creation in God's sovereignty. In contrast to God, human nature is finite, limited, bound, and dependent on its Creator, so humans are not God and cannot be worshiped. The image of God as a strong likeness to God in humans provides a capacity for reason, morality, and the unique ability to love others "or an innate sense of God."[11] What makes human beings uniquely different from other creatures is that humans stand in the middle of spiritual and physical nature. This uniqueness is why humans need to worship. A human soul and body together form an integral being and, when humans are in a relationship with God, cannot be separated. The human being is always one thing, one creature, in life before God.[12]

God is relational. The image of God consists of being social and self-relational: "Our created finitude means that we need each other, that we receive the gift of learning to live with and for another, and above all, that we need God."[13] The *imago Dei* in humans reflects the capacity that humankind has to relate to God and one another, in addition to the God-given authority and responsibilities toward the rest of creation (Gen 1:26; Ps 8:4–8).

Humans are creatures, part of the whole creation. But humans are uniquely created in God's image.[14] This unique characteristic makes it possible for humankind to have a *substantial view* of God's image that allows humans to relate to God in a way that other creatures cannot—to have a *relational view*, to be communal (in a loving relationship with others) and have a *functional view* of that *imago Dei* as caretakers of and stewards over nature.

---

11 Felker-Jones, *Practicing Christian Doctrine*, 105.

12 Felker-Jones, *Practicing Christian Doctrine*, 100.

13 Felker-Jones, *Practicing Christian Doctrine*, 99.

14 Felker-Jones, *Practicing Christian Doctrine*, 105.

These three views of God's image in humans are essential in ministry because they are the Trinity model of relationship and unity. Understanding and applying these views will help churches have a diverse communal life with no biases and will dissolve any politics and policies that divide and denigrate others. These ideas also will help families have a healthy relationship with God, with one another, and with the rest of nature. And as a result, we will experience healthy spiritual, emotional, and physical people in collective service. But to achieve this vibrant communal life, we will need to understand the true nature of our sin and its remedy to foretaste what it means to bear God's image.[15]

In contrast to God, humans are finite, and this makes humans interdependent. Humans need God.[16] Unlike God, humans are limited, bound, and dependent, and they must never be worshiped because they are not God.[17] In contrast to the rest of nature, humans are kind of middle creatures because, according to Felker-Jones, humans stand in the middle of the spiritual and physical creation, and human beings are bodily and spiritually united (psychosomatic unity). This concept is vital because humans cannot split into parts to connect to God; instead, humans interact with God with their integral being. Christian theological anthropology rejects any dualistic doctrine such as materialism.[18] It also rejects holistic dualism, which denies the spiritual and physical natures of humanity.[19]

The First Adam as an Image of the Whole

When humankind sinned in Genesis 3, the image of God in humanity was distorted and broken. Sin tarnished the image of God in humans as well as the inherent goodness of nature. It deeply fractured the relationships between God and humans, between different humans, and between humans and the rest of creation. In short, sin is always

15 Felker-Jones, *Practicing Christian Doctrine*, 107.

16 Felker-Jones, *Practicing Christian Doctrine*, 99. Our created finitude means that we need each other, through which we receive the gift of learning to live with one another, and, above all, that we need God.

17 Felker-Jones, *Practicing Christian Doctrine*, 99.

18 Felker-Jones, *Practicing Christian Doctrine*, 102.

19 Felker-Jones, *Practicing Christian Doctrine*, 103.

a violation of bond. The unfaithfulness of the first human creatures led them away from God's Word, taking them to disobedience, which was the main reason for humanity's fall.[20] The original sin affected and infected humanity and the rest of creation (Rom 8:22).[21] Romans 5:12 says, "Therefore, just as sin entered the world through one man, and death through sin, and in this way death came to all people because all sinned" (NIV).

Does all this mean that we can no longer talk about the *imago Dei* in humans because of our sinful nature? Humans inherited transgression and death from Adam. But from and through the Second Adam, Jesus the Son of God, humanity inherits righteousness and eternal life! Adam's story is every human's story because he stands in a legal relationship representing the entire human race.[22] But humanity is still making its personal choice by executing its own decisions and sin, and they are responsible for it. No one denies that humans have the freedom of choice to do what they most want to do. In this sense, humans have *liberum arbitrium* (free will). When humans do not want God leading their lives, they practice a *liberum arbitrium captivatum* (captive free will), which leads them to sin. Human beings require *liberum arbitrium liberatum* (liberated free will), which can only come through God.

The Second Adam as an Image of the Whole

Christ's righteousness is applied to the rest of humans if we believe in Jesus's death and resurrection and we live our human lives through him. Human wickedness is not the end of humankind's story; instead, we have good news that humanity experiences new creation in Christ. Human *imago Dei* is restored through the work and obedience of the Second Adam, Jesus Christ: "For God was pleased to have all his fullness dwell in him [Jesus], and through him to reconcile to himself all

20 John Calvin, *Institutes of the Christian Religion*, II.I. 4.

21 Calvin, *Institutes*, II. I. 8. Original sin, therefore, seems to be a hereditary depravity and corruption of our nature, diffused into all parts of the soul, which first makes us liable to God's wrath, then also brings forth in us those works that the Scripture calls "works of the flesh" (Gal 5:19–21, NRSV).

22 Felker-Jones, *Practicing Christian Doctrine*, 112.

things, whether things on earth or things in heaven, by making peace through his blood, shed on the cross" (Col 1:19–20, NIV).

The great love of God is this: that the Sovereign Lord did not let sin define humans; instead, Jesus Christ defines our humanity.[23] God's work as Creator, Redeemer, and Sustainer gives rise to viewing human beings as creatures created in God's image, an image distorted by sin, and redeemed by the work, death, and resurrection of Jesus Christ that will be completed at the eschaton.

Historical Jesus Perspectives and Some Heresies in General

Throughout the church's history, the most controversial debate in Christology has concerned the person and work of Jesus Christ. Some modern theologians have determined that it is not logical to conceive Christ as both human and God, and they seek to investigate the life of the historical Jesus based on this perspective. In the early church, if the challenge was accepting the full deity of Jesus, the Hellenistic problem was his full humanity.[24] The heresy of Docetism is the Greek challenge to Christ's full humanity. The Docetists held that Christ's humanity is merely an appearance instead of real. For them, Jesus only seemed to be human.

In the book *Incarnation: The Person and Life of Christ*, Thomas F. Torrance argues that the whole picture of the person, life, and work of Jesus, including his task of revelation, redemption, and reconciliation, can only be understood in the light of his two natures, human and God in one person, through the profound significance of Christ's virgin birth into humanity.

Torrance discusses the significance of the virgin birth: "The Once and For All Union of God and Man: Christ's Birth into our Humanity." Even the Gospels are witnesses of the virgin birth of Jesus, and they present it in their point of view, intending to highlight that Jesus

---

23 Felker-Jones, *Practicing Christian Doctrine*, 115. "Who is the 'image'? The answer is, 'Jesus Christ.'" As we practice theological anthropology, we learn that *true* human being is a gift, and we receive it through Christ by the power of his resurrection. We will learn, in the power of the Holy Spirit, to be faithful bearers of the image of God, to be transformed, body and soul, into Christlikeness.

24 Michael Scott Horton, *The Christian Faith: A Systematic Theology for Pilgrims on the Way* (Grand Rapids, MI: Zondervan, 2011), 471.

comes from above. Matthew and Luke portray the virgin birth of Jesus and his childhood, but Mark does not. Perhaps Mark omitted Joseph's appearance to emphasize quite explicitly Jesus's divinity. All this about the virgin birth is significant because through this sign, grace comes to utter humanity. From the first epistle of John 5:18, "We know that anyone born of God does not sin, but he who was born of God keeps himself" (NKJV). That is, it is from Christ's unique virgin birth once and for all that our new childbirth depends, where the new creation is shared, and this is the heart of baptism.

The miracle of the virgin birth marked a new beginning for humankind. In the book of Galatians, the apostle Paul reaffirms that humans partake of Christ in baptism and his Spirit of sonship. According to Torrance, the virgin reveals that the second Adam comes from heaven and comes into existence from a woman: "As such, Jesus Christ is the firstborn of the new creation, the head of a new race in perfect union with God."[25] Torrance argues that we cannot disconnect the virgin birth from the resurrection because a relationship exists between the birth of Jesus of the Virgin Mary and the resurrection of Christ from a virgin tomb. The latter event brought a new life, a metamorphic life for humankind. The real human by God's union with man restored the distorted image of God caused by sin, and the empty tomb points to God's revelation through our humanity. However, the birth of Jesus was no act of human cooperation. All this is why the man in the person of Joseph is set aside.

According to Torrance, we can perceive in absolute intensity what took place in the life of Israel: "the election of the one as the instrument of the divine love for the redemption of all."[26] The Triune God made a covenantal relationship with Israel to portray God's Word, but they could not accomplish it, so we see the Word made flesh in the unity of the person and work of Christ. This continuous union in the life of Jesus is the ultimate fulfillment and the complete integration of God's Word and will in our humanity.

---

25 Thomas F. Torrance, *Incarnation: The Person and Life of Christ* (Downers Grove, IL: InterVarsity Press, 2008), 94.

26 Torrance, *Incarnation*, 109.

God became a revelation to the nations through Israel. The Triune God establishes a covenant relationship with Israel, saying, "I will be your God, and you will be my people." Jesus is the fulfillment of this covenant in his nature because he is the One who is God with us and fulfills the human side of the pact. Jesus is coming from Israel's seed because he fulfills the promise; he is the covenant's climax. In Christ, God communicates to humanity his very self, and he is the eternal election of love and the everlasting covenant. We know God through Christ's deeds and the relationship of the Son with the Father. Torrance continues pointing to the person of Christ, who is the atoning sacrifice on the cross because Jesus enters our flesh as a mediator, standing in our place, showing the faithfulness of covenant grace and the love of God in front of the unfaithfulness of humans. The Son is the judge and the judged one at the same time; he is both God choosing and the chosen man. In the Son, God binds humanity forever to himself and condemns sin in his holy flesh life, and at the same time, he sanctifies human beings to God. Torrance says that the life and work of Jesus as the Son of God restored humans' communion with God. The person and deed of Christ and the continuous union to his life make it possible to humanize the inhumanity after the fall by restoring the divine Sonship, the image of God.

The person and life of Christ, according to Torrance, is characterized by obedience, prayer, and faithfulness to the Father. Jesus is the perfect example of the utter submission to the Triune God's purpose of creation and redemption. Torrance presents the Spirit's role in the person and life of Christ through his human development and ministry. The Spirit of Christ is the same Spirit that Jesus pours out to the church.

In the book *Christian Theology*, Millard J. Erickson describes how Christ's mystery inspired some modern theologians to search for the historical Jesus with the expectation of discovering that the real Jesus was different from the Christ who appears in the Gospels and to Paul in Acts.[27] Erickson continually portrays those points of view, saying that the earthly Jesus was increasingly described as a basic good man, a great spiritual teacher, but not the preexistent Second Person of the

27 Millard J. Erickson, *Christian Theology* (Grand Rapids, MI: Baker, 1998), 679.

Trinity, the One who operates miracles.[28] Erickson also presents other researchers, led by Rudolf Bultmann. Bultmann concluded that the story of Jesus is surrounded by myth and that the point of understanding Christianity is reinterpreting the legend to learn how Jesus influenced his disciples and people around him.[29]

Rosemary Radford Ruether describes the role of Jesus in the redemptive plan of salvation for the whole of humanity as quite different in feminist theology. Ruether argues that Jesus's performance in the redemption history is a root story for the redemptive process in which we must all be engaged, but he does not and cannot do it for us.[30] Instead, she presents her theological point that Jesus is only the foundation of the redemptive process that we must all be committed to being part of.

According to Ruether, Jesus's "story can model what we need to do, but it happens only when all of us do it for ourselves and with one another."[31] Humans liberate themselves by continuing Jesus's example of opposing the religious and political structures on behalf of the oppressed, particularly on behalf of women. In this way, according to Ruether, following Jesus's praxis will lead us to overcome hierarchical social structures. Jesus's story resonates with Christian feminists as echoing and founding their own story.

According to Ruether, the patriarchal system is sin, and redemption is the liberation from that patriarchal structure. Ruether's desire is that the church would call people to repent from that hierarchical structure and patriarchy, and she urges the church to see its calling to redemption as liberation from patriarchy. Ruether insists that this Christian feminist theological position is the real gospel of Jesus.

---

28 Erickson, *Christian Theology*, 679. "Among the more famous early 'lives of Jesus' were those produced by David Strauss, *A New Life of Jesus*, 2nd ed. (London: Williams & Norgate, 1879), and Ernest Renan, *Life of Jesus*, trans. and rev. from the 23rd French ed. (New York: Grosset & Dunlap, 1856)."

29 Erickson, *Christian Theology*, 677.

30 Rosemary Radford Ruether, "C. Rosemary Radford Ruether (1936–)," in *A Journey through Christian Theology*, ed. William P. Anderson (Minneapolis: Fortress Press, 2010), 397.

31 Ruether, "C. Rosemary Radford Ruether (1936–)," 397.

Ruether does not present any idea of Jesus sacrificing his life to redeem and reconcile humanity with the Father. The human being does not obtain redemption by Jesus's suffering and death, which represents the victory of oppressors who wanted to silence him. Instead, we need to imitate Jesus's example of protesting against injustice and defending life.

The soteriological issue from Christian feminist theology that struck me the most is that it invalidates the redemptive work of Jesus's suffering and death on the cross on behalf of humans. I have the perception that Ruether believes that Jesus rose in a religious movement to overcome the ecclesial patriarchy and establish a subversive legacy of power against the ethical and social structures that marginalized the poor and despised, mostly women. I wonder where the eschatological hope and view from Jesus's resurrection is. What are Ruether's perspectives on the Trinity, Christology, and Creation? Ruether's feminist theology is missing the incarnation part of Jesus in the human redemption story.

This feminist theology denies the cross and the atoning sacrifice of Jesus, the Son of God, to redeem humanity and the rest of creation. To counteract this Christian feminist theology, we have to present the God of covenants and look back to the Old Testament background. God, through Moses, delivered the covenant to the people with his commands and warrants. To seal this pact, Moses took blood and threw it upon the people of Israel, expressing words for them to obey (Exod 24:1–8). They could not fulfill their commission, and they were banished from their promised land. Like Adam and Eve, they could not meet their calling of a spiritualized christological faithfulness and obedience, and they were expelled from the garden. As Michael Scott Horton expresses it, "There is nothing that the covenant people can do to reconcile themselves to God."[32]

The new covenant has been fulfilled in Jesus Christ.[33] The key to counteracting feminist theology is the Last Supper that Jesus provided to his disciples, saying, "Drink from it, all of you; for this is my blood of the covenant, which is poured out for many for the forgiveness of sin" (Matt 26:26–28, NRSV). In Leviticus, an animal victim is presented as

32 Horton, *The Christian Faith*, 493.

33 1 Cor 11:25; Heb 9:15; 12:24.

a substitutional sacrifice for the convict, and in Isaiah 53, the prophet singles out the suffering servant that has its fulfillment in Jesus's suffering and death on the cross. Jesus is the Lamb of God provided in our place. Also, we see Jesus's exaltation through his resurrection, beginning a new creation and kingdom that ultimately will be accomplished at the eschaton. In his ascension, he was seated by his Father's right hand. The passion, cross, and resurrection are the real gospel of Jesus.

Yes, Jesus's ministry focused on the oppressed and needy, mostly seen as women. His ministry focused attention on the forsaken and marginalized, and in so doing, it modeled the true religion, the real relationship that God expects us to have with each other. Yes, women bear the image of God like men. Both of them were created in the image of God, according to Genesis 1:27. After the fall, sin distorted the creation's goodness, and Jesus, the second Adam, representing the whole of humanity, restored and redeemed it by his blood.

This feminist theology does not provide what we need for ministry because it does not give ultimate hope, an eschatological future in which the kingdom of God is established. Instead, it portrays Jesus's sacrificial redemption as mythological. No hope, no salvation, no resurrection to experience a new creation. Where will be our faith and assurance for now and our eschatological future?

What Is Normative Christology?

Christ's work reflects the pattern of the One for the sake of the many, conforming to Genesis. Also, Christ's deeds are fulfilled at the eschaton, in line with the book of Revelation. Sin brought the curse that had a universal effect. The Triune God already had a plan to redeem the whole of humanity. After the fall, the plan of salvation started to unfold a pattern of significant elections on behalf of humankind. In Genesis 1–11, we encounter the big picture of the development of that pattern. In Genesis 12, the model narrows to a particular one as God establishes a covenantal relationship intended for all humanity but portrayed in one person. God singles out Abraham to bless him and to be a channel of blessing to the nations: "The Abrahamic blessing is more than the blessing of creation because it is designed to contend with and to overcome its opposite: God's curse."[34]

God becomes a revelation to the nations through Israel. The Triune God establishes a covenant relationship with Israel, saying, "I will walk among you and be your God, and you shall be my people" (Lev 26:12, NKJV). Jesus is the fulfillment of this covenant in his nature because he is the One who can embody the perfect God with us and fulfill the human side of the pact.

Jesus comes from Israel's seed and fulfills God's covenant. Jesus is the perfect image of God in humanity, the ideal covenant partner, and an exact model of the relationship with God. All this is why "you are in Christ" instead of "you are in covenant."

To understand Christ's work, we have to refer to Christ's threefold offices as Prophet, Priest, and King. Jesus is the telos of the covenant. In his role as Prophet, Jesus proclaimed the Word of God to Israel. He is the Word of God, incarnated. According to Horton, prophets proclaim the truth, and Jesus is the truth. Jesus, as Priest, embodies the temple himself. In his Priesthood ministry, he continues his office as a Mediator and Intercessor for humanity to the Father. Jesus's priesthood comes not through the line of Aaron but through Melchizedek. In Jesus's resurrection and ascension, his Kingship is established, and his Father exalts him. Jesus's Kingship began at the creation and is assured of his obedience to the cross. It will bring fulfillment of life at the eschaton. As Horton puts it, "The Son reflects the Father's glory in eternity as well as in time."[35]

The work of God at the cross is the saving plan of God toward humanity. The cross is not something that overtakes Jesus, but something he undertakes.[36] The cross is a key context in which we see the contrast and complexity of humanity and divinity. The cross is the place of victory. Through the cross, Jesus took all the barriers away that prevent human beings from relating to God freely, and he provided restoration of the fullness of life.

---

34 Richard Bauckham, *Bible and Mission* (Grand Rapids, MI: Baker, 2003), 35.

35 Horton, *The Christian Faith*, 522.

36 John 10:18: "No one takes it from me, but I lay it down of my own accord. I have power to lay it down, and I have power to take it up again. I have received this command from my Father" (NRSV).

Jesus is the redeemer who set us free from slavery to sin. God does not owe anything to the devil; instead, Jesus set us free from sin. The cross reminds us that we depend on and we need Christ to conquer sin. Jesus is the perfect lamb offered in sacrifice for many. The cross does not connect to lots of shame. The cross was God's provision of salvation to creation, and this event is the blessing from the One to the many. God is a God of the covenant, and here at the cross, God is accomplishing in Christ the pact made to Abraham, Isaac, and Jacob. Reconciliation is not just for us but for all creation.[37] The sacrifices of Christ on the cross restored our relationship with God. The work of Jesus on the cross is more than just forgiveness, but establishes a formative, restored, new relationship with God through the Spirit. Humanity cannot be saved by itself. Jesus, in the representation of us, died on the cross to undo the damage of sin. Jesus bears in our place the punishment of sin, so God is satisfied. The cross is the ultimate expression of the love of the Trinity toward us.

Through his ministry, the work of Jesus provided a bit of that victory consummated on his resurrection, ascension, the descending of the Spirit in Pentecost, and Christ's triumphant return in glory.[38] Jesus is risen from the dead by the power of the Spirit, and we will experience the same at the end of ages.

Jesus did not remain dead at the tomb; he has risen in body and spirit. He rose in a physically transformed, glorified new body, giving us the guarantee of a newly embodied life after death (humans will not be mere immortals), and our bodies will be transformed like his to enjoy the glorious future with Christ at the eschaton. In Jesus, the kingdom has come, and this is sustaining us in between times. Jesus's resurrection is the affirmation of the goodness of God's creation, especially of human bodies. God has a glorious future for the whole of

---

37 Romans 8:20–23: "For the creation was subjected to futility, not of its own will but by the will of the one who subjected it, in hope that the creation itself will be set free from its bondage to decay and will obtain the freedom of the glory of the children of God. We know that the whole creation has been groaning in labor pains until now; and not only the creation, but we ourselves, who have the first fruits of the Spirit, groan inwardly while we wait for adoption, the redemption of our bodies" (NRSV).

38 Horton, *The Christian Faith*, 522.

creation. Jesus's resurrection is the guarantee of the glorious new creation at the eschaton. Jesus is present and lives in our hearts by the Holy Spirit. Bodily, Jesus is by the right hand of the Father.

God exalted Jesus in the ascension. The ascension is the guarantee of the return of Jesus in glory. It is the establishment of his kingdom, restoring Israel's inheritance that will have its fulfillment at the eschaton; Jesus's ascension is the blessing warranty not only over Israel but also over all nations on earth at the eschaton. In Jesus's heavenly exaltation, he continues performing all three offices. As a prophet, Jesus continues to proclaim God's Word through his body, the church. Jesus's priesthood continues in heaven by interceding for us to the Father. Christ reigns in grace now and will return in judgment and justification, and his kingdom will be consummated in everlasting glory.[39]

Conclusion

This study explored how giving less importance to Jesus's humanity negatively affects the church's identity, life, and work. When the church recognizes Jesus's integral being in both essences, it will understand Christ's work more deeply, both theologically and practically, in terms of how the church participates in the Triune God's redeeming plan for all of creation. Ignoring Jesus's incarnation and its consequences for practical theology in the church, a thin Christology brings confusion, identity crisis, and a tarnishing image of God in ministry, hurting the progress of the church's mission and causing disunity in the body of Christ. In my Pentecostal tradition experience, I notice that in practice, we emphasize Jesus's divine essence more than his humanity even though we theologically believe Jesus bears both natures. I explore how one Pentecostal tradition's position toward discerning Jesus's dual natures has implications for its practice of discipleship. Even though I did not come out with many conclusions, I had the opportunity to help our bishop recognize the need to structure our biblical and unanimous theological standard for a healthy spiritual and physical community and ministry growth.

39 Horton, *The Christian Faith*, 533.

3

Profetas of Evangelism

ELIEZER VALENTÍN-CASTAÑÓN

THIS ESSAY WILL EXPLORE a definition of evangelism from a prophetic, liberating, and Wesleyan perspective. Still, we must recognize that as we engage in this exploration, we run up against a misguided understanding of evangelism in most of Christianity that is antithetical to Jesus's teachings and lifestyle. In other words, I will argue that we have come to accept the gospel of Jesus the Messiah as an imperial theological discourse, which condones, endorses, and sustains the powers of domination and oppression of this world. Although this imperial Christian discourse speaks of a God of love and compassion, when we look at its application, what we find is the liberating "good news" proclaimed by Jesus being used as a weapon of oppression in the arms of the powers and principalities of this world: the principalities (*archas*), the authorities (*exousias*), the world-powers (*kosmokratoras*), as we read in Ephesians 6:12.[1] In this imperial Christian tradition, we have come

1 For a powerful discussion on these forces see the work of Walter Wink, *Naming the Powers: The Language of Power in the New Testament* (Philadelphia: Fortress Press, 1987), 13–98. Also, the work of Michael J. Gorman, *Apostle of the Crucified Lord: A Theological Introduction to Paul and His Letters* (Grand Rapids, MI: Eerdmans, 2004), 506–28. And also, Justo L. González, *Three Months with Paul* (Nashville: Abingdon Press, 2006), 164–65. For additional analysis see Dieter Georgi's essay "God Turned Upside Down," 148–57; Helmut Koester's essay "Imperial Ideology and Paul's Eschatology in 1 Thessalonians," 158–66; and Neil Elliott's essay "The Anti-Imperial Message of the Cross," 167–83, in *Paul and Empire: Religion and*

to place Jesus at the service of the world's empires, the powerful, and every economic ideology that supports personal gain at the expense of humanity's well-being.[2]

Through the imperial Christian message, we have turned Jesus's proclamation into the sanctioner of the status quo in every generation.[3] This imperial Christianity turned Jesus into the "glorious king," the one who is all powerful and perfect. This imperial Jesus substituted the peasant Jew who rose from an impoverished working-class family, who came from an unknown little hamlet called Nazareth, and who was crucified by the Roman forces occupying Palestine for proclaiming an anti-imperialist message of human liberation, of God's salvation. Over the centuries, this imperial Christianity turned the anti-imperialist Jesus into one who seems to have accepted the offer Satan made to him in the desert.[4] The Jesus most of us have come to know in the Christian world seems to have bowed down to Satan, therefore, to all the powers and principalities of this world.

This imperial-victorious Christianity has created a vision of the Godhead as an all-powerful (omnipotent), all-knowing (omniscient), and ever-present (omnipresent) being—a God who is so beyond us (so transcendent), that God becomes out of reach for us mere mortals. This

---

Power in Roman Imperial Society, ed. Richard A. Horsley (Harrisburg, PA: Trinity Press International, 1997). See also Nicholas Thomas Wright's work *Paul: A Biography* (San Francisco: HarperOne, 2018), 298–301.

2 See Franz J. Hinkelammert, *The Ideological Powers of Death: A Theological Critique of Capitalism* (Maryknoll, NY: Orbis, 1986), 150–52.

3 See Leonardo Boff, *Pasión de Cristo, Pasión del Mundo* (Bogotá: Indo-American Press Service, 1973). See also the work of Samuel Silva Gotay, *El pensamiento cristiano revolucionario en América Latina y el Caribe: Implicaciones de la teología de la liberación para la sociología de la religión* (Río Piedras, Puerto Rico: Ediciones Huracán, 1983). And, Gustavo Gutiérrez's work, *Teología de la liberación: Perspectivas* (Salamanca, Spain: Editorial Sígueme, 1972). This matter comes alive every time church leaders quote Romans 13 as a way to justify the actions of states, emperors, and those in power; it almost calls us to a blind obedience to the *archas*, the *exousias*, the *kosmocratoras* of this world (Eph 6:12) under the guise of obedience to God.

4 "Again, the devil took him to a very high mountain and showed him all the kingdoms of the world and their splendor. 'All this I will give you,' he said, 'if you will bow down and worship me'" (Matt 4:8–9, NIV).

imperial Christianity presents us with a God who is distant and unconcerned with our human frailties. This ideation of the Godhead has left us convinced that God, whom we are told loves us, is only interested in us if we are concerned with a "spiritual holiness" that will lead us out of this world and into the perfect world where God resides (in heaven). This theological discourse has presented us with a reading of Matthew's heaven as a place far, far away.[5] Although this idea of heaven is sustained in antiquity,[6] the fact is that in the New Testament, heaven, as the final destination for our salvation, is not actually the final place for those who believe. In the New Testament, God has brought heaven to earth (e.g., Matt 2:1–11; John 1:14; 2 Cor 5:18–20; Phil 2:1–8). Therefore, God's place is now present among us because God is among us; God has pitched his tent among us (as the Greek says in John 1:14). This is what the incarnation has done. The amazing act of God's salvation establishes that God's new place of residence (ergo heaven) is among us.

On the other hand, the neo-Platonic imperial theology of the Godhead expressed in the desire to maintain heaven as something separate from us certainly fits a political ideology of alienation, where human

---

5 While Matthew primarily uses the term *kingdom of heaven* (more than thirty-two times), and other Gospel writers (notably Luke) use the term *kingdom of God*, it is clear that these two expressions mean exactly the same thing (compare Matt 5:3 with Luke 6:20). The term *kingdom of God* occurs four times in Matthew (12:28; 19:24; 21:31; 21:43), fourteen times in Mark, thirty-two times in Luke, twice in the Gospel of John (3:3, 5), six times in Acts, eight times in Paul, and once in Revelation (12:10). In the past, some have tried to maintain a distinction between the kingdom of heaven and the kingdom of God; see Matthew Henry, *An Exposition of the Old and New Testament* (New York: R. Carter & Brothers, 1856), 4:158; C. I. Scofield, ed., *The Scofield Reference Study Bible* (New York: Oxford University Press, 1996), 1003; Michael Pearl, *Eight Kingdoms: And Then There Was ONE* (Pleasantville, TN: No Greater Joy Ministries, 2006). However, the vast majority of theologians today recognize the terms as synonymous; see the works of William MacDonald, *Believer's Bible Commentary* (Nashville: Thomas Nelson Publishers, 1995); J. Dwight Pentecost, *Things to Come* (Grand Rapids, MI: Zondervan, 1970); Charles C. Ryrie, *Basic Theology* (Wheaton, IL: Victor Books, 1991); and others.

6 See especially chapter 5 of Paul B. Sumner, "The Divine Council in Second Temple Judaism and the New Testament" (PhD diss., Pepperdine University, April 1991), www.hebrew-streams.org/works/hebrew/divinecouncil-ch5.pdf.

beings have to be concerned only with getting to heaven, where they will be saved. In a way, this is the epitome of neo-Platonic theology, which makes God's dwelling, heaven, God's prison; according to this imperial theological understanding, a perfect God can only be perfect when separated from humanity's imperfection and corruption.

This imperial Christian theology has also used the Gospel of John to justify this view of the Godhead, a God that is more concerned with Godself than with humanity's misery: "The hour is coming, and is now here, when the *true worshipers* will worship the Father in *spirit and truth*, for *the Father seeks* such as these to worship him. God is spirit, and those who worship him must worship in spirit and truth" (4:23–24, NRSV, italics mine).[7] I am not suggesting that this is what John was trying to convey to readers in the early church. My argument is that the text has been used to that end.

This passage has been used with the purpose of making people believe that if they are to reach God, they can only do it through prayer, fasting, reading of Scripture, worship, retreats, and so on, because these are the instruments to encounter the divine.[8] We are left with the clear message that the only way to reach this God is by moving to a level of existence that is beyond our means, which God makes available through constant "spiritual" disciplines, which then will elevate us to the mystical plane where the Godhead resides. In other words, it is only by being in constant alienation from the world that we find the true God "who art in heaven" (Matt 6:9).

We have been told that these are the things Christians must care about because they will take us to heaven—again, a mystical place out of this reality. So, if we love Jesus, have faith in Jesus, everything will

---

7 Other Scripture used with this intention (though I am not suggesting this is the right use of the passages) include Ps 51:17; 145:18; Isa 57:15; Matt 15:8, 9; 2 Cor 3:17; Phil 3:3; and more.

8 See articles such as David Mathis, "Worship in Spirit and Truth," Desiring God, January 5, 2014, www.desiringgod.org/articles/worship-in-spirit-and-truth; "How Can I Worship the Lord in Spirit and Truth (John 4:23-24)? What Is True Worship?," Compelling Truth, accessed November 13, 2019, www.compellingtruth.org/true-worship-spirit-truth.html; or C. H. Spurgeon, "Sermon #3464: True Worship" (sermon, Metropolitan Tabernacle, London, September 1, 1870), www.spurgeongems.org/vols61-63/chs3464.pdf. These are just illustrations of this view.

be taken care of by this God once we get to heaven. Heaven is our destination and our reward; it is where salvation will actually occur, for this world is corrupt and, after all, belongs to the devil (as the passage in Matt 4:1–10 seems to imply).[9]

Notwithstanding, in many Christian communities, spiritual disciplines are only tangentially connected to addressing worldly concerns because as concerned as God can be for our worldly challenges, the reality is that these challenges are temporary inconveniences until we make it to heaven. After all, all human suffering is fleeting until we make it to heaven.[10] And yet, this imperial Christianity has developed a theology that will accommodate these conditions and argued that they are due to our sinful nature; therefore, there is not much we can do about them. This imperial theology sustains the notion that things will get better someday. In the meantime, we live and wait until we get to heaven. At the end, the world as we know it will be consumed, and the "kingdom of God" will be established on earth at the *parousia*.

We must give St. Augustine, the bishop of Hippo, the honor of starting to frame this theology for Christianity. From Augustine's understanding we must realize that these worldly challenges and human experiences are the result of our totally corrupted nature.[11] According to John Calvin, a great follower of St. Augustine, there is no glimmer of the nature of God.[12] Therefore, whatever we can do to

---

9 See, for example, the autobiography of Cardinal Robert Sarah, *God or Nothing: A Conversation on Faith* (San Francisco: Ignatius Press, 2015); Andrew Murray's work *The Spiritual Life: Undeniable Ways to Conquer the Flesh and Grow in Christ* (Apollo, PA: Ichthus Publications, 2015); and many others.

10 I am not trying to be cynical in this representation. I do not mean to imply that Christians do not care for human suffering. Many Christians do. The point I am making here is that the theology we use in many of our imperial churches is only concerned with taking us to heaven, whereas the point of the incarnation is how to bring heaven (the place where God is) to earth (the place God gave God's all to save, as expressed by Paul in Phil 2:5–11).

11 For a great description of Augustine's thought see Justo L. González, *A History of Christian Thought*, vol. 2, *From Augustine to the Eve of the Reformation* (Nashville: Abingdon Press, 1975).

12 For an in-depth description of Calvin's doctrine of total depravity, as espoused by the Synod of Dordrecht, see Herman Hanko, Homer Hoeksema, and Gise J. Van

ameliorate the impact of human suffering and pain is fine, as long as we do not pretend to work to end the suffering in the world, because only God can do that.[13] Although we understand only God can ultimately end evil in the world, this theology will lead Christians to inaction and resignation; we must endure suffering for a little while longer until the end comes, when God will make all things new.

However, it is within this context that John Wesley would criticize his Christian generation as the Christianity of the Constantinian Church, the church of the empire with its concomitant theological construction, a church that turned Jesus into a puppet of the empire. In "Sermon 66: The Signs of the Times," Wesley said:

> Thousands of those who bear the name of Christ are now given up to an undiscerning mind. The god of this world hath so blinded their eyes, that the light cannot shine upon them; so that they can no more discern the signs of the times, than the Pharisees and Sadducees could of old. A wonderful instance of this spiritual blindness, this total inability to discern the signs of the times mentioned in Scripture, is given us in the very celebrated work of a late eminent writer; who supposes, the New Jerusalem came down from heaven, when Constantine the Great called himself a Christian. I say, called himself a Christian; for I dare not affirm that he was one, any more than Peter the Great. I cannot but believe, he would have come nearer the mark, if he had said, that it was the time when a huge cloud of infernal brimstone and smoke came up from the bottomless pit! For surely there never was a time wherein Satan gained so fatal an advantage over the Church of Christ, as when such a flood of riches, and honour, and power broke in upon it, particularly on the Clergy![14]

Baren, *The Five Points of Calvinism* (Grandville, MI: Reformed Free Publishing Association, 1976), www.prca.org/fivepoints/index.html.

13 Although I agree with the principle that only God can bring human suffering to its final end, the fact of the matter is that the God that was in Jesus has called us to join God in God's mission to save the world.

14 John Wesley, "The Signs of the Times," *The Sermons of John Wesley*, sermon 66, §2, ¶7, Wesley Center Online, http://wesley.nnu.edu/john-wesley/the-sermons-of-john-wesley-1872-edition/sermon-66-the-signs-of-the-times/. See also the same

But Wesley is not the only one to make this criticism of the Christian church. Other Christian authors like Justo González are critical of the imperial church, which made the Christian religion the official religion of the Roman Empire.

> [During the reign of Constantine] these new conditions also had their negative consequences. In the first place, there soon began mass conversion that inevitably detracted from the depth of conviction and the moral life of the church. Secondly, the imperial protection made it easier for the powerful to join the church and to seek to retain and exert their power within the community of faith. Finally, the same protection, which gave Christians the possibility of developing their theology to an extent that was previously impossible, also implied the possibility of imperial condemnation or favor to one theological position or another, and this in turn gave theological controversies a political dimension that they had not previously had.[15]

---

sentiment expressed by John Wesley in a letter he wrote on January 4, 1749, to Dr. Conyers Middleton: "Because, 'after the empire became Christian' (they are your own words), 'a general corruption both of faith and morals infected the Christian Church; which by that revolution, as St. Jerome says, "lost as much of her virtue as it had gained of wealth and power"' (page 123). And this very reason St. Chrysostom himself gave in the words you have afterwards cited: 'There are some who ask, Why are not miracles performed still? Why are there no persons who raise the dead and cure diseases?' To which he replies, that it was owing to the want of faith and virtue and piety in those times." John Wesley to Dr. Conyers Middleton, 4 January 1749, Wesley Center Online, accessed November 13, 2019, http://wesley.nnu.edu/john-wesley/the-letters-of-john-wesley/wesleys-letters-1749/. John Wesley, sermon 2, "The Almost Christian" (St. Mary's, Oxford, July 25, 1741), http://wesley.nnu.edu/john-wesley/the-sermons-of-john-wesley-1872-edition/sermon-2-the-almost-christian/.

15 Justo González, *A History of Christian Thought*, vol. 1, *From the Beginnings to the Council of Chalcedon* (Nashville: Abingdon Press, 1987), 262. See also Justo González, *The Story of Christianity*, vol. 1 (New York: HarperCollins, 2010), 147–48. "This situation changed drastically with the advent of Constantine and the peace of the church. Now one could be both a good Roman and a good Christian. Following the lead of the emperor, the Romanized classes flocked to the church. Others from the same social strata who had been converted earlier saw this as a

This critique of the church raised by many Christians throughout the centuries also explains how the gospel the church has been proclaiming has left some important components out, which I believe to be essential to the full sense of what it means to evangelize from a Latin-prophetic, liberating, and Wesleyan perspective.[16]

In this exploration I believe we should start with the oldest records available to us today: the Pauline letters. From the late 40s CE and until his martyrdom in the 60s CE, Paul wrote letters to the churches that he founded (or guided). These are the earliest Christian writings that the church has, and in them Paul speaks of "the gospel" (*euangelion*) (1 Thess 1, 2, 3). Yet it seems as if Paul's understanding of the gospel (the *euangelion tou theu*) he preached was pretty much consistent with the stories contained in the Synoptic Gospels. Paul speaks of the good news (the gospel) as the proclamation of the good news of God or about God—that is to say, what God is doing in the world today. This is where our challenge to the imperial Christian theology begins.[17]

---

positive development, for their earlier decision was now corroborated by that of other important people. But Christians from the lower classes tended to see the new developments as a process of corruption of the church. What these Christians had always hated in the Roman empire was now becoming part of the church. Soon the powerful—those who controlled politics and the economy—would also control the church."

16 See, for example, Johannes Roldanus, *The Church in the Age of Constantine: The Theological Challenges* (New York: Routledge, 2006); Richard J. Mouw: *The Challenges of Cultural Discipleship: Essays in the Line of Abraham Kuyper* (Grand Rapids, MI: Eerdmans, 2011); and H. A. Drake, *Constantine and the Bishops: The Politics of Intolerance* (Baltimore: Johns Hopkins University Press, 2002); among others.

17 *Encyclopaedia Britannica Online*, s.v. "Biblical Literature: The Meaning of the Term Gospel," accessed February 8, 2019, www.britannica.com/topic/biblical-literature/New-Testament-literature; Rudolf Bultmann, *History of the Synoptic Tradition*, rev. ed. (New York: Harper & Row, 1963), and Rudolf Bultmann, *The New Testament and Mythology and Other Basic Writings* (Philadelphia: Fortress Press, 1984). See also Charles Harold Dodd, *The Meaning of Paul for Today* (London: Allen and Unwin, 1920), https://archive.org/details/meaningofpaulfor008866mbp/page/n13; Charles Harold Dodd, *The Gospel in the New Testament* (London: The National Sunday School Union, [1926]); and Charles Harold Dodd, *The Epistle of Paul to the Romans: Moffatt New Testament Commentary* (New York: Harper & Row, 1932).

It was Paul who said that he proclaimed the *euangelion tou theu* (the good news of God) in Romans 1:1–4: "Paul, a servant of Jesus Christ [the Messiah], called to be an apostle, set apart for the *gospel* of God," and goes on to describe this "gospel" in what was, by that time, traditional language, such as: "which he promised beforehand through his prophets in the holy scriptures, the *gospel* concerning his Son, who was descended from David according to the flesh and was declared to be Son of God with power according to the spirit of holiness by resurrection from the dead, Jesus Christ [Messiah] our Lord" (NRSV, italics mine). This gospel is the power of God for salvation to everyone who has faith, "for in it the righteousness of God is revealed through faith for faith" (1:17, NRSV).

Here people will say, with the traditional imperial orthodoxy, that the apostle was talking about faith *in* Jesus. I argue, however, that that is not what the apostle is referring to in these verses. Here Paul implies that it is by the message of faith, the faith that Paul preached, the faith that has come to us through Jesus, that is, because of Jesus. Jesus's faithfulness to God allows us, those *who have the faith of Jesus*, to find the salvation promised beforehand through the prophets.[18]

---

18 Here I avail myself of the discussion in biblical and theological circles of a different understanding for interpreting Paul called "the New Perspective," that is, a new perspective on understanding Pauline theology. The main exponents of the New Perspective begin with E. P. Sanders, *Paul and Palestinian Judaism* (London: SCM Press, 1977). This study drove the wedge between the modern understanding of Second Temple Judaism and the Judaism exemplified by Luther and the Reformation. New Perspective scholars believe that Luther, Calvin, and other reformers got the teachings of Second Temple Judaism wrong. According to the Protestant reformers the Jews of Jesus's and Paul's period believed in a works righteousness and therefore in justification by works. However, Sanders and other Christian thinkers, going back to the sources, came forward with a resounding rejection of this idea. In other words, "justification by works" was not the belief held by scribes and Pharisees of the first part of the first century. As a matter of fact, the New Perspective authors have come to the conclusion that Second Temple Jews believed in a grace-based salvation, not in a works-based salvation. Certainly, this grace-based salvation was not what the reformers understood as "salvation by grace through faith." For them, salvation was based on grace because Jews of the Second Temple period understood that Israel was chosen collectively; that is, they were elected solely on the basis of God's grace, not on the basis of

For Paul, therefore, to have the faith of Jesus, to receive the good news was a matter of following Jesus and accepting his teachings and his way of life, not merely an assent to the proposition that Jesus is Lord. This is what Paul understood by following Jesus; that is why he emphasized the things he taught his followers were essential: "For I received from the Lord what I also handed on to you" (1 Cor 11:23, NRSV). So, Paul passed on to us his understanding of what this message from God to the world was.

Thus, Paul's commission was simple: "I became its servant by the commission God gave me *to fully proclaim to you the word of God, the mystery* that was hidden for ages and generations but is now revealed to His saints. To them God has chosen to make known among the Gentiles the glorious riches of this mystery, which is the Messiah in you, the hope of glory" (Col 1:25–27, Berean Study Bible).

So if we are reading this passage correctly, Paul tells us that the mystery that has been hidden for generations was that God had intended from the beginning to save the world; that the Gentiles are part of this community of God as much as Jews are; that Jews and Gentiles are one people under God, for we have all been made by the one and only true God (Rom 1:1–6; 3; 8; 9; 10:12–15; Gal 3:28; 5:6; 1 Cor 12:12–13; Eph 2:13–22; 4:4; Col 3:11; and many more). This is why the Gospel of John makes the declaration, "For *God so loved the world* that he gave his only Son, so that everyone who believes in him may not perish but may have eternal life" (3:16, NRSV). And, as John will declare, "God's love was

the Jews being something special. For Second Temple Jews, being part of the community of Israel meant having the Scriptures and the covenant; having the markers of that covenant (i.e., circumcision, dietary laws, special days, and so on) led this community to believe that Jewish righteousness was based on the ethnic identity connected with these outward markers. Therefore, Jewish leaders taught that the people of the covenant were only those who showed these markers (see some of this as Paul describes it in Rom 2:17—3:8). For a continuing exploration on this matter see, in addition to Sanders's work, N. T. Wright, *Justification: God's Plan and Paul's Vision* (London: SPCK, 2009); James D. G. Dunn, *The New Perspective on Paul*, rev. ed. (Grand Rapids, MI: Eerdmans, 2007); and Michael J. Gorman, *Becoming the Gospel: Paul, Participation, and Mission* (Grand Rapids, MI: Eerdmans, 2015). This is not an exhaustive list of resources but a simple one that offers a good place to start.

revealed among us in this way: God sent his only Son into the world so that we might live through him. In this is love, not that we loved God but that he loved us and sent his Son to be the atoning sacrifice for our sins" (1 John 4:9–10, NRSV).

And, as Paul declared in Romans 8:31–37:

> What then are we to say about these things? If God is for us, who is against us? He who did not withhold his own Son, but gave him up for all of us, will he not with him also give us everything else? Who will bring any charge against God's elect? It is God who justifies. Who is to condemn? It is Christ Jesus, who died, yes, who was raised, who is at the right hand of God, who indeed intercedes for us. Who will separate us from the love of Christ? Will hardship, or distress, or persecution, or famine, or nakedness, or peril, or sword? As it is written,
>
> > "For your sake we are being killed all day long;
> > we are accounted as sheep to be slaughtered."
>
> No, in all these things we are more than conquerors through him who loved us. (NRSV)

This is the tradition we find in the Synoptic Gospels as well. Notwithstanding, I find that for many Christians the earthly life of Jesus is hardly noted or is altogether missed; we could probably go from the birth story and jump to the death and resurrection stories without having to say anything about what Jesus did and taught. In both extremes of this narrative (birthday to resurrection and glorification) we find the presentation of a glorious and victorious Jesus who suffers of an anemic humanity. In the Christian imperial narrative about Jesus we seem to miss his life as an ordinary construction worker (Mark 6:3) who lived in poverty (like most of the people who listened to him), a traveling preacher who did not have enough to eat or a place to lay his head (Luke 9:58), a preacher rejected by the religious and political authorities of his time (Mark 14:53–65) and by the Roman Empire, which killed him (Mark 15:6–27; Luke 23:7–15).

Still, for the purposes of a theology of evangelism that is prophetic, liberating, and Wesleyan, we must look at these Gospel narratives to find out what Jesus meant by the good news of the kingdom of God.

What Jesus preached was the good news of the kingdom of God (Το Ευαγγέλιον της Βασιλείας του Θεού).

Jesus's words and actions, his own being, illustrated for his disciples the truth about the kingdom of God. This is what Jesus shared with his disciples, the mystery of the kingdom of heaven (Matt 13:11). This mystery Jesus speaks about is the same mystery, I will argue, that Paul wrote about in his letters to the early followers of Jesus (Rom 11:25; 16:25; 1 Cor 2:10; Col 1:26–27; 2:2). This mystery shows with clarity that "God was in the Messiah reconciling the world to God-self" (2 Cor 5:19). The mystery that this revelation concludes is that God was calling every single human being, not just a few, to be part of the people of God: "There is neither Jew nor Gentile, neither slave nor free, nor is there male and female, for you are all one in Christ Jesus. If you belong to Christ, then you are Abraham's seed, and heirs according to the promise" (Gal 3:28–29, NIV; see also Rom 10:5–17; Eph 2:4–22).

Thus, we can see that the mystery of the good news of the kingdom of God is that God has declared that everyone has an entry to God, to become part of God's called and chosen people. Still, what is the kingdom of God all about? We start getting this picture in the synoptic tradition where Jesus said, "Repent, for the kingdom of heaven is at hand" (Matt 3:2, ESV; 4:17; Mark 1:15). The call to repentance was not only for personal sins but for our collective sins as well. The call to repentance was a call to accept the new order that Jesus, from God, was offering his fellow Jews and the entire human family. This new way brought an order of life, where we are called to love each other and care for each other, therefore introducing a new ethic: that of Love. This is not an ethic based on ethnic affiliation, or national identity, or religious identity, or any other identifier, but rather, this is an ethic that applies to everyone and is based on the power of God's love.

The first thing we find in the Gospels' narratives is that the present and coming kingdom of God was central to the message of Jesus. His teaching was designed to show the human race that they were called to be part of this new thing that God was bringing (Matt 5:20; 7:21). This is the reason the opening narratives in Matthew and Luke usher us into a story in which the Messiah is introduced in an announcement to a young peasant girl named Mary. This does not even compare with the story of Moses, who was born to a slave family in Egypt but reared in the house of Pharaoh in privilege and power. No, Jesus comes to a lowly woman, not a powerful woman, nor to a family with means. God is starting to show that this is all about God's work of love in the world and for the world.

Then the heavenly host shows up to make the official announcement that the Messiah, the savior of the world (whom the magi were talking about to Herod), was going to be born in Bethlehem of Judea, and cradled in a manger (a basket where animals fed), that is, inside a dirty and smelly stable filled with animals. This Messiah would be born in the same conditions of poverty and want that countless other children in the world were being born. There is no special treatment for the savior of the world, for the son of God. Then we are told of the people who are the special guests for this most auspicious occasion; they are not the powerful and mighty, as it should be when someone of importance is born. On the contrary, Jesus is welcomed into the world by the lowliest: the meek and unclean shepherds (Luke 2:8–20), who were working at night taking care of their flocks. And, as if this is not outrageous enough, he is then welcomed by a group of gentiles, the magi (Matt 2:1–11). He is not welcomed by the religious elite of Israel (who are not even moved to curiosity when the magi barge into town announcing the birth of the new king), not even by the leaders of the synagogue. No, he is welcomed by gentiles, people who practice magic and consult with the stars, a profession that was forbidden in Israel and considered a sin by many. So, by God's design, Jesus is welcomed into the world by sinners, outcasts of society, and undesirable foreigners.[19] God is certainly doing something new.

Jesus is not introduced as one who had power or any special gifts; no, he is introduced as a defenseless child (as millions of other children were at that time) who has to escape from political persecution for fear that he might be killed by the powerful Herod. Then, his birth is not followed by a communal celebration but rather by a massacre of children perpetrated by the authorities, principalities, and world powers of his age (King Herod). The son of two peasants from an unknown little town in Galilee named Nazareth was just living what millions of

19 This introduction is only changed in the Gospel of John, where Jesus is presented as a divine being who takes the form of a human being (John 1).

others had experienced before him, and since (Luke 1:26—2:40; Matt 1–2). Jesus's birth is the first message in the Gospels' narratives where we are made succinctly aware that the power in the story resides with God and no other. This is the first miracle of God's love. Thus, these stories were intended to show that the kingdom of God had come (Matt 12:28), not by human power but by the will of God, by God's loving mercy and grace.

In this sense, the good news of the gospel begins with the revelation that Jesus is the one who inaugurates the kingdom, and to do that he begins his messianic ministry by revealing what his missional agenda was going to be: "The Spirit of the Lord is on me, because he has anointed me to proclaim good news to the poor. He has sent me to proclaim freedom for the prisoners and recovery of sight for the blind, to set the oppressed free, to proclaim the year of the Lord's favor" (Luke 4:18–19, NIV).

If that was not clear enough, when John the Baptist asks Jesus if he is the one who was to come, he sends word to him, saying (again, reaffirming what we had read above), "Go back and report to John what you hear and see: The blind receive sight, the lame walk, those who have leprosy are cleansed, the deaf hear, the dead are raised, and *the good news is proclaimed to the poor*" (Matt 11:4–5, NIV, italics mine; also, Luke 7:18–22).

Indeed, in his kingdom message Jesus teaches something the people have not heard before; he speaks of love, of the liberating power of love, and how by engaging in this radical act of loving the other, the world will be transformed, because that is the will of God:

> You have heard that it was said, 'You shall love your neighbor and hate your enemy.' But I say to you, Love your enemies and pray for those who persecute you, so that you may be children of your Father in heaven; for he makes his sun rise on the evil and on the good, and sends rain on the righteous and on the unrighteous. For if you love those who love you, what reward do you have? Do not even the tax collectors do the same? And if you greet only your brothers and sisters, what more are you doing than others? Do not even the Gentiles do the same? Be perfect, therefore, as your heavenly Father is perfect. (Matt 5:43–48, NRSV)

The implication of this passage is clear: to be perfect like our Father in heaven we must love even those we do not like, especially those who are not like us. Yet this is not all that Jesus has to say about the kingdom of God; the entire Sermon on the Mount is an illustration of how we are to live our lives as citizens of the kingdom. He teaches his disciples that when we live according to the values of the kingdom (Luke 6) it will have consequences for the entire world. In Matthew 25 we find Jesus's greatest expression of the kingdom's values and what happens when they are put into practice:

> Then the king will say to those at his right hand, "Come, you that are blessed by my Father, inherit the kingdom prepared for you from the foundation of the world; for I was hungry and you gave me food, I was thirsty and you gave me something to drink, I was a stranger and you welcomed me, I was naked and you gave me clothing, I was sick and you took care of me, I was in prison and you visited me." Then the righteous will answer him, "Lord, when was it that we saw you hungry and gave you food, or thirsty and gave you something to drink? And when was it that we saw you a stranger and welcomed you, or naked and gave you clothing? And when was it that we saw you sick or in prison and visited you?" And the king will answer them, "Truly I tell you, just as you did it to one of the least of these who are members of my family, you did it to me." (25:34–40, NRSV)[20]

The values expressed in this parable of the judgment to the nations are values that reflect what ought to be our way of life, how we ought to care for each other, especially for the least among us. Caring and loving the least, those who have been impoverished, are the central values of the kingdom of God.

---

20 See John O. Gooch, ed., *Grace upon Grace: The Mission Statement of The United Methodist Church* (Nashville: Graded Press, 1990), 10: "In the gospel we see Christ Jesus: preaching good news, healing the sick, calling the righteous to the new commitments to the kingdom, feeding the hungry, raising the dead, overturning the tables of corruption, teaching the signs of the Kingdom, liberating the captives, giving sight to the blind, dying on the cross, rising from death, and living among his people."

As a matter of fact, even the prayer Jesus taught his disciples follows the underlying principle that the kingdom of God is a reality that is lived in the world, in the here and now. This is why Jesus's prayer is so important to his discourse. In Matthew 6:9–13, Jesus calls his disciples to pray in this fashion:

> Our Father in heaven, hallowed be your name. Your kingdom come. Your will be done, on earth as it is in heaven. Give us this day our daily bread. And forgive us our debts, as we also have forgiven our debtors. And do not bring us to the time of trial, but rescue us from the evil one. (NRSV)

The first section praises and honors God, which reminds us of the Jewish prayer the Shema, then he calls for something that in our imperial theological heritage will make no sense; the prayer calls for the kingdom of God to come to earth, and that God's will be done here on earth as it is in heaven. In other words, there should be no difference between the will of God being obeyed in heaven and on earth. Clearly, Jesus is not teaching his disciples to pray so that they can get to "a heaven" out of the realm of this world. Jesus is not teaching his disciples that God's will is a matter for heaven only, but rather, it is a matter for earth as well. Then we are taught to call for God's will to become a reality in this world, in the tangible reality of our lives. But this is not the end of the prayer: Jesus tells us that as we ask God to forgive our sins, we must be willing to forgive those who sin against us (those who trespass against us, those who sin against us); in other words, God's forgiveness is conditioned by our own openness to offer forgiveness to those who have done wrong to us (see verse 14). By forgiving the other, we do not have room for vengeance or revenge. Here we find that another key value of the kingdom of God is forgiveness.

In addition, this prayer teaches us to ask for our needs, our daily sustenance, what we need to live, and to live in the will of God every day. Clearly, we do not need to have so much that it becomes a waste of God's resources; we only need what is necessary to have a fruitful and full life in God right here in this world, in this plane of tangible realities, not in a heaven somewhere in a realm that is unknown.[21] After praying for our daily sustenance and asking for forgiveness, we are asked to request from God deliverance from evil. Nothing in this prayer requests a way out of this world or to wait for a life after death in order to begin to live our saved lives. On the contrary, through this prayer, Jesus simply continues to affirm what he had already stated earlier: "Do not think that I have come to abolish the law or the prophets; I have not come to abolish but to fulfill" (Matt 5:17, NRSV; see also Heb 12:27). Indeed, to live in the will of God is to live according to the commandments God gave the band of slaves who were liberated from slavery in Egypt.

Now, we are called to live in this kingdom, the one we have prayed for, the same kingdom that God has inaugurated through Jesus. It is this Jesus who shows us how to live and fulfill the law,[22] which is the expression of the kingdom of God. It is this new kingdom that Jesus calls us to embrace: "So if anyone is in Christ, there is a new creation: everything old has passed away; see, everything has become new! All this is from God, who reconciled us to himself through Christ" (2 Cor 5:17–18, NRSV). This living in the kingdom of God, in this new creation, the place that God has prepared, the place where God makes salvation available and real—this is the place where heaven and earth come together; they have been brought together in the person of Jesus, for he embodies the final coming together of heaven and earth. As N. T. Wright argues when commenting on Ephesians 1:10:

> Chapter 1 verse 10 is a verse that the church in the Western world has studiously ignored. "Please do not do this!" Rather, note carefully what Paul says in verse 10, "God's plan for the fullness of

21 Let me be clear, I am not saying that heaven is not real. My argument is that by taking God's salvation to heaven (i.e., beyond this world), salvation has been used as a tool for alienating people from living here in this world, alienating people struggling to make of this world the place that God intended the world to be. Our going to a heavenly place after death is not in question; what is in question is the making of "a heaven" the place of salvation while forgetting that God gave us this world as our home and our responsibility to make it the paradise God desires.

22 This is the law that both Jesus and Paul recognize to be God's gift to humanity (Matt 22:34–40; Rom 3:31; 7:12–14; 1 Tim 1:8; and others).

> time was to gather up all things in Christ, things in heaven and things on earth." . . . We have lived in a culture that has long separated heaven and earth, which thinks of heaven as "somewhere up there a long way away." In this view, heaven is a place that maybe we'll go one day but has not got much to do with who we are down here. We don't get that message when we read the Bible. We inherited our view from a Western philosophical and intellectual tradition. Two hundred years ago, this tradition decided that we would send God away into His "heaven," out of sight. This was ultimately for our own convenience, so that we could run the world the way we wanted without interference.[23]

We must be clear that as followers of Jesus we have been called to live in a world in which heaven and earth have already come together once and forever: the kingdom of God is among you, as Jesus tells us (Luke 17:21). This is why Paul speaks to the churches he founded (or worked with), not about how one gets to heaven, but rather, about how to live as citizens of the kingdom right here on earth, as is the case with Romans 12:1–2, 9–21:

> I appeal to you therefore, brothers and sisters, by the mercies of God, to present your bodies as a living sacrifice, holy and acceptable to God, which is your spiritual worship. Do not be conformed to this world, but be transformed by the renewing of your minds, so that you may discern what is the will of God—what is good and acceptable and perfect. . . .
>
> Let love be genuine; hate what is evil, hold fast to what is good; love one another with mutual affection; outdo one another in showing honor. Do not lag in zeal, be ardent in spirit, serve the Lord. Rejoice in hope, be patient in suffering, persevere in

---

23 See N. T. Wright, "Ephesians: What We Get Wrong about Life after Death," N. T. Wright Online: Renewing Minds through Biblical Teaching, accessed February 8, 2022, https://ntwrightonline.org/ephesians-get-wrong-life-death/. See also Wright, "The Letter to the Ephesians" (presentation, Scottish Church Theology Society conference, January 2013), 5, https://ojs.st-andrews.ac.uk/index.php/TIS/article/view/1215.

> prayer. Contribute to the needs of the saints; extend hospitality to strangers.
>
> Bless those who persecute you; bless and do not curse them. Rejoice with those who rejoice, weep with those who weep. Live in harmony with one another; do not be haughty, but associate with the lowly; do not claim to be wiser than you are. Do not repay anyone evil for evil, but take thought for what is noble in the sight of all. If it is possible, so far as it depends on you, live peaceably with all. Beloved, never avenge yourselves, but leave room for the wrath of God; for it is written, "Vengeance is mine, I will repay, says the Lord." No, "if your enemies are hungry, feed them; if they are thirsty, give them something to drink; for by doing this you will heap burning coals on their heads." Do not be overcome by evil, but overcome evil with good. (NRSV)

Paul concludes this description on how to live as citizens of the kingdom (heaven and earth in one place) by calling the Roman church to

> owe no one anything, except to love one another; for the one who loves another has fulfilled the law. The commandments, "You shall not commit adultery; You shall not murder; You shall not steal; You shall not covet"; and any other commandment, are summed up in this word, "Love your neighbor as yourself." Love does no wrong to a neighbor; therefore, love is the fulfilling of the law. (13:8–10, NRSV)

The people of God who have been called to live in the reality of God's kingdom have not been told to wait until they get to "a heaven" far away; no, they are called to live right here right now in this new reality that God has created for the world. This is also why Paul argues that to live by the Spirit is an experience to be lived in this world. We live in this new heaven and earth that God has forged through Jesus right here and now. That is the reason the fruit of the Spirit, which Paul speaks about in Galatians 5, is not about how one prepares to go to "a celestial heaven," but rather, how one lives in relationship to others, in relationship to the people that God loves. As one reads in verses 16–21, one might conclude that Paul is talking about getting away from the desires of the flesh: "fornication, impurity, licentiousness, idolatry, sorcery, enmities, strife, jealousy, anger, quarrels, dissensions, factions, envy, drunkenness, carousing, and things like these" as a way to escape this world. However, the fact is that Paul does not pursue the idea of escaping from a sinful world to a holy place in "heaven"; rather, Paul refers to how Christians are to live their lives in community in the world. The desires of the flesh refers almost entirely to how these desires affect human relations.

As a matter of fact, Paul makes it clear that "those who do such things will not inherit the kingdom of God" (Gal 5:21, NIV). People who live like this cannot inherit the kingdom because these acts, these behaviors, are a contradiction to what it means to live in community and to care for each other. In other words, "Do nothing out of selfish ambition or vain conceit. Rather, in humility value others above yourselves" (Phil 2:3, NIV).

On the other hand, Paul goes on to tell us that those who will inherit the kingdom of God are the people who live by the Spirit, that is, the people who live with "love, joy, peace, patience, kindness, generosity, faithfulness, gentleness, and self-control" (Gal 5:22–23, NRSV). These are the people who will not satisfy the desires of the flesh, which he just described in the preceding verses. These are the people who let themselves be guided by the Spirit (verse 25) to live as people of the kingdom. These are the people who will "not be conformed to this world" but will be "transformed by the renewing of [their] minds" (Rom 12:2, NRSV).

These passages do not send the followers of Jesus to live in the crummy world while waiting for their time to get to heaven. No! Paul reminds the followers of Jesus that to live as citizens of the kingdom of heaven there is a way to live right in the present reality on earth, not right here.

Finally, Paul reminds us that those who follow Jesus are the people who love like Jesus loved, to the point of giving one's life for the other (John 15:12–13). This is captured with such power and resolve in 1 Corinthians 13, where Paul highlights, in one of the most famous biblical passages, how bound we are to this heaven-and-earth new reality we have come to receive through Jesus. The followers of Jesus, those who live according to the values of this kingdom that Jesus has inaugurated, are the people who *do not* rest on their speaking skills (verse

1), or their gift to prophesy and their ability to understand mysteries, or their faith to move mountains (verse 2), or their possessions, or their sacrifices (verse 3). On the contrary, they rest on their love for the other. As a matter of fact, all the expressions Paul mentions about how to love relate to its impact on other human beings (verses 4–7). And, after all is said and done, love is the only thing that will remain: no special skills, no human or spiritual prowess, no creedal statements, no doctrinal orthodoxy. In the kingdom inaugurated by Jesus, we have only to love God and other human beings. That is what matters (verse 13).

Therefore, the mission of Jesus is presented to us in his message about the kingdom of God he came to inaugurate. So, as we seek to proclaim the good news of the kingdom, the gospel of Jesus the Messiah, we have been confronted by numerous views and interpretations of what Jesus's mission was all about. David Bosch describes a variety of ways in which this mission has been defined throughout the centuries. First, he argues that the mission to which we are called to participate in has been seen "primarily in soteriological terms: as saving individuals from eternal damnation." Second, Jesus's mission has been understood in "cultural terms: as introducing people from the East and the South to the blessings and privileges of the Christian West." Third, it has been "perceived in ecclesiastical categories: as the expansion of the church (or of a specific denomination)." Lastly, it has been defined as "salvation-historically: as the process by which the world—evolutionarily or by means of a cataclysmic event—would be transformed into the Kingdom of God."[24]

The different approaches to the mission of God through Jesus reveal the ideological forces behind the movements that promoted these various definitions. From a Latino perspective, all of these modalities have been used in order to Christianize Latinos. In other extremes, some of these definitions have served as ways to sanction the exploitation, oppression, exclusion, and annihilation of nations. Some of these definitions of evangelism have served to benefit the ideological powers of death and exclusion, which have benefited the interests of the wealthy, the powerful, and the principalities who rule this world.

---

24 David J. Bosch, *Transforming Mission: Paradigm Shifts in Theology of Mission* (Maryknoll, NY: Orbis Books, 2001), 10, 389–93.

The missionary efforts of Protestantism during the nineteenth century did not distance themselves from the missionary practices that the Catholic Church had used during Spanish colonization in Central and South America[25] or the British colonization in the North. The reality is that the evangelistic efforts of Protestant missions to Latin America and the Caribbean were done in partnership with the liberal capitalist movements that were exploring new commercial markets in the southern hemisphere.[26]

This unholy union has had negative repercussions that are still felt today. Protestant missionaries are seen in Latin America not only as religious groups, but also as groups that foment submission to the powers of death (apolitical submission to the authorities), especially those that are pro–United States. These groups, by and large, have received support from conservative Christians and nonreligious organizations that promote US economic interests, Protestants who are under the illusion that the United States and US-style democracy are the expression of God's kingdom on earth.

A clear example of this unholy union can be seen in the "missionary" work that took place in Puerto Rico by the end of the nineteenth century. Missionaries arrived in Puerto Rico at the invitation of the US Department of War.[27] Sadly, these missionaries saw their evangelistic efforts connected to the interest of the invading forces, as well as their desire to Christianize the heathens on the island.

---

25 A powerful illustration of this experience was captured in the movie *The Mission*. In this movie a group of Jesuits became the defenders of the Brazilian natives and the hierarchy, which was deeply intertwined with the economic interests of the Portuguese government that sanctioned the killing of their own priests and the natives whom they were protecting. See Enrique D. Dussel, *A History of the Church in Latin America: Colonialism to Liberation (1492–1979)*, trans. Alan Neely (Grand Rapids, MI: Eerdmans, 1981), chap. 4.

26 Orlando E. Costas, *The Integrity of Mission: The Inner Life and Outreach of the Church* (New York: Harper & Row, 1979), 64.

27 See Carlos F. Cardoza-Orlandi, "Nos llamaron 'mulatos, fiesteros, pero redimibles': Antropología misionera y definición del protestantismo en Puerto Rico," in *Más Voces: Reflexiones Teológicas de la Iglesia Hispana*, ed. Luis G. Pedraja (Nashville: Abingdon Press, 2001), 124. See also Costas, *The Integrity of Mission*, 64.

The penetration of the US government and big business in the Caribbean raises concerns as to how the evangelistic task pursued by American missionaries was linked to the economic and geopolitical plans of the US government. In a document of the International Missionary Council, they declared:

> The Evangelical Church entered Puerto Rico upon the crest of the wave of foreign power and institutions. Missions appeared in response to the conviction of the Church in the United States that it had a responsibility for the spiritual ministry of the new dependency. . . . *Like other agents of occupation* from the United States, church representatives were supplied with ample funds. Church buildings, schools, hospitals, parsonages, and the education and salaries of pastors and teachers were provided. . . . No one questioned . . . the source of funds with which [institutions] were established.[28]

Orlando Costas comments that the "negative impact that this alliance has had upon the younger churches, their members and the nations of which they are part has been far greater than what many of us would like to admit."[29] The fact of the matter is that, according to Cardoza-Orlandi, the relationship between the sociopolitical and the Protestant missionary enterprise reveals the ideological character of the missionary enterprise. A proposed cultural transformation emerges through the institutions that promote and communicate values intertwined with the Protestant faith and the American model of liberal democracy.[30]

---

28 International Missionary Council, *The Church in Puerto Rico's Dilemma* (New York: International Missionary Council, 1942), 57. As cited in Cardoza-Orlandi, "Nos llamaron 'mulatos, fiesteros, pero redimibles,'" 125, italics mine.

29 Costas, *Integrity of Mission*, 64.

30 Cardoza-Orlandi, "Nos llamaron 'mulatos, fiesteros, pero redimibles,'" 123. Costas comments that "in a real sense, the missions functioned as a social and ideological arm of the colonial and imperial powers," 63. See also Costas, *Integrity of Mission*, 64–65. Also, Thomas A. Langford's study guides for *Grace upon Grace: The Mission Statement of The United Methodist Church*, 19. See also Rodney Clapp, *A Peculiar People: The Church as Culture in a Post-Christian Society* (Downers Grove, IL: InterVarsity Press, 1996), 171.

This is, in the final analysis, the crude reality of what many Latin American countries have experienced at the hands of missionaries and their mission boards. In the case of Puerto Rico, not only did missionaries preach their gospel of salvation, but they also preached the "gospel" of cultural superiority and of cultural assimilation.[31] We were offered the gospel of economic bliss if we would accept the "American" (US) institutions and system of government.[32] The missionaries' purpose might have been honest, but the mechanisms to achieve it, and what had to be sacrificed, were too costly.

It is in this context that we were introduced to the gospel of Jesus the Christ, the Christ of the colonizing forces, the Christ of the invading forces. It is in this context that we met the Christ of the oppressor. This is what we found in their christological message, in the evangelistic message received.

Therefore, our Latin American understanding of the meaning of Christ has been mediated by centuries of an oppressed and oppressive Christ; it is this characteristic that is deeply embedded in the conscience of the excluded and exploited in our hemisphere. That is, Latin America (and its counterparts in the United States) has lived through the experience of the "Christ of the cross, of the death that conquers."[33] This was the Christ introduced to us by the oppressor, by

31 The stories from retired Puerto Rican Methodist clergy in this particular point are very telling. A few pastors remember that when they were young the style of preaching that their pastors used to copy was that of their "spiritual" fathers: US preachers. This is not unusual, since we all seek to emulate our mentors. However, what has been very revealing is the fact that these older pastors comment that what was fascinating among the Creole leadership was not only that they copied the style of preaching, but that they also copied the accent of the US preacher. Since the US preachers spoke Spanish with an English accent, Puerto Rican preachers copied the US preachers' Spanish accent.

32 See the statement written by General Nelson Miles to the people of Puerto Rico after the US army had taken control of the island: Idsa E. Alegria Ortega, *La comisión del status de Puerto Rico: Su historia y significación* (Rio Piedras, Puerto Rico: Editorial Universitaria, 1982), 3.

33 Saúl Trinidad, "Christology, Conquista, Colonization," in *Faces of Jesus: Latin American Christologies*, ed. José Míguez-Bonino, trans. Robert R. Barr (Maryknoll, NY: Orbis Books, 1984), 60.

the conquistador. Saúl Trinidad tells us that this Christ "has become the archetypical beggar, some sort of scarecrow, a compendium of miseries and a sample of humiliations."[34] This is the Christ that we have received through the evangelistic message of Western Christianity. Therefore, our Christology has to surpass the limitations of an ideological construct that has been serving the powers and principalities of this world; a Christology that serves as a sanctioner of oppression, exploitation, and exclusion. That is to say, we must present a gospel to the world that is not at the service of the powers of this world or at the service of the powerful and wealthy.

Our evangelism—and our Christology, therefore—must be one that promotes and sustains the liberating message Jesus preached and taught his early disciples, a message that identifies, like Jesus, with the suffering and pain of God's "little" ones. True evangelism must present to the world a liberating evangelism, an evangelism that is immersed in community, in the midst of the excluded and marginalized.[35]

It is only through a liberating evangelism, which implies a liberating Christology, that the church can proclaim the good news that can bring real redemption and liberate God's people to live as citizens of the kingdom of God. As we recognize that in Christ we find God's full revelation (Col 2:9) we are able to comprehend what his mission was all about, as Bosch makes clear for us:

> Our mission has no life of its own: only in the hands of the sending God can it truly be called mission, not least since the missionary initiative comes from God alone. . . . Willingen [Conference, 1952] recognized a close relationship between the *missio Dei* and mission as solidarity with the incarnate and crucified Christ. Whereas the Willingen meeting was convened under the theme "The Missionary Obligation of the Church," the addresses

---

34 Trinidad, "Christology, Conquista, Colonization," 60. See also Hugo Assman, "La actuación historica del poder de Cristo," *La nueva frontera de la teología en América Latina*, ed. Rosino Gibellini (Salamanca, Spain: Ediciones Sígueme, 1977), 142–43. Also Lamberto Schuurman, "Christology in Latin America," in *Faces of Jesus*, 162–82.

35 See Leonardo Boff, "Liberación de Jesucristo por el camino de la opresión," in *La nueva frontera de la teología en América Latina*, 106.

> delivered at the meeting were published under the title *Missions Under the Cross* (1953). Thus, next to the affirmation that the mission was God's, the emphasis on the cross prevented every possibility of missionary complacency.[36]

Jesus's mission is God's, and God's mission is the salvation of the world.[37] God was in Christ reconciling the world to Godself (2 Cor 5:18, my paraphrase), and thus showing God's love and God's solidarity and liberation to the oppressed and excluded of the world (John 3:16–18; Luke 4:18–19). The church's missionary activities "are only authentic insofar as they reflect participation in the mission of God."[38] This implies a reaching out to the world out of love; love for God's creation and for every living being. "Evangelism as the mission of the Church . . . has to be service to the *missio Dei*, representing God in and over against the world, pointing to God, holding up the God-child before the eyes of the world in a ceaseless celebration of the Feast of the Epiphany. In its mission, the church witnesses to the fullness of the promise of God's reign and participates in the ongoing struggle between that reign and the powers of darkness and evil."[39]

We may participate in God's mission only if we show God's love to the world, especially to the excluded. We must act in love toward God's children. Without a sacrificing love in the life of a believer, God cannot be present. Thus, Wesley says:

> It is so to love God, who hath thus loved you, as you never did love any creature: so that ye are constrained to love all men as yourselves; with a love not only ever burning in your hearts, but flaming out in all your actions and conversations, and making your whole life one 'labour of love,' one continued obedience to those commands, 'Be ye merciful, as God is merciful'; 'Be ye holy, as I the Lord am holy'; 'Be ye perfect, as your father which is in heaven is perfect.'[40]

36 Bosch, *Transforming Mission*, 390.

37 Bosch, *Transforming Mission*, 390.

38 Bosch, *Transforming Mission*, 391.

39 Bosch, *Transforming Mission*, 391.

40 John Wesley, "The Marks of the New Birth," §4 in *Sermons I*, ed. Albert Outler, vol. 1 of *The Bicentennial Edition of the Works of John Wesley* (Nashville: Abingdon

Likewise, Gustavo Gutiérrez says that God first loved us and made us by love to love others.

> "Dios nos amó primero" (1 Jn 4:19) [*missio Dei*]. Todo parte de allí. Ese don está en el origen de nuestra existencia y marca nuestras vidas. Hemos sido hechos por amor y para amar. Por eso sólo amando podemos realizarnos como personas, es así como damos respuesta a la iniciativa de amor de Dios.[41]

Jesus came to bring liberation to the poor and the oppressed; Jesus announced that "the kingdom of God is at hand for the poor."[42] Jesus showed that his approach to the kingdom is not generic, but it is indeed universally partial to the impoverished, those to whom the gospel has been preached.[43] This describes Jesus's allegiance; it is Jesus's praxis that makes his life so crucial because he lived what he preached. Jesus lived, died, and was raised from the dead to bring liberation to every human being that accepts to live his way, loving sacrificially.[44]

What makes this christological approach different from imperial Christologies is, precisely, the emphasis on Jesus's life and practice of love. Traditional Christologies approach Jesus from the official faith statements of the church,[45] that is, from a confessional perspective or

---

Press, 1984), 428.

41 Gustavo Gutiérrez, *Beber en su propio pozo* (Salamanca, Spain: Ediciones Sigueme, 1986), 142.

42 Boff, "Liberación," 90.

43 See Matt 11:2–5 and Luke 7:19–22, where the Gospel writers witness to the fact that the evidence of Jesus's ministry was in his actions.

44 God's way, God's household rules, are clearly described by M. Douglas Meeks in *God the Economist: The Doctrine of God and Political Economy* (Minneapolis: Fortress Press, 1989).

45 Rudolf Bultmann, *Theology of the New Testament* (New York: Scribner's, 1951), 33–37. See also James Breecher, *The Silence of Jesus: The Authentic Voice of the Historical Man* (Philadelphia: Fortress Press, 1987), 5–11. Here I have some difficulties with Gerald O'Collins's work, *The Tripersonal God: Understanding and Interpreting the Trinity* (New York: Paulist Press, 1999), because in his analysis of the Trinity the discussion focuses on a dogmatic interpretation of the Godhead completely devoid of any historical connections to human reality. As the author says, "Christianity stands or falls with Trinitarian faith" (6), therefore leaving God unaffected again. See especially chapter 2 of O'Collins. In opposition to O'Collins,

from a dogmatic standing. Others approach Jesus from an existentialist or pragmatic utilitarian standpoint that is only interested in what he can teach us today. Does he have anything for "me"? However, what makes the person of Jesus crucial for our understanding of his message about the kingdom of God is his practice of love, his way of living in the world.[46]

An evangelism that is prophetic, liberating, and Wesleyan, then, is a gospel that shows a Jesus who brings liberation to all creation out of love: "Christ the savior liberates man from sin, which is the ultimate root of all disruption of friendship and of all injustice and oppression."[47] Through Christ we are made truly free, but this freedom is not something that one possesses; it is not an object. To be free is to be able to be in relationship with others, to be free for the other, because only when we are in relationship we are truly made free.[48]

This freedom to serve, this freedom to be for the other, is Jesus's way. Jesus showed us the way that we ought to pursue in order to live as citizens of the kingdom: "In the gospel we see Christ Jesus: preaching good news, healing the sick, calling the righteous to the new commitments to the kingdom, feeding the hungry, raising the dead, overturning the tables of corruption, teaching the signs of the Kingdom, liberating the captives, giving sight to the blind, dying on the cross, rising from death, and living among his people."[49]

This is good news! This is the evangelism that is liberating, prophetic, and Wesleyan: to bring salvation to a broken world is more than wishful thinking or doctrinal acquiescence; it implies a commitment to the world that God loves, and to its people; to announce the good news of the kingdom of God to the impoverished, oppressed, and destitute.[50]

---

see Justo L. González's work, *Mañana: Christian Theology from a Hispanic Perspective* (Nashville: Abingdon Press, 1990), esp. chap. 6.

46 Jon Sobrino, *Jesus in Latin America*, trans. Robert R. Barr (Maryknoll, NY: Orbis Books, 1987), 64.

47 Gutiérrez, *Teología de la Liberación*, 68–69.

48 Gutiérrez, *Teología de la Liberación*, 67. See Gutiérrez's quote of Dietrich Bonhoeffer's work *Creation and Fall.*

49 The United Methodist Church, *Grace upon Grace: The Mission Statement of The United Methodist Church* (Nashville: Graded Press, 1990), ¶7.

50 Langford's study guides for Gooch, ed., *Grace upon Grace*, 10.

This fulfills what Jesus implied is the evangelistic mission of the church in Matthew 25:35–36: "I was hungry and you gave me food, I was thirsty and you gave me something to drink, I was a stranger and you welcomed me, I was naked and you gave me clothing, I was sick and you took care of me, I was in prison and you visited me" (NRSV).[51]

The judgment to the nations that Jesus speaks about in this passage tells us what it means to live for the other, what it means to live in the will of God; it tells us what is good about the kingdom of God that Jesus proclaimed. Indeed, we are called to care for the other, regardless of who they are or where they come from; as a matter of fact, Jesus is identified as the other, the one we are called to care for. An evangelism that does not insist on the centrality of social and personal transformation is not faithful to the message Jesus preached and taught. As Jon Sobrino says, "A view of Jesus from his practice makes for a more obvious discovery and a better explanation of his determinate social placement, the stand point from which he observes the totality of his surrounding reality, and the persecution and fate that came upon him."[52]

As a matter of fact, a proclamation of the gospel that does not insist on transforming the structures of sin and the systems of oppression in the church and society is not living a holy life. As Bosch reminds us, "The *missio Dei* is God's activity, which embraces both the church and the world, in which the Church may be privileged to participate."[53]

Therefore, the proclamation of God's acts of salvation through Jesus's life is confirmed through us when we live out Jesus's message in the world.[54] When we affirm that it is Jesus who liberates the

51 Matthew 25:35–36 provides a vivid description of the church's obligation for social justice and compassionate ministry.

52 Sobrino, *Jesus in Latin America*, 68.

53 Bosch, *Transforming Mission*, 391. God will use not only Christians to achieve God's plan of salvation. We have been invited to be part of this process. However, history shows that our participation has not always been on the side of God's mission. Therefore, God will not depend on us for his mission to be accomplished.

54 Costas, *Integrity of Mission*, 74. See also S. Paul Schilling, *Methodism and Society in Theological Perspectives* (Nashville: Abingdon Press, 1960), 204. Schilling says, "Rooted in God, salvation thus comes to full flower in the life of righteousness and love toward God and all whom God loves. This means that salvation is for truly Christian faith inevitably social. Men do not live alone, and they cannot

oppressed and excluded of the world, it is not a metaphor to illustrate a profound spiritual truth.[55] It is the heart of the gospel. It is the heart of God's liberating action in the world. This is prophetic evangelism.

be saved in isolation. They must be saved as whole persons, and this means as persons-in-community, with all manner of interlocking connections" (204).

55 Leonardo Boff, *Jesus Christ Liberator: A Critical Christology for Our Times*, trans. Patrick Hughs (Maryknoll, NY: Orbis Books, 1989), 52–53, 142, 152–53. See also Sobrino, *Jesus in Latin America*, 13, 14–15.

4

Profetas in Cross-Cultural Mission

JOSEPH A. OCASIO

GENERALLY SPEAKING, MOST AMERICANS tend to combine all Hispanics into one cultural group because of the common Spanish language. In fact, more than seventeen distinct nationalities are represented in the United States, with each group containing unique cultural and language variations. There are, however, commonalities within all Hispanic cultures that can facilitate a missional strategy for the purpose of connecting cross-culturally. The challenge of ministering to Hispanic groups across the country rests in three basic premises: how to minister within a diversity of distinct Hispanic nationalities whose dominant language is Spanish, how to cope with the exponential growth of the Hispanic communities and its impact on the local church, and how to engage the issue of the migrant diaspora that is changing the demographics of entire communities.

It is becoming increasingly necessary to minister cross-culturally between various multilingual communities. The need for bilingual ministries has been growing as a result of an increase in the Hispanic population. Many English-dominant churches have had to add Spanish-language ministries in order to address this growth. Additionally, because of language, Hispanic ministers are able to minister cross-culturally and connect multiple generations for the purpose of maintaining family unity under the same roof. Although this position is not limited only to Hispanic Americans, this condition will only increase since Hispanics are the largest ethnic minority group in this country. This new reality requires that the American church foster an incarnational missional ethos by "embodying the culture and life of a target group in order to meaningfully reach that group of people from within their culture."[1] This chapter will provide a snapshot of the Hispanic American cultural context and provide practical considerations to help inform the church's missional mandate to cross cultural borders that are no longer outside the borders of the United States but are just outside the doors of the local church. As a School of Prophets, the church must first capture the essence of the Hispanic theological and cultural nuances to help shape a missional approach within this community.

Understanding Hispanic Theological Perspectives

In order to properly understand a culture, it is important to become a student of culture. Creating a Hispanic missional strategy requires a contextualized understanding of the Hispanic community. The Hispanic American culture has been an intricate part of the formation of the United States for the past five hundred years. In fact, "long before the Pilgrims landed on Plymouth Rock, Hispanics were a presence in these lands."[2] Within this context, it becomes even more complex because "Hispanics did not cross the border of the territories that they had occupied for five centuries, the border crossed them."[3]

Over the years, attempts have been made to create structures within the church to address the overwhelming number of different cultural groups represented in the United States. The Roman Catholic and evangelical churches address the missional strategy from two different perspectives. The Roman Catholics emphasize cultural diversity, "while evangelical churches emphasize the commonly shared identity of born-again Christians."[4] The main emphasis of the Roman Catho-

1 Alan Hirsch, *The Forgotten Ways: Reactivating the Missional Church* (Grand Rapids, MI: Brazos Press, 2008), 281.

2 Ana María Pineda, "The Challenge of Hispanic Pluralism for the United States Churches," *Missiology* 21, no. 4 (October 1993): 437.

3 Pineda, "The Challenge of Hispanic Pluralism for the United States," 438.

4 Kathleen Garces-Foley, "Comparing Catholic and Evangelical Integration Efforts," *Journal for the Scientific Study of Religion* 47, no. 1 (March 2008): 18.

lic Church is to articulate the principle of inculturation. Inculturation "refers to the ongoing dialogue between the gospel and culture and the belief that though the gospel transcends any particular culture, it can only be encountered through culture."[5] This was a move away from a "melting pot" society and brought the idea of cultural pluralism to the church in order to "ensure that pluralism, not assimilation and uniformity, is the guiding principle in the life of communities in both the ecclesial and secular societies."[6]

The evangelical church differs in that the focus remains primarily on evangelism, and when new immigrants began to arrive en masse after 1965, the evangelicals maintained the ethnic church model. Church growth specialist C. Peter Wagner popularized the "homogenous unit principle."[7] Underlying this principle is the notion that "since people prefer to be with people like themselves, the most effective way to form new churches is to focus on homogeneous groups."[8] In the 1990s, a shift began to take place toward a more multicultural model emphasizing reconciliation, because "reconciliation between diverse peoples and evangelism go hand-in-hand. . . . Evangelism must be cross-cultural in order to fulfill the commandment to preach to all nations."[9]

Although the Roman Catholic and evangelical churches have proceeded down the path of reconciliation and diversity, understanding the diverse cultural landscape requires more than a change in mindset; it requires an intimate understanding of a culture's theological underpinnings. For the Hispanic community, the theology of *orthopathos* (i.e., divine suffering) can be considered a theological framework from which to understand the Hispanic cultural condition.

Paul, in Philippians, emotionally describes orthopathos as a foundational concept in this way: "That I may know Him and the power of His resurrection and the fellowship of His sufferings, being conformed to His death; if by any means I may attain to the resurrection from the dead" (Phil 3:10–11, NKJV). The prophetic church must align itself

5 Garces-Foley, "Comparing Catholic and Evangelical Integration Efforts," 19.

6 Garces-Foley, "Comparing Catholic and Evangelical Integration Efforts," 19.

7 Garces-Foley, "Comparing Catholic and Evangelical Integration Efforts," 20.

8 Garces-Foley, "Comparing Catholic and Evangelical Integration Efforts," 20.

9 Garces-Foley, "Comparing Catholic and Evangelical Integration Efforts," 21.

with the reality of what role orthopathos plays within the Hispanic community. As the apostle Paul instructs the Philippian church, "Your attitude should be the same as that of Christ Jesus: Who, being in very nature God, did not consider equality with God something to be grasped, but made himself nothing, taking the very nature of a servant, being made in human likeness" (Phil 2:5–7, NIV). Jesus became human in order to connect with the pathos of humanity. Connecting with the Hispanic community requires a commitment to walk in the shoes of a Hispanic theological reality.

Embracing this primal spiritual ethos requires a missional church that models itself around "its real purpose of being an agent of God's mission to the world."[10] In other words, the church is not only the product of the mission, "but obligated and destined to extend it by whatever means possible,"[11] and "the Church does not 'do' mission; rather, the Church 'is' mission."[12] The incarnation of Christ requires that the church must also experience the pathos of the community it serves.

Samuel Solivan presents this theological perspective that represents the plight, hope, and contributions of Hispanic Americans to their churches and communities. Solivan argues that "orthopathos is the understanding of theology as the proper relationship between correct belief (orthodoxy) and proper ethics or action (praxis)."[13] Solivan asserts that orthodoxy "as a correct doctrine has done little to address the issues of oppression and injustice among the poor and disenfranchised people."[14] Correct doctrine has not contributed to mitigating the plight of the widow, the alien, and the orphan.

Although orthopraxis reflects a context of action, "orthopraxis in the United States is often reduced to a critical reflection on the [social] praxis of others and is not a direct contact or engagement with those

10 Hirsch, *Forgotten Ways*, 82.

11 Hirsch, *Forgotten Ways*, 82.

12 Patrick Franklin, "Bonhoeffer's Missional Ecclesiology," *McMaster Journal of Theology & Ministry* 9 (December 2007): 97.

13 Samuel Solivan, *Spirit, Pathos and Liberation: Toward an Hispanic Pentecostal Theology* (Sheffield, UK: Sheffield Academic Press, 1999), 11.

14 Solivan, *Spirit, Pathos and Liberation*, 11.

who suffer."[15] Orthopathos addresses the reality of the Hispanic American condition. Solivan describes "Hispanic theology [as] a survival theology that challenges 'what is' with 'what is to come,' a faith experience that dares to sing the songs of Zion even in a foreign land."[16] Paul puts it this way: "That is why, for Christ's sake, I delight in weaknesses, in insults, in hardships, in persecutions, in difficulties. For when I am weak, then I am strong" (2 Cor 12:10, NIV). There is a Spanish phrase, *Estamos en la Lucha* ("We are in the Battle"), that describes the reality of orthopathos with an understanding that, within a foreign land, whether accepted or rejected, God's promises will still come to pass.

Therefore, orthopathos is "the power of the Holy Spirit in one's life that transforms *pathos* [suffering] and despair into hope and wholeness. Orthopathos is that holistic, liberating process that engenders hope in their suffering."[17] It is that internal drive within humanity to persevere in hardship through the difficulties of life because the Holy Spirit is the guarantee from Christ for the hope that is available now and the hope that is to come. Connecting missionally within the culture requires that "those of us who seek to speak on behalf of the sufferer must return to that place of suffering."[18] People "who allow themselves to be in touch with and touched by the pain and suffering of others humanize and deobjectivize them."[19] Solivan asserts that "this contact provides an entrée to the voices and vision of the disinherited and a location for legitimate discourse by those whom orthodoxy seeks to save and orthopraxis seeks to represent."[20] Unless the church connects with the orthopathos of the community, a missional strategy will lack the connectedness required to effectively communicate the gospel of Christ.

Mahatma Gandhi's identifying with the suffering poor drove him to "strip off his European clothes, dispossess himself of material things, and seek companionship with the poor and suffering. 'A leader,' he said,

---

15 Solivan, *Spirit, Pathos and Liberation*, 11.

16 Solivan, *Spirit, Pathos and Liberation*, 11.

17 Solivan, *Spirit, Pathos and Liberation*, 27.

18 Solivan, *Spirit, Pathos and Liberation*, 37.

19 Solivan, *Spirit, Pathos and Liberation*, 11.

20 Solivan, *Spirit, Pathos and Liberation*, 11.

'is only a reflection of the people he leads.'"[21] In other words, Gandhi preferred to identify himself with the "untouchables" of his community rather than the upper class in order to embrace the orthopathos of that community.

Mother Teresa described it this way: "I see the face of Jesus in disguise," as she looked upon the dying beggars in the streets whom she then invited to her home in Calcutta, "sometimes a most distressing disguise."[22] Mother Teresa, like Gandhi, understood "that the direction of charity is not condescending, but rather ascending: in serving the weak and the poor, we are privileged to serve God himself."[23]

The implication of orthopathos does not discourage the Hispanic from embracing hope, but in fact, it propels the Hispanic toward hope more intently. Embracing the orthopathos of a community provides the passion the church needs to affect a missional strategy cross-culturally. Jesus Christ experienced humanity's orthopathos so that humanity within every context could experience the same hope that Christ provided.[24] A missional strategy must connect with the orthopathos of a community as a theological foundation of understanding the Hispanic culture.

Understanding Hispanic Cultural Context

Orthopathos is a theological reality of marginalized Hispanic Americans, who hold their identity, hope, and trust in God: "There are times in the history of persons and people, particularly times of crisis . . . when the awakening of a sense of heritage becomes a potent determinant of destiny."[25] Pluralism, rather than assimilation, lends itself to a more practical understanding of multiculturalism: "To expect all groups to likewise assimilate is pure naïveté. Many groups have great difficulty, cling to their ethnicity, and provide a safe haven as repositories of

---

21 Philip Yancey, *Soul Survivor: How Thirteen Unlikely Mentors Helped My Faith Survive the Church* (New York: Doubleday, 2003), 57.

22 Yancey, *Soul Survivor*, 57.

23 Yancey, *Soul Survivor*, 57.

24 Phil 2:6–8.

25 John A. MacKay, *Heritage and Destiny* (New York: Macmillan, 1943), 1.

history and culture."[26] The missional approach of the church must accept and embrace this ongoing reality for the twenty-first century and push toward a multicultural and multilingual missional strategy. Although many unique cultural differences exist between the dominant culture and the Hispanic culture in particular, two are presented as primary considerations for a missional strategy: language as a marker of cultural identity and the tension of a growing population on New Mestizaje.

Language as a marker of cultural identity for many ethnic groups in the United States has been the primary source for xenophobia, bias, and controversy. What the dominant culture does not understand is that the Spanish language is very much part of the Hispanic culture: "It is a 'living language,' which has been infused by the contributions and vitality of the Amerindian and African cultures."[27] Language in any culture has the profound "political power implicit in its unifying force"[28] to provide a sense of self-worth, comfort, and connection to one's cultural roots.

Solivan points out that the culture in the United States has a "monocular vision" by "universalizing the English language as the only appropriate means of intelligent discourse."[29] This creates a perception that English is the only language through which "one acquires civility, intelligence and self-worth. The arrogance of this position is evident in the English-only movement."[30] But "consistent with a self-understanding as a nation of immigrants, but equally consistent with a socio-history of oppression and racism in North American society, the public awareness that is emerging about Hispanics is shrouded in ambiguity."[31] Eldin Villafañe observes that for Hispanic people, the Spanish language serves as a means of strength and unity within the community. At the same time, many individuals, in a xenophobic move, are attempting to pass legislation of "English only" as the official

26 MacKay, *Heritage and Destiny*, 11.

27 Eldin Villafañe, *The Liberating Spirit: Toward an Hispanic American Pentecostal Social Ethic*, 2nd ed. (Grand Rapids, MI: Eerdmans, 1993), 16.

28 Villafañe, *Liberating Spirit*, 16.

29 Solivan, *Spirit, Pathos and Liberation*, 115.

30 Solivan, *Spirit, Pathos and Liberation*, 115.

31 Villafañe, *Liberating Spirit*, 16.

language of the United States, and others are questioning the validity of bilingual education.[32]

The reality is that as more Hispanics enter this country, the need for Spanish-speaking people will remain high. It is estimated that only 19 percent of Hispanics in the United States do not speak English, and that number is getting lower.[33] Bilingualism is likely to continue as a cultural norm within the United States, because Spanish is already part of the American culture. Justo L. González advises the Hispanic church to respect others who have a different facility or experience with the Spanish language. "Let us not so idolize our culture that we oppress another Hispanic who does not speak as we do, or even one who has never learned how to speak Spanish because the pressures of society were too great."[34] According to Solivan, "One of the important roles Spanish-speaking churches play in the urban centers of the United States is that of the guardian of the culture and language of the community, thereby providing a means of affirming and empowering this marginalized community through the maintenance of its people's self-worth and dignity."[35]

Creating a missional strategy requires the church to acknowledge and accept the multilingual challenge because "twenty-first-century leaders need to develop a multiple consciousness and a multi-vocal discourse."[36] Like those early disciples, "we have to be conversant in more than one cultural language in order to grow and sustain these congregations that give us a chance to engage in real community and develop ethics of truth telling with one another."[37] Making a commitment to communicate cross-culturally allows relationships to pass surface assumptions and move toward real intimacy.

A second area affecting the cultural condition within the Hispanic community is a continuously growing population of Mestizo people.

---

32 Villafañe, *Liberating Spirit*, 16.

33 Villafañe, *Liberating Spirit*, 9.

34 Villafañe, *Liberating Spirit*, 20.

35 Solivan, *Spirit, Pathos and Liberation*, 117.

36 Jacqueline J. Lewis, "On Earth as It Is in Heaven: Rehearsing the Reign of God," *Theology Today* 65, no. 1 (April 2008): 4.

37 Lewis, "On Earth as It Is in Heaven," 4.

Mestizaje is an interesting phenomenon occurring in the United States, in which second- and third-generation immigrant groups lose identity with their parents' culture and at the same time are treated as foreigners within the dominant culture. Hispanic Americans born on US soil are considered "not from here," or "from there." Father Virgilio P. Elizondo, widely recognized for his popularizing of Mestizo studies, describes it from the Mexican American perspective; he realizes that "the current *Mestizo* does not fit conveniently into the analysis categories used by either parent group. The *Mestizo* may understand them far better than they understand him or her. To be an insider-outsider, as is the *Mestizo*, is to have closeness to and distance from both parent cultures."[38]

This is a unique position for Hispanic Americans who are trying to find identity between cultures, because they "feel as though they live at the border, the place where two cultures meet, which is not contained within either culture. Elizondo claims that, 'the Mestizo is not allowed to feel at home anywhere.'"[39]

For example, Mexican Americans and mainland-born Puerto Ricans are not considered Mexican or Puerto Rican. In this, "intersection of two spheres defines a unique point, common to both spheres yet not contained within either."[40] Although this new community of Hispanic Americans is connected to two cultures, the implications create an opportunity to act as a natural bridge to communicate cross-culturally: "Hispanic Americans can be intermediaries between the North American church mission boards and our Latin American brothers and sisters."[41] By creating a potentially new "Galilean" group within the dominant culture, "the bilingual, bicultural identity weaves Latin American and North American cultural traditions together into a new fabric."[42] Just as the first Mestizaje transformed the culture in the Caribbean, Latin American, and South American cultures, this new Mestizaje will continue to affect the American community moving

38 Villafañe, *Liberating Spirit*, 59.

39 John P. Rossing, "Mestizaje and Marginality: A Hispanic American Theology," *Theology Today* 45, no. 3 (October 1988): 296.

40 Rossing, "Mestizaje and Marginality," 297.

41 Solivan, *Spirit, Pathos and Liberation*, 42.

42 Rossing, "Mestizaje and Marginality," 297.

forward and will be an important factor when considering a missional strategy for the church to engage this growing reality.

How does the church consider issues of language and culture? Does the prophetic voice of the church choose one or the other? Or does it broaden its view to embrace a larger picture of Christ's church in communion with the Spirit? Given a theological and cultural challenge, the following sections will dive into practical missional considerations for engaging the Hispanic community theologically and in context.

Cultivating Strategies to Engage the Hispanic Community

Realigning the Missional View of the Church

The challenge in developing a Hispanic missional strategy first begins with educating the local church on crossing cultural norms: "ethnic churches seek to maintain a culture different from the broader multicultural society or denomination in which they reside because they are strongly attached to their national culture, not in the first place because of theological or biblical convictions."[43] This ethos does not have room to embrace a culture's theological or contextual conditions. Religion continues to "remain one of the most enduring institutions in which racial and ethnic sorting continues in most communities today both within and outside the United States."[44] Ethnic immigrant or language groups in the United States tend to remain separate from the dominant culture because they are, as Matthew Todd puts it, "decidedly disinclined to evolve into non-ethnic churches or to embrace non-ethnic evangelism. These churches (and they can be of any ethnicity) function largely as culture clubs."[45] Although Todd may have a good point, his position does not take into consideration the societal factors. He also does not take into account the propensity

43 Matthew Todd, "The Challenge of Jesus's Great Commission to Ethnic Churches," *Direction* 37, no. 2 (Fall 2008): 238.

44 Gregory Stanczak, "Strategic Ethnicity: The Construction of Multi-Racial/Multi-Ethnic Religious Community," *Ethnic & Racial Studies* 29, no. 5 (2006): 859.

45 Todd, "Challenge," 239.

for denominations to be identified with specific ethnicities or groups because "labels create a cultural expectation of whether they are 'white' or 'black' churches."[46]

Todd does acknowledge the benefits of such a condition when he states that in his observations, "ethnic churches tend to be successful in reaching immigrants of their own ethnicity. Ethnic churches are like midwives, helping first-generation Christians move from the safety of their native culture into the culture of their new home, while helping them keep their faith."[47] This is an unavoidable condition so long as many new immigrants are entering the United States and tending to gravitate first toward ethnic Hispanic churches because of the common language or culture.

Furthermore, Todd asks the question, "So how do you bring a people so invested in their cultural identity to begin to invest in cross-cultural/intercultural outreach?"[48] The solution, according to Todd, is to do a better job of teaching the church that God loves the entire world, not just one group over another. But the challenge in cross-cultural ministry lies not in assimilating various ethnic groups into a community, but rather in creating the impetus by which cultural groups can cooperate within a kingdom mentality. In other words, there are times when it would be more appropriate to maintain ethnic churches but not at the expense of rejecting or not accommodating persons of different ethnic or language backgrounds.

A Hispanic missional strategy should not emphasize proselytizing a group of people simply to incorporate them into an English-speaking church, but to minister to the community in a way that keeps the family structure intact. That is the challenge. The following sections will define the various types of multiracial congregations and how neighborhood and demographic changes are factors in developing a Hispanic missional strategy.

---

46 John Dart, "Hues in the Pews: Racially Mixed Churches an Elusive Goal," *Christian Century*, February 8, 2001, http://hirr.hartsem.edu/cong/articles_huesinthepews.html.

47 Todd, "Challenge," 239.

48 Todd, "Challenge," 242.

Navigating Neighborhood Changes

Historically, large metropolitan cities have been the melting pot of diverse cultures. Today, the Hispanic population is growing in more and more small cities and towns due to many different factors. Churches that are not intentional in creating a Hispanic missional strategy will miss great opportunities for ministries. The main impetus of this analysis focuses on the causation of multiracial congregations to ask the question, "Why, in the face of so many counteracting forces, do some congregations transform from uniracial to multiracial (or begin as multiracial)?"[49] Answering this will provide a better understanding in order to develop an overall missional strategy within communities in transition.

Emerson and Kim identify two main variables that underlie the development of a multiracial congregation. The first variable is the "primary impetus for change."[50] This is primarily the guiding force behind a congregation's decision to reach cross-culturally. This could include the church's mission, its survival amid a changing neighborhood, or denominational mandates. The second variable is identifying "the source or origin of the minority population."[51] In other words, it takes into account the population around the church, the appeal of culture within the church, and the merging of two or more congregations. It is within this framework that Emerson and Kim identify seven specific types of multiracial congregations.

1. *Neighborhood embracing* congregations change because it's their mission to reach whosoever within an existing community.
2. *Neighborhood charter* congregations initially began as multiracial congregations.
3. *Niche embracing* congregations focus on reaching new ethnic groups within their region.

49 Emerson and Kim, "Multiracial Congregations: An Analysis of Their Development and a Typology," *Journal for the Scientific Study of Religion* 42, no. 2 (June 2003): 220.

50 Emerson and Kim, "Multiracial Congregations," 220.

51 Emerson and Kim, "Multiracial Congregations," 220.

4. *Niche charter* congregations intentionally establish multiracial congregations in specific multiethnic communities.
5. *Survival embracing* congregations are forced to transform due to ethnic changes within the community, or they simply close down.
6. *Survival merge* churches are two or more ethnic groups merging due to lack of resources.
7. *Mandated* are congregations forced to become multiracial due to outside denominational influences or mandates.[52]

Emerson and Kim conclude that both niche charter and niche embracing are most likely to sustain a multicultural emphasis, whereas survival merge and mandated are the least likely to survive change.

Identifying and moving in a multicultural direction is easier said than done. They conclude that "unless a congregation engages in vigorous efforts—cultural, symbolic, organizational, and networking—to remain multiracial, it will eventually become uniracial."[53] The natural inclination in churches is to become uniracial, and that is why, in order for change to take place, it must be intentional. The next section will provide some general considerations that contribute toward creating a sustained Hispanic missional strategy.

Churches That Are Intentionally Cross-Cultural

Kevin Dougherty and Kimberly Huyser identify external and internal factors that are typically present within multiracial church congregations: "While the external environment creates opportunity for racial diversification in congregations, findings demonstrate racially diverse leadership, charismatic worship, and small groups as internal congregational features also relevant to diversity."[54]

The external environments are not consistent throughout the United States. The West Coast, for example, has a higher percentage of desegregated churches as compared to older metropolitan areas in the

52 Emerson and Kim, "Multiracial Congregations," 221–24.

53 Emerson and Kim, "Multiracial Congregations," 225.

54 Kevin D. Dougherty and Kimberly R. Huyser, "Racially Diverse Congregations: Organizational Identity and the Accommodation of Differences," *Journal for the Scientific Study of Religion* 47, no. 1 (March 2008): 23.

Midwest and the South. But some common aspects remain that are related to the external environments, conducive to racial desegregation. For example, "the interest in and presence of racial and ethnic diversity in congregations systematically rise in more densely populated, urban areas."[55] As such, "diversity inside a congregation appears highly contingent on the diversity outside its doors."[56] Although the external environment may play an important factor in creating an atmosphere conducive for a racially desegregated congregation, it still requires internal factors to cultivate an integrated congregation.

In order to review the internal factors, Dougherty and Huyser pose an important question: "Why are particular congregations able to accommodate worshippers from different races in a society where religious life is largely segregated?"[57] They argue that "in order to bridge racial and ethnic boundaries, being multiracial has to become a part of a congregation's identity."[58] It has to answer the question, "Who are we?" External factors are not sufficient in and of themselves to create this atmosphere, but "overcoming embedded customs of social distance requires a purposeful effort on the part of any formal organization in a racialized society" in order to be effective.[59] Integrating cultural groups requires a change in the ethos of the church; "it requires cultivating a shared, collective identity that transcends participants' personal ethnic identities."[60] The church serves as a bridge connecting each ethnic group while embracing the beauty of each culture.

In multicultural churches that were studied, Dougherty and Huyser identify five internal structural strategies:

1. *Programming*: These congregations emphasize racial reconciliation programs as part of their missional strategy.
2. *Leadership*: These churches have diverse leadership or the pastor's ethnicity is different than the dominant culture, which will contribute to creating a diverse membership in the church.

55 Dougherty and Huyser, "Racially Diverse Congregations," 24.
56 Dougherty and Huyser, "Racially Diverse Congregations," 24.
57 Dougherty and Huyser, "Racially Diverse Congregations," 25.
58 Dougherty and Huyser, "Racially Diverse Congregations," 25.
59 Dougherty and Huyser, "Racially Diverse Congregations," 26.
60 Dougherty and Huyser, "Racially Diverse Congregations," 26.

3. *Worship*: Congregations that emphasize experiential, charismatic worship will have more racially diverse membership.
4. *Informal Relations*: The ability to accommodate diversity will increase informal connections within members of the congregation.
5. *Small Groups*: Congregations using small groups will be more likely to possess racially diverse participants than will congregations without small groups.[61]

George Yancey and Michael Emerson's method for defining the reason churches become open to a multicultural approach comes from a slightly different viewpoint. They identified four important factors motivated by external opportunities that influence the church to pursue a multicultural mission. The first factor involves the important role or influence of leadership: "These leaders, whether clergy or laity, develop a vision for multiracial congregations and were able to convince the attendees to work toward fulfilling that vision."[62] As the leader goes, so will those who follow.

The second factor involves the role of evangelism: "*Evangelical multiracial churches* have become integrated because of attempts to proselytize members of other races, which can be seen in the high loading of evangelism and outreach programs."[63] It is the desire to win people to Christ that drives these churches to become multiracial. One of the pastors stated, "Our goal is not to integrate. Our goal is not to segregate. Our goal is simply to reach people with the gospel of Christ. Souls don't have ages, sizes, shapes, colors, and other cultural indicators."[64]

The third factor in their research is the demographics of the community. These churches "are multiracial because of racial integration within the residential area of the church."[65] These churches become multiracial by intentionally "incorporating racial changes in the

61 Dougherty and Huyser, "Racially Diverse Congregations," 27–29.

62 George Yancey and Michael Emerson, "Integrated Sundays: An Exploratory Study into the Formation of Multiracial Churches," *Sociological Focus* 36, no. 2 (May 2003): 117.

63 Yancey and Emerson, "Integrated Sundays," 118.

64 Yancey and Emerson, "Integrated Sundays," 120.

65 Yancey and Emerson, "Integrated Sundays," 118.

neighborhood and/or because the church is in a transition from one racial group to another."[66] These are churches that recognized and embraced changes in the community and are proactive in their efforts to stay in step with the changes in the community.

The last factor involves social networks that develop between church members "through inter-racial marriages or friendships."[67] In this environment, many smaller subgroups that are diverse may form for the purpose of familiarity or common interests and then assemble together as one church for the Sunday-morning worship. Unique groups are maintained for this familiarity and common interest but not to the detriment of embracing diversity within the church. But it is important to stress the importance of leadership that is necessary to create and maintain momentum within a cross-cultural missional strategy.

Churches That Work Alongside Ethnic Cultures

In developing inclusive communities, Daniel Mulhall poses an interesting question: "How do you take distinct cultural communities and nationalities and make them into one parish?"[68] Mulhall provides six practical suggestions based on his experience and discussions with groups of people from various cultures and ethnic groups. With the rapid growth in population to over 300 million and increasing waves of immigrants entering the United States from many countries, mostly from Central or Latin America, a great demand is being placed on the local churches: "Pastors and other parish leaders face the difficult task of helping these new-comers feel welcomed and at home, while at the same time helping other parishioners to be welcoming and to accept the changes taking place in the parish."[69] In that context, "before a parish can pray together as one community, it first has to develop the intercultural and cross-cultural relationships that will allow it to become one community."[70]

---

66 Yancey and Emerson, "Integrated Sundays," 118.

67 Yancey and Emerson, "Integrated Sundays," 118.

68 Daniel S. Mulhall, "Building Inclusive Communities," *America* 196, no. 4 (February 5, 2007): 20.

69 Mulhall, "Building Inclusive Communities," 20.

70 Mulhall, "Building Inclusive Communities," 21.

Mulhall suggests that the following are required in order to bring distinct cultural communities together into one church: (1) Know your people by performing a demographic study with the existing congregation; (2) set up a multicultural advisory committee by getting the various groups to participate in leadership and allowing them to choose their own representatives for the committee; (3) work for the complementarity of cultures, which can be accomplished by ensuring that all "procedures need to be structured so that all people are treated equally, and fairly, with dignity and respect";[71] (4) "develop structures to deal with cultural tensions" before they develop;[72] (5) "encourage conversation and interaction" in order to learn each other's culture;[73] and (6) listen, which "without judging or comparing or offering solutions may be the most important skill one can learn for working across culture."[74] Mulhall reminds us that "they need us to build bridges across cultural chasms, to open doors to closed organizations and closed minds, and to help them understand how 'the system' works so they can participate fully in it."[75] Mulhall provides a practical framework from which to begin positive communications cross-culturally, but it requires that both sides are willing to communicate openly and establish a common community for all races entering the church.

If the church is to become a School of Prophets, it must be willing to cross cultural borders and engage the community missionally: "Our fallenness sometimes renders us incapable of grasping the scope of the new spiritual family—that it includes redeemed people from every nation."[76] It was the intent of this chapter to provide a snapshot of the Hispanic community as an example of the many diverse cultures represented in the United States. The reality is that ministering in the United States is complex and challenging. It requires more than good

71 Mulhall, "Building Inclusive Communities," 22. He adds, "We need to move from the concept of welcoming the stranger to welcoming home a missing family member" (22).

72 Mulhall, "Building Inclusive Communities," 22.

73 Mulhall, "Building Inclusive Communities," 22.

74 Mulhall, "Building Inclusive Communities," 22.

75 Mulhall, "Building Inclusive Communities," 22.

76 Todd, "Challenge," 238.

intentions; it requires a love and passion to cross cultural borders. It requires leadership to embrace the reality that the "determining factor is Scripture, which requires us to pull ourselves outside of our comfort zones."[77] This is what Jesus did.

With the many Hispanic nations represented in this country, Walter Contreras, Hispanic coordinator of the Evangelical Covenant Church, correctly says, "I have had to learn to be a Mexican, how to be a Puerto Rican, how to accommodate my speech patterns and social skills."[78] Embracing a Hispanic missional strategy requires work, dedication, and more importantly, the Holy Spirit. But it must first begin with a willing desire to serve: "Then I heard the voice of the Lord saying, 'Whom shall I send? And who will go for us?' And I [Isaiah] said, 'Here am I. Send me!'" (Isa 6:8, NIV). Isaiah saw the need and responded to the call.

---

77 Elfriede Wedam, "Multiracial Congregations in America: Looking for a More Realistic Picture of What the World Looks Like," Hartford Institute for Religion Research, accessed February 8, 2022, http://hirr.hartsem.edu/cong/articles_multiracialcongs.html.

78 Walter Contreras quoted in Roldolpho Carrasco, "Catching Up with Hispanics," *Christianity Today* 45, no. 14 (November 12, 2001): 67.

5

Profetas in Social Action

JOSEPH A. OCASIO

THE PROPHETIC ROLE OF the church requires a contextualized theology specific to the Hispanic culture: "There can be no monolithic view of the relation of Christ to culture, for there is no ideal culture. God's kingdom culture embodied in the church always takes particular form in concrete contexts."[1] Samuel Solivan adds, "A Hispanic-American theology, to be authentic, must hold itself accountable to the Hispanic-American communities' *Mestizo* [new race] composition."[2] It is a role that defines what the church does and how it lives out its mandate to sustain a new community.

Eldin Villafañe correctly states, "Without a doubt, this century, perhaps as no other, the Spirit has been challenging the church in 'rethinking identity and vocation.'"[3] This involves the assimilation of the various elements or roles of a missional church. Separating or focusing on selective areas at the expense of the whole will dilute the full potential impact of a missional church. Veli-Matti Kärkkäinen writes, "The reason is simple: since all members have the Spirit no one of them

1 Brad Harper and Paul Louis Metzger, *Exploring Ecclesiology: An Evangelical and Ecumenical Introduction*, 1st ed. (Grand Rapids, MI: Brazos Press, 2009), 207.

2 Solivan, *Spirit, Pathos and Liberation*, 41.

3 Villafañe, *Liberating Spirit*, 216.

can monopolize his leading."[4] Therefore, "since the Spirit's leading is a privilege of all members, the structures of a charismatic fellowship have to arise through the interaction of all its members."[5]

It is within a "charismatic structure that Kärkkäinen describes the four basic tasks of the church: "first, the fellowship of mutual edification [*Koinonia*], second, fellowship of service to each other and to the world [*Diakonia*], third, fellowship of witness [*Kerygma*], and fourth, fellowship of worship [*Leitourgia*]."[6] If the church is to be fully functional, it is imperative that each area of ministry be intentionally activated and guided by the Holy Spirit in order to be fully effective in creating a missional strategy within the Hispanic context.

According to Murray W. Dempster, "within this context of church mission, ministry programs of both evangelism and social concern are needed in order for the church to bear an authentic witness to the gospel."[7] Martin Luther King Jr. puts it this way:

> The gospel at its best deals with the whole man, not only his soul but also his body, not only his spiritual well-being but also his material well-being. A religion that professes a concern about the souls of men and is not equally concerned about the slums that damn them, the economic conditions that strangle them, and the social conditions that cripple them, is a spiritually moribund religion.[8]

The mission of the church "brings people, nations and the whole world into the eschatological reign, in which God gives priority to the poor, the sick, the downtrodden, and the widows and calls us to participate

---

4 Veli-Matti Kärkkäinen, *Toward a Pneumatological Theology: Pentecostal and Ecumenical Perspectives on Ecclesiology, Soteriology, and Theology of Mission* (Lanham, MD: University Press of America, 2002), 118–19.

5 Kärkkäinen, *Toward a Pneumatological Theology*, 118–19.

6 Kärkkäinen, *Toward a Pneumatological Theology*, 119.

7 Murray W. Dempster, "Evangelism, Social Concern, and the Kingdom of God," in *Called and Empowered: Global Mission in Pentecostal Perspective*, ed. Murray W. Dempster, Byron D. Klaus, and Douglas Peterson (Grand Rapids, MI: Baker Academic, 1991), 24.

8 Martin Luther King Jr., *Strength to Love* (Minneapolis: Fortress Press, 2010), 159.

in self-giving service."[9] Therefore, implementing a Hispanic missional strategy for the church must embrace the unity and interdependent relationship of the four essential functions of the church. The first missional aspect is koinonia and its implication for a missional strategy.

Koinonia: The Spirit's Communion with the Community

Koinonia can be described as "fellowship, association, community, communion . . . as exhibiting an embodiment and proof of fellowship."[10] In Acts 2:42, the newly baptized believers "devoted themselves to the apostles' teaching fellowship, to the breaking of bread and the prayers" (NRSV). In this text, Luke captures the consequence of a Spirit-led koinoniac experience that was to become an example for a missional church today. Without the Spirit, koinonia simply becomes a social club with ritualistic activities. Without an outward focus of the koinoniac expression, the church will not be able to fulfill its God-given mission to the world.

The church must be intentional in koinonia: "The church, then, is the 'sign,' 'instrument' and 'foretaste' of what is to come, as God's eschatological reign spreads throughout the world."[11] *Koinonia* is not a term used to justify an inward focus of a church to maintain a social club status that is static, but to be a vehicle by which the koinoniac of the church moves outward as a *communitas* to evangelize the community. *Communitas* is a "unique experience of togetherness that only really happens among a group of people inspired by the vision of a better world who actually attempt to do something about it."[12]

Communitas within the framework of koinonia and empowered by the Holy Spirit can become a change agent within a community.

9 Peter Althouse, "Towards a Pentecostal Ecclesiology: Participation in the Missional Life of the Triune God," *Journal of Pentecostal Theology* 18, no. 2 (2009): 234.

10 Bible Study Tools, s.v. "Koinonia," accessed February 9, 2022, www.searchgodsword.org/lex/grk/view.cgi?number=2842.

11 Althouse, "Towards a Pentecostal Ecclesiology," 234.

12 Hirsch, *Forgotten Ways*, 277–78.

Without the outward focus of koinonia, the salt would lose its flavor and no longer be useful in the kingdom of God. The church must build "its own spiritual life in order to create a caring environment in which people are empowered to grow as persons as well as to build a basis for mobilizing active participation in programs of evangelism and social concern."[13] The church, "as God's colony in a human world, . . . is both a model and a sign of redeemed and transformed relationships. It is a koinonia of the Spirit and koinonia with fellow Christians."[14] In other words, the church becomes a community of the Spirit and a *communitas* to the world by demonstrating the Spirit's expectations.

Villafañe insists that the church's demonstrations display "to the Hispanic community and the world, loving and just structures of relationships."[15] This includes the removal of "deeply entrenched moral biases, value preferences, and social prejudices" that can be expressed through sexism, classism, or racism, which is antithetical to the Holy Spirit's missional expectation of the church.[16] As Murray correctly describes, "All dividing walls of the old social order are forever undermined in the koinonia that the Spirit creates. In replicating the kingdom ministry of Jesus through the charismata, the Holy Spirit creates koinonia, which witnesses to the inclusive scope and the egalitarian nature of God's reign."[17]

Additionally, an important kerygmatic connection to koinonia manifests itself through evangelism. It expresses the importance that each function of the church is interconnected in creating an authentic missional *communitas*. Orlando Costas makes the point that true koinonia is the validation of kerygma because "it gives credibility to the message of love that is proclaimed by the community of faith."[18] Koinonia must become the model by which it overcomes all social barriers within the community. Koinonia within a missional church must demonstrate in action what it claims in word.

---

13 Dempster, "Evangelism," *Called and Empowered*, 27.

14 Villafañe, *Liberating Spirit*, 216–17.

15 Villafañe, *Liberating Spirit*, 217.

16 Dempster, "Evangelism," *Called and Empowered*, 29.

17 Dempster, "Evangelism," *Called and Empowered*, 29.

18 Villafañe, *Liberating Spirit*, 218.

Dempster further articulates this connection between kerygma and koinonia by making four points: "First, when the church's koinoniac ministry is brought into line with Jesus' kingdom ministry, it validates the truthfulness of the church's kerygmatic announcement that God's reign has already broken into history in the ministry of Jesus Christ."[19] In order to make an impact, koinonia must become more than simply an ideology of a missional theology; it must become a "visible 'interpretation' of what it means for the church to say that the eschatological kingdom can already be experienced as a foretaste of the future needs to be found in the life of the community."[20]

The second point Dempster makes is that the church is a countercultural institution that must function as the vehicle from which to usher in the present and future reign of God. The church in its "koinonia already embodies a social criticism of the existing social order that is dominated by the economic interests of the powerful and the national interests of political rulers."[21] It requires the church to assume a nonconformist position against the weight of social pressures that are contrary to God's teaching. It is the Holy Spirit that empowers the church to withstand the tides of tolerance, "and this nonconformity to the world's dehumanizing values, from a Pentecostal kingdom perspective, takes meaningful form in the church's koinonia."[22]

The dehumanizing values of the world can cause individuals to deny their identity for the purpose of gaining acceptance by society at the expense of losing a multicultural, multilingual, and multiracial identity. On the other hand, according to Solivan, "the development of community and identity as a Hispanic-American people provides our conjunctive orientation. We must be both Hispanic and American. We can contribute in a unique way to the pluralism, which so characterizes the United States."[23] The church, in essence, becomes the conduit by which the Holy Spirit releases koinonia, which transcends any

19 Dempster, "Evangelism," *Called and Empowered*, 29, 30.

20 Dempster, "Evangelism," *Called and Empowered*, 30.

21 Dempster, "Evangelism," *Called and Empowered*, 30.

22 Dempster, "Evangelism," *Called and Empowered*, 30.

23 Solivan, *Spirit, Pathos and Liberation*, 122.

racial, social, or cultural differences and instead embraces the new life in Christ together in unity.

Dempster's third point is that "through its koinonia the church demonstrates that it understands its social responsibility to function 'as a bearer of moral tradition.'"[24] The local church, as guided by the Holy Spirit, is the moral compass by which society is to gauge true love and justice. If the church cannot reflect the proper koinonia as intended by God, society will be inclined to define morality based on its own presuppositions and interpretations of social justice.

The last point Dempster makes is that the church is a signpost that points toward God's future reign. The vocation of the church is "displaying in its own life the justice doing and peacemaking of God," that is, demonstrating the hope that is to come by expressing it in the present reality.[25] Koinonia in action requires more than just gathering together as church; it requires connecting with the community as part of an overall missional strategy to build relationships cross-culturally.

Kerygma: The Spirit's Communication with the Community

Kerygma can be described as "the message or proclamation [the preaching] of the heralds of God or Christ."[26] First Corinthians 2:4 says, "And my message and my *preaching* were not in persuasive words of wisdom, but in demonstration of the Spirit and of power" (NASB). In this text, Paul qualifies the kerygma or proclamation not as mere truth, but as truth that is supported by the testimony and demonstration of the Holy Spirit's power. Kerygma without the Holy Spirit is simply another religious ideology. The proclamation of the good news of Jesus Christ is the heart of the kerygmatic ministry: "the church is anointed by the Holy Spirit for the express purpose of empowering its preaching with the same power with which Jesus was anointed for his proclamation. With this transference of the Spirit's anointing, the church is enabled

24 Dempster, "Evangelism," *Called and Empowered*, 31.

25 Dempster, "Evangelism," *Called and Empowered*, 31.

26 Bible Study Tools, s.v. "Kerugma," accessed February 9, 2022, www.searchgodsword.org/lex/grk/view.cgi?number=2782.

to proclaim the message of the good news of the kingdom."[27] The point is that "God's preferential agents for evangelization are those rejected by the dominant society."[28] Those who experience the *orthopathos* of Christ in the present are more empathetic in crossing cultural borders within the community.

The Holy Spirit empowers the kerygmatic focus of the church as it did with the apostle Peter, who, after being filled with the Holy Spirit, stood up with the power of the Spirit to respond to questions about hearing praises to God in their own languages.[29] In this Spirit-led kerygmatic event, Peter preached his first sermon, resulting in the conversion of more than three thousand people. In Peter's exuberance and with the power of the Spirit, a fruitful kerygmatic experience launched the church. The apostle Paul describes God's modus operandi when he states that God chose the foolish things, weak things, lowly things, and despised things.[30] According to Daniel Rodríguez, "God didn't choose the economically and educationally privileged, or the upwardly-mobile middle-class Jews, but the unschooled and ordinary Galileans (Acts 4:13)."[31]

In 1906, a fresh pouring of the Holy Spirit brought about a revival at the Azusa Street Mission, which was led by an African American pastor named William J. Seymour. Cecil M. Robeck Jr. describes what happened in 1906 as follows: "The revival reached out to the rest of the world with a rapidity that is hard to imagine. It was like a fire lit by dry tinder when nobody was looking. It exploded—billowing up and scattered its sparks in every direction."[32] In 1914, Charles Shumway, a member who was there at the very first meeting, said, "The whole company was immediately swept to its knees as by some mighty power."[33]

---

27 Dempster, "Evangelism," *Called and Empowered*, 24–25.

28 Daniel A. Rodríguez, "No Longer Foreigners and Aliens: Toward a Missiological Christology for Hispanics in the United States," *Missiology* 31, no. 1 (January 1, 2003): 59.

29 Acts 2:6–41.

30 1 Corinthians 1:26–31.

31 Rodríguez, "No Longer Foreigners and Aliens," 59.

32 Cecil M. Robeck Jr., *The Azusa Street Mission and Revival: The Birth of the Global Pentecostal Movement* (Nashville: Thomas Nelson, 2006), 187.

33 Robeck, *The Azusa Street Mission*, 68–69.

The empowering of the Spirit brought the same exuberance at Azusa Street that Peter experienced. This resulted in the same compelling desire to proclaim the gospel as heralds sent by God. The outcome of the Azusa Street revival launched a worldwide movement that continues today, with more than 600 million people around the world part of the Pentecostal/charismatic movement. Although the Spirit provided the fire, it was through men and women, from every race and ethnic background, young and old, whom the Lord used as vehicles from which the "fire" of the gospel would spread around the world.

As noted by Dempster, "evangelism is the traditional name that we give to the objective of the church's kerygmatic ministry because in this activity the church invites people to respond to the 'evangel' being preached."[34] This call to conversion defines the objective of the kerygmatic function. Stephen Charles Mott describes conversion as a "redirection of life, characterized by a new allegiance at the center of the personality and by a new direction in social relationship."[35] Brian Kelly is "convinced that the concept of spiritual journey or pilgrimage is the best model for envisioning the conversion process."[36] He describes a process of conversion that includes a spiritual quest, the encounter and the continual process of transformation.[37] Dempster adds that "salvation, within this frame of reference, is personally experienced in this conversion to God's reign and the attendant radical overthrow of the old self-centered kingdom."[38] Dempster correctly describes the practical aspect of delivering the "evangel" as well as describing the experience of the respondents. Although personal, individual salvation is important, it is still just one aspect of the kerygmatic experience.

The other aspect involves the expected social ramifications resulting from the kerygmatic experience that not only lead the respondent toward the not-yet hope of God's kingdom, but also ground the new believer in the here-and-now reality of God's kingdom in the present.

---

34 Dempster, "Evangelism," *Called and Empowered*, 25.

35 Dempster, "Evangelism," *Called and Empowered*, 25.

36 Brian M. Kelly, *One Step Closer to Christ: Evangelism as Spiritual Pilgrimage Together* (Scotts Valley, CA: Barnabas Missions Unlimited, 2000), 18.

37 Kelly, *One Step Closer*, 18.

38 Dempster, "Evangelism," *Called and Empowered*, 25.

Although Christ is preached, Villafañe points out that "kerygma has a prophetic cutting edge. . . . This means that the Hispanic Pentecostal church must not be content to preach and witness just to individual-personal sins, but must see the larger spiritual conflict."[39] Any missional strategy must preach from the whole Bible to the whole person because "no area is exempt in personal or social life from the kerygmatic task."[40] Just as koinonia is connected with the kerygmatic task, so kerygma is connected with the *diakonic* [service] necessity to serve one another.

The church must proclaim love and justice but also address the social issues such as abortion, education, health, AIDS, immigration, discrimination, and so on. Villafañe adds, "Let there be no mistake, the kerygma is nothing less and nothing more than the full liberation that Jesus Christ brings."[41] The church witnesses this reality by word and deed under the power of the Holy Spirit. Villafañe correctly describes the full kerygmatic experience from the individual and social aspects by pointing to practical areas in which the church can also participate as ambassadors of Christ's reign in the present. Without an outward social connection to the community, the role of the church devolves into a continuation of the status quo.

The maintenance-mode hope is that more people will find their way into the physical structure of the church. The redemptive strategy of God includes both humanity and this world. Rethinking kerygma eschatologically will compel the church to get ready for the actual return of Christ, who is to reign in this world and bring all things back to order. The hope is not that the church would go to heaven; rather, the church expects Christ to return. Jesus will return. The kerygmatic function of the church should reflect a desired response from the Master: "Well done, good and faithful servant!" (Matt 25:23, NIV). The Master is referring to the kerygmatic mission for this world in the "here and now" because his glory already resides in heaven.

Through the Spirit, the kerygmatic missional strategy must be outward in focus in the present world while preparing for the return of the King who will reign in this world. Creating a Hispanic kerygmatic

39 Villafañe, *Liberating Spirit*, 220.

40 Villafañe, *Liberating Spirit*, 220.

41 Villafañe, *Liberating Spirit*, 220.

strategy must include identifying where the individual is in his or her spiritual journey. It also must include an accurate interpretation of the hearer's culture with a thorough understanding of the language in which the unbeliever can best hear. Lastly, it requires a truthful translation of the faith story into a language the unbeliever can hear and understand.[42]

In summary, "one of the most effective ways the church validates the gospel is by translating the 'truths' it proclaims in the kerygma into the way it structures and lives out its own congregational life."[43] This section emphasized not only the role of the kerygmatic word but also the role of the kerygmatic deed. The following section on *diakonia* will focus on how a missional strategy requires the church to serve the world.

Diakonia: The Spirit's Connection with the Community

Diakonia can be described as "service, ministering . . . the ministration of those who render to others the offices of Christian affection especially those who help meet needs by either collecting or distributing of charities."[44] Ephesians 4:12 says, "For the equipping of the saints for the work of *service*, to the building up of the body of Christ" (NASB). This text describes the role of leadership and the responsibility of preparing believers for the ministry of *diakonia*. In describing *diakonia*, Villafañe notes that "the diaconal mission of the church reaches out to all; no human need escapes its concern."[45] It must be an authentic expression of love through serving the community: "Whatever form our diaconal mission takes, whatever be its social strategy: social service, social education, social witness, or social action; it ever needs to be reminded that action really receives its character from prayer."[46]

42 Kelly, *One Step Closer*, 22.

43 Dempster, "Evangelism," *Called and Empowered*, 27.

44 Bible Study Tools, s.v. "Diakonia," accessed February 9, 2022, www.searchgodsword.org/lex/grk/view.cgi?number=1248.

45 Villafañe, *Liberating Spirit*, 221.

46 Villafañe, *Liberating Spirit*, 221.

In regard to the Hispanic church, Frank D. Macchia rightly asserts that "Pentecostal communities in Latin America have been so successful as centers of hope and new opportunities for the poor that one Pentecostal scholar could quip that Pentecostals do not have a social policy for renewal, they are a social policy."[47] It is a theology of *orthopathos* that enables a Hispanic missional strategy to be connected to its community through *diakonia*. Unfortunately, Pentecostals "in general have been less attuned to the social structures and cultural realities that implicitly support poverty and racism."[48] The church has not been sensitive to the sighs of the Holy Spirit, who desires "these powers to be overthrown so that God's people might recognize more of the divine grace implicit in creation, a grace that is fulfilled, but by no means eclipsed, by redemption and healing through the gospel of Christ."[49]

Diakonia is more than the immediate needs of the poor and marginalized in society. Dempster correctly states that "the Church's diakonic ministry, stated bluntly, is more than a theologically based version of the international Red Cross."[50] Generally speaking, most outreach programs that churches administer are more kerygmatic in purpose. The intent of serving or ministering is salvation focused in nature with the intent on being *diakonic*. Simply meeting a need is replaced with a hidden agenda to save people.

The primary discussion to this point has been about *diakonia* in terms of social welfare, because "social welfare focuses on the welfare of people; this aspect of the church's social services 'aim at removing or alleviating their suffering by direct treatment of themselves and their environmental circumstances."[51] But Dempster describes another aspect of *diakonia* as social action. This differs from social welfare in that "social action has the goal of changing or reforming basic conditions in society which cause human need."[52] In other words, social

47 Frank D. Macchia, *Baptized in the Spirit: A Global Pentecostal Theology* (Grand Rapids, MI: Zondervan, 2006), 280.

48 Macchia, *Baptized in the Spirit*, 280.

49 Macchia, *Baptized in the Spirit*, 280.

50 Dempster, "Evangelism," *Called and Empowered*, 32.

51 Dempster, "Evangelism," *Called and Empowered*, 33.

52 Dempster, "Evangelism," *Called and Empowered*, 33.

welfare attempts to alleviate the symptomatic problems of the community, whereas social action attempts to draw out the underlying causation that brought about the symptoms. It is in this area of social action from which justice can be sought out. Villafañe adds:

> Scripture teaches that justice is a standard, a plumb line to which all humans must conform in their relationships. Listen to the words of Isaiah 28:17: "I will make justice the measuring line and righteousness the plumb line." Scripture presents us a rich and nuanced understanding of justice. At heart it speaks to us of a concept of justice that I want to underline—that is, justice as "fidelity to the demands of relationship."[53]

It is this understanding of justice that is found in the book of Amos, where the focus of God's wrath was centered on the injustice of the wealthy and powerful toward the poor and weak of society: "But let justice roll on like a river, righteousness like a never-failing stream!" (Amos 5:24, NIV). According to Villafañe, the lesson is clear: "idolatry is at the heart of social injustice and the eventual downfall of a nation. Social injustice, not sexual immorality *per se*, is the central criterion by which to judge a ruler or nation."[54] Dempster defines a Christian social action as "changing the system." Although the social welfare programs of the church are an important part of the *diakonic* ministry, they "need to be complemented by social action in order to express the kind of service that God intends to render to the world in his reign of love, justice, and shalom."[55]

The fallacy of the separation of church and state has created a culture of complacency within American churches. The Hispanic Pentecostal church, by virtue of its status within the dominant society, has had to address issues directly and often without the support of many Pentecostal groups. Dempster argues that the church must be clear regarding its role to support God's mandates or man's unjust laws: "Taking clues from Amos, many Pentecostal groups—with their

---

53 Eldin Villafañe, *Beyond Cheap Grace: A Call to Radical Discipleship, Incarnation, and Justice* (Grand Rapids, MI: Eerdmans, 2006), 66.

54 Villafañe, *Beyond Cheap Grace*, 74.

55 Dempster, "Evangelism," *Called and Empowered*, 35.

heritage of status quo quietism, or their new found alliance with right-wing political agendas—also need to heed the warning that Christian faith can be transformed into an ideology that may unwittingly serve the cause of oppression."[56]

Within the area of social action are a few areas that need attention. The first thing that the church must realize is that it "needs to desacralize the state and its system of laws as the ultimate source of human rights by reminding political authorities of their God-given obligation to guarantee justice for all peoples."[57] Unjust laws according to God's precepts are still unjust. Churches must be vocal in this area as representatives of God's kingdom.

A second thing the church may participate in is the political process: "Working for creative reform through politics is a necessary strategy in the promotion of social justice because some desirable societal changes can be brought about only through government initiative."[58] The church must also intervene in the political process, "not for the sake of its own self-serving interests but on behalf of the voiceless and disinherited members of society," who cannot be fairly represented.[59] The idea of separation of church and state is a humanistic ideology, yet the Pentecostal church has opted to avoid encouraging Christians to participate in the political arena.

A third thing the church may use to promote social change is "instituting its own social programs that function as instruments of human justice."[60] By pursuing this area of involvement, it may break the stereotypical mindset that social issues are to be addressed strictly through political means. Dempster states that the church "can demonstrate that significant social change does not necessarily involve government intervention in all cases."[61] The church can reclaim the role of serving the community as change agents for social issues.

---

56 Murray W. Dempster, "Pentecostal Social Concern and the Biblical Mandate of Social Justice," *Pneuma* 9, no. 2 (Fall 1987): 142.

57 Dempster, "Evangelism," *Called and Empowered*, 35.

58 Dempster, "Evangelism," *Called and Empowered*, 36.

59 Dempster, "Evangelism," *Called and Empowered*, 36.

60 Dempster, "Evangelism," *Called and Empowered*, 37.

61 Dempster, "Evangelism," *Called and Empowered*, 37.

But in a more practical manner, each individual church may define common issues from which to connect ecumenically with other churches to collaborate on social issues that are common to the body of Christ. The American emphasis on individualism has affected the church in a negative manner by creating a Lone Ranger mentality. Hearing descriptions of churches as "independent" or "sovereign" implies a group disconnected from the overall body of Christ. A complete *diakonic* ministry will involve cooperation and colaboring efforts from followers of Christ regardless of denominations or liturgical differences. The true strength of the church lies in its oneness in Christ.

Patrick Franklin explains that "while proclamation is crucial to the Church's mission, it must never be separated from embodiment of the gospel in concrete action and loving service."[62] But in order to develop a Hispanic missional strategy, a more comprehensive *diakonic* emphasis must also include a social action emphasis. Bonhoeffer notes "that when Jesus says, 'You are the salt of the earth,' he means they will be his witnesses in the totality of their existence, both in word and deed, proclaiming and acting. The disciples do not possess the salt; they themselves are the salt."[63] The *diakonic* aspect of a missional strategy must go beyond religion and connect outwardly to the *orthopathos* of the community. The next section will discuss the final piece of the puzzle, which is the glue that unites the other three aspects of the church. The last section will address *leitourgia.*

Leitourgia: *The Spirit's Worship with the Community*

Leitourgia can be described as "a service or ministry of the priests relative to the prayers and sacrifices offered to God . . . a gift or benefaction for the relief of the needy."[64] Second Corinthians 9:12 says, "For the ministry of this *service* is not only fully supplying the needs of the saints, but is also overflowing through many thanksgivings to God" (NASB). In this text, Paul describes *leitourgia* not only in supplying the needs of the saints, but by worshiping God through the many types

62 Franklin, "Bonhoeffer's Mission Ecclesiology," 101.

63 Dietrich Bonhoeffer, *The Cost of Discipleship* (New York: Touchstone, 1995), 116.

64 Bible Study Tools, s.v. "Leitourgia," accessed February 9, 2022, www.searchgodsword.org/lex/grk/view.cgi?number=3009.

of thanksgivings. According to Simon Chan, "worship is a 'creative response' to God's self-revelation."[65] Villafañe comments that

> the whole Scripture is a commentary on the worshiping life and vocation of God's people. Jesus reminded the Samaritan woman that worship must be in spirit and in truth (John 4:23–24). Worship in the 'cultos' must be complemented by worship in the 'barrios' of the world. . . . From Amos to Isaiah God's people are challenged to place their worship praxis—offerings, fasting, music, liturgy—within the context of just action (diakonia) to the poor and the oppressed. There is a deep spiritual relationship of service (social justice) and solidarity with the oppressed and true worship.[66]

Villafañe points out the "spiritual relationship" between koinonia, *diakonia*, and *leitourgia*. Developing worship praxis must take into consideration a theological perspective toward a liturgical theology. Performing rituals without a thorough grasp of their theology will mitigate the effectiveness and impact of the liturgical role of ministry. Justo Gonzáles describes *leitourgia* as worshiping from the context of being an exile or pilgrim:

> Christian worship is, among other things, the place where we catch a glimpse of that future—a glimpse that both supports us in our pilgrimage and judges us in our attempts to be too settled. In the Eucharist, as we share food, we commit ourselves to a life of sharing, "until he comes" (1 Cor. 11:26). In baptism, we are grafted into the resurrected body of Jesus, and thus share in his resurrected life. In preaching, we announce to ourselves and to the world God's promised Reign of love, peace, and justice. In singing, we practice for the day when we shall "laud and magnify" God's glorious name "with angels and archangels, and with all the company of heaven," as we now say at communion.[67]

---

65 Simon Chan, *Liturgical Theology: The Church as Worshiping Community* (Downers Grove, IL: InterVarsity Press, 2006), 13.

66 Villafañe, *Liberating Spirit*, 219.

67 Justo L. González, *Alabadle!: Hispanic Christian Worship* (Nashville: Abingdon Press, 1996), 19.

González paints a wonderful picture of Christian worship and adds that "for worship to be all of these things, however, we must have a clear sense that we are a pilgrim people; that we can never be fully installed in this world or in this society and its present order; that for us, as a second-century Christian would say, 'every foreign land is a homeland, and every homeland is foreign.'"[68] Therefore, *leitourgia* from a Hispanic context resembles the following:

> Part of what we as Hispanics bring to worship—and part of our contribution to the worship life of the church at large—is the painful experience of not quite belonging, which is the counterpart of the joyful experience of belonging to God and God's Reign! Our very existence, and the witness of our churches in our barrios, is an invitation to the entire church to become a pilgrim people, and to learn to worship "on the march."[69]

According to Solivan, "an examination of Pentecostal worship is the lens through which one can best see and understand Pentecostalism. . . . Pentecostals are best understood in the context of worship and its relation to evangelism and mission."[70] Hispanic Pentecostal liturgy reflects three important aspects that contribute to its contextualized worship.

The first is the belief in the "priesthood of all believers," or the ministry of the laity. There is a communal sense to the worship in which laypeople, clergy, children, young adults, and the elderly can have an opportunity to play a role in worship. According to Solivan, "what [are] most important are the leading of the Holy Spirit and the affirmation of a person's ministry and/or gifts, and the use of these gifts for the edification of the congregation."[71] The phrase *a royal priesthood*, "drawn from Exodus 19:6, reinforces the liturgical purpose of the church."[72] The second aspect is that Hispanic Pentecostal worship is noncreedal in

68 González, *Alabadle*, 19.

69 González, *Alabadle*, 19.

70 González, *Alabadle*, 45.

71 González, *Alabadle*, 50.

72 Rodríguez, "No Longer Foreigners and Aliens," 62.

stance: "Their sole basis of authority for informing worship is Scripture as interpreted and applied by the community."[73]

The third aspect is within its nonliturgical tradition. That is, it does not follow specific rituals or patterns, but is led by the Spirit under the supervision of the pastor. A liturgy does exist, but it is informal in execution. This creates four general principles: "an openness to the leading of the Holy Spirit; an environment of expectation that the Holy Spirit will meet us as we worship; and openness to be free to praise God and God's word as it addresses us in worship; and passionate and participatory worship."[74]

Leitourgia is in essence the totality or encompassing aspect from which kerygma, koinonia, and *diakonia* flow: "Through Jesus, therefore, let us continually offer to God a sacrifice of praise—the fruit of lips that profess his name. And do not forget to do good and to share with others, for with such sacrifices God is pleased" (Heb 13:15–16, NIV). Chan writes, "To see the preaching of the gospel in the world as a liturgical act means that it is first and foremost a service rendered to God."[75] In other words, every component of a missional strategy within the community is a form of worship unto the Lord. The proclaiming of the good news, serving the community, and coming together as a community can all be regarded as a form of worship unto the Lord. Creating any missional strategy in the church must first be considered an act of worship accomplished by the power of the Holy Spirit.

Crossing cultural borders was the plan of God from the beginning as Jesus confirmed in Acts 1:8: "But you will receive power when the Holy Spirit comes on you; and you will be my witnesses in Jerusalem, and in all Judea and Samaria, and to the ends of the earth" (NIV). By contextualizing the four functions of the church to reach a broader population, the church realigns its ethos to better engage a diverse community. Developing a Hispanic missional strategy within the culture of the church requires the Holy Spirit and a willing spirit to extend a hand of friendship within this growing and evolving community.

---

73 González, *Alabadle*, 50.

74 González, *Alabadle*, 52.

75 Chan, *Liturgical Theology*, 44.

6

Profetas to the Nation

GIRIEN RICARDO SALAZAR

ALMOST 250 YEARS HAVE passed since the American Experiment began, and since then individuals rich and poor, great and small, religious and nonreligious have strived to influence policy at every level of government, especially national. Tocqueville wrote, "The cares of political life engross a most prominent place in the occupation of a citizen in the United States, and almost the only pleasure of which an American has any idea is to take a part in the Government, and to discuss the part he has taken."[1] What Tocqueville keenly observed was that American citizenship and political engagement go hand in hand. In America, one group that has a long history of political engagement is Christian ministers. Whether because or in spite of the Bill of Rights' religious clauses or various interpretations of the "wall of separation" that exists between the church and the state, Christian clergy of numerous denominational backgrounds and political persuasions continue to partake in the "pleasure" of American politics.[2]

---

1 Alexis de Tocqueville, *Democracy in America, The Complete and Unabridged Volumes I and II* (New York: Bantam Books, 2004), 291.

2 The words, "Congress shall make no law respecting an establishment of religion, or prohibiting the free exercise thereof," are widely considered the "religion clauses" of the US Constitution, the former part of the phrase considered the Establishment Clause and the latter part the Free Exercise Clause.

Clergy political engagement—what is perceived by many to be an audacious yet delicate dance between that which is sacred and that which is secular—is now in full force among Hispanic Christians in the United States and is led by organizations such as the National Hispanic Christian Leadership Conference, Hispanic Action Network, and National Latino Evangelical Coalition. More than ever before, Hispanic pastors in America are charged with becoming astute in their role as political leaders of their communities and cognizant of the expectations that come with it. Fortunately, pastors do not have to look far to gain a rudimentary understanding of the type of model their political engagement efforts will likely or should resemble; they may look to academic studies and mainstream Christian thought.

In academic studies on clergy, a political engagement model can be used to describe not only the political role that the congregation, denomination, and broader community bestow on the minister or permit the minister to assume, whether assertively or passively, but can also describe the clergy's attitude toward political activity. James Guth and colleagues stated, "In real life pastors play their roles as citizen, religious professional, and institutional leader simultaneously, and it is often difficult to separate them."[3] Yet, even with this difficult task, contemporary studies consistently demonstrate that politically engaged ministers generally function through an engagement model that characterizes American ministers as political prophets.

Ted G. Jelen observed that the political role that stands out among the political activities of pastors, particularly within their congregations, is the role of opinion leader.[4] In many ways, pastoral opinion leaders have functioned much in line with how leadership scholar James M. Burns classified political opinion leaders, men and women existing in a dynamic leader–follower relationship and navigating a myriad of political opinions in order to shape public opinion, or in the minister's

3 James L. Guth et al., *The Bully Pulpit: The Politics of Protestant Clergy*, Studies in Government and Public Policy (Lawrence: University Press of Kansas, 1997), 194.

4 Ted G. Jelen, "Notes for a Theory of Clergy as Political Leaders," in *Christian Clergy in American Politics*, ed. Sue E. S. Crawford and Laura R. Olson (Baltimore: Johns Hopkins University Press, 2001), 25.

case, congregational opinion.[5] Much in line with the concept of opinion leadership, the political roles of American ministers have been characterized as that of "advisor" in the seventeenth century, "opinion molder" in the eighteenth century, and "articulator of national identity" in the nineteenth century.[6]

Yet Jelen moved beyond the nonreligious language for his eventual characterization of politically engaged American ministers: "The political [opinion] role that clergy assume within their congregations can be considered analogous to the role of 'prophet' in the Hebrew Scriptures."[7] Jelen described the Roman Catholic priest as a "distant prophet" for his ways of teaching congregants about political issues through persuasion and reason,[8] and Djupe and Gilbert described a minister of the Evangelical Lutheran Church of America and Episcopal Church as a "prophetic representative" for his or her ways of battling moral reform issues in the community.[9] It is true that as a "prophet" congregants expected the minister to provide a moral critique of the political realm,[10] functioning as a religious political critic, advisor, or opinion leader, but in contemporary studies the prophetic engagement model is used also to describe the minister as one who desires to see Christian principles actualized beyond his or her faith community and within the broader civil construct. According to Mary Sawyer, the prophetic engagement model increasingly emerged within the African American community during and following the civil rights movement, which inspired their efforts in moral persuasion, calls for civil disobedience, and eventually

---

5 James M. Burns, *Leadership*, First Harper Perennial Political Classics Edition (New York: Harper Perennial, 2010), 257–65.

6 Neal E. Wise, "Clergymen in the 95th Congress: A Case Study of Religion in Politics" (PhD diss., Graduate Theological Union, 1982), 13.

7 Jelen, "Notes for a Theory," 25.

8 Ted G. Jelen, *The Political World of the Clergy* (Westport, CT: Praeger, 1993), 106–9, see also 145–46.

9 Paul A. Djupe and Christopher P. Gilbert, *The Prophetic Pulpit: Clergy, Churches, and Communities in American Politics* (Lanham, MD: Rowman & Littlefield, 2003), 126–48.

10 Djupe and Gilbert, *The Prophetic Pulpit*, 7, see also 90.

the seeking of public office in order to affect public policy, when clergy desired to see their faith principles influence the broader community.[11]

Inasmuch as the aforementioned contemporary studies document the American minister's preferred prophetic attitude of political engagement, Hispanic ministers should note that the prophetic posture is also promoted within conventional Christian thought in America. Stephen Carter, Yale University law professor and Christian author, urges today's Christians to position themselves with a distinctly "prophetic voice" in American politics, one that calls the political world to account, points individuals in the direction of God's will, and, indifferent to the identity of the ruler, concerns itself with whether rulers rule correctly. For Carter, the prophetic role of Christians is a role subversive to cultural norms and is most pure when proclaiming what the Lord requires of a nation.[12] The prophetic voice is a concept that is also embraced by Jim Wallis, the founder of Sojourners and a Christian theologian. He envisions the future of American politics to be a debate between moral values, values brought to the forefront by those who carry the witness of the biblical prophets and Jesus. Wallis defines the work of political prophets as diagnosing present political issues, articulating moral truth, and pointing the way to a just solution that works on behalf of the common good, what he calls "prophetic faith."[13] Christian Hispanic ministers are now among those who advocate for and participate in prophetic political activism. Samuel Rodriguez, Hispanic minister and president of the National Hispanic Christian Leadership Conference, argues that what America needs above all else is a prophetic movement, an outpouring of the Holy Spirit and a forward-looking application of truth to power, what he calls "The Lamb's Agenda" or "the prophetic center." For Rodriguez, Christian political engagement must be

11 Mary M. Sawyer, "Theocratic, Prophetic, and Ecumenical: Political Roles of African American Clergy," in *Christian Clergy in American Politics*, 74; see also 66–67, 75.

12 Stephen L. Carter, *God's Name in Vain: The Wrongs and Rights of Religion in Politics* (New York: Basic Books, 2000), 28–31.

13 Jim Wallis, *God's Politics: Why the Right Gets It Wrong and the Left Doesn't Get It*, 1st ed. (San Francisco: HarperSanFrancisco, 2005), vxiii; see also xxi, xxv, 71–72.

an exercise of prophetic witness that results in vertical (spiritual) and horizontal (communal) transformation.[14]

A cursory presentation of academic studies and mainstream Christian thought reveals a preferred (maybe natural) inclination of American ministers toward prophetic political activism. However, Hispanic ministers in America must now begin to ask themselves, "What does it mean to take on a prophetic model of political engagement in the nation?" It is a question worth asking. One may take a deeper survey into the findings of contemporary scholars and arguments of Christian thought leaders, or, as is customary among Christians, one can turn to the Bible from which the role and understanding of the biblical prophet first emerged. Wallis himself believes that a politics of God begins with understanding the prophets—what subjects they addressed, to whom they spoke, and for whom they spoke.[15] This is not merely an optional exercise but a necessary task if Hispanic ministers should seek to better understand the biblical role of prophets in ancient Israel and embrace their own roles as *profetas* to the nation.

Biblical Observations of the Prophet Samuel's Role with Israel

Hispanic ministers who seek to understand what it means to serve as *profetas* in politics would benefit greatly from an observation of the biblical account of the prophet Samuel in the first book of Samuel for at least two reasons. First, many biblical scholars, including Eric C. Rust, note that "Samuel, whose training had been for the priesthood, was now called of God to be a prophet."[16] As such, Hispanic pastors, priests, and ministers who sense a call to assume a prophetic mantle could readily identify their own spiritual calling with that of the priest and prophet Samuel. Second, Peter C. Ackroyd observes that the first book of Samuel is the first place in the Bible in which the Hebrew

14 Samuel Rodriguez, *The Lamb's Agenda: Why Jesus Is Calling You to a Life of Righteousness and Justice* (Nashville: Thomas Nelson, 2013), 19; see also 187, 34.

15 Wallis, *God's Politics*, 32.

16 Eric C. Rust, "The First and Second Books of Samuel," in *The Layman's Bible Commentary*, ed. Balmer H. Kelly, vol. 6 (Atlanta: John Knox, 1978), 87.

word for prophet—*nabi*—is applied.[17] In other words, Hispanic ministers can look to the prophet Samuel's call and prophetic activity as a paradigm on which to build a primary understanding of the prophetic role and against which other prophetic paradigms can be compared, including modern ones. Although numerous biblical observations can be made concerning the prophetic call and role of Samuel, the current study will limit its observations to certain passages on Samuel's life that arguably present foundational ideas about the prophetic role as a model of political engagement in the nation: Samuel's call (1 Sam 3:1—4:1) and Samuel's anointing of Saul as king (8:1—10:27).

The Nation Prophet's Purpose

One foundational observation concerning the prophet's role comes to light in what appears to be the early stages of Samuel's ministry and the final days of Eli's. The fact that the boy Samuel was ministering to the Lord before Eli (3:1) clearly indicates that Samuel's ministerial practices at this time were preparing him to be a priest, a faithful minister in the house of the Lord, as was his teacher Eli. In the words of David H. Jensen, Samuel was "learning the priestly craft from a seasoned veteran."[18] Samuel was performing the priestly tasks that he witnessed Eli perform and was functioning in the capacity in which Eli had entrusted and empowered him, behaviors that seemed to demonstrate Samuel's heart of service and obedience in preparing himself for life as a priest. However, one night in the temple, the Lord repeatedly called Samuel by name and entrusted him with a message to deliver to Eli (3:4–10). Rust says, "By its threefold repetition the experience was proved to be real and not hallucinatory, and Eli was convinced that Samuel was being called by the Lord himself,"[19] and Ronald F. Youngblood comments, "the Lord called out Samuel's name twice, imparting

---

17 Peter C. Ackroyd, *The First Book of Samuel*, ed. Peter C. Ackroyd, A. R. C. Leaney, and J. W. Packer, *The Cambridge Bible Commentary: New English Bible* (Cambridge: Cambridge University Press, 1971), 45.

18 David H. Jensen, *1 & 2 Samuel, Belief: A Theological Commentary on the Bible* (Louisville, KY: Westminster John Knox, 2015), 36.

19 Rust, "The First and Second Books of Samuel," 87.

a sense of urgency and finality."[20] There was no doubt about it: the Lord had called Samuel, and it was the Lord who had given the young priest words to deliver to his teacher.

The moment the Lord himself orally imparted a word to Samuel to deliver to Eli was the moment of demarcation of a change in ministry for young Samuel. David T. Tsumura writes that 3:4–21 "clearly shows that in the beginning the word of the Lord was lacking in the nation, but at the end it was supplied," and later in the text, "here Samuel is playing his role as the prophet of the Lord for the first time by delivering God's message as the one who was called by Him, received His message, and was sent as His messenger."[21] Even Ackroyd contends, "Now a new era begins, the era of prophecy."[22] Samuel would become Israel's first ever prophet (*nabi*), which literally meant that Samuel would act as one appointed to proclaim the message of God himself.[23] In the Bible, *prophecy* is a word used to describe the message of men who spoke to the nation of Israel under the inspiration of the Spirit of God and involved "the knowledge and communication of spiritual truths" in a way that could not be done by human reason alone but through hearing and discerning the very words of God: "In declaring his message . . . the prophet is always conscious of the fact that he speaks as God's mouthpiece, that his word is the word of Him who is the Lord of history."[24] "Samuel," Lyle M. Eslinger writes, "begins the chapter as a priestly servant and ends as a prophet."[25]

Hispanic ministers who seek to engage in politics through a prophetic posture would benefit from understanding the foundational

---

20 Ronald F. Youngblood, "1 & 2 Samuel," in *The Expositor's Bible Commentary*, ed. Frank E. Gaebelein, vol. 3, *The Expositor's Bible Commentary with the New International Version* (Grand Rapids, MI: Zondervan, 1992), 591.

21 David T. Tsumura, *The First Book of Samuel*, ed. R. K. Harrison and Robert L. Hubbard Jr., *The New International Commentary on the Old Testament* (Grand Rapids, MI: Eerdmans, 2007), 173; see also 181.

22 Ackroyd, *The First Book of Samuel*, 42–43.

23 Paul P. Enns, *The Moody Handbook of Theology* (Chicago: Moody, 1989), 65.

24 *The New International Dictionary of the Christian Church*, s.v. "Prophecy" (Grand Rapids, MI: Zondervan, 1978).

25 Lyle M. Eslinger, *Kingship of God in Crisis: A Close Reading of 1 Samuel 1–12*, Bible and Literature Series 10 (Decatur, GA: Almond, 1985), 143.

concept that the voice of the prophet has a different purpose than the voice of the priest. It appears the Lord was not in search of a priest who would only speak to God on behalf of men, but of a prophet who would also speak to men on behalf of God. During Eli's ministry Israel was a theocracy. God was king, and the final word and interpretation on God's laws and judgments were administered through the judges, a role that Samuel eventually assumed, though not until some twenty years after his prophetic call (7:15).[26] His role as a judge was interrupted by Israel's demand for a king (8:5). Perhaps it was for this reason, because the Lord foreknew that the Israelites would reject him as king, that he prepared a way for his voice to be heard even when a new form of governance would arise.

The renowned judges of Israel governed Israel from the time of Joshua to Eli; Samuel was the last. Tsumura notes that although 4:1 indicates that "the word of the Lord through [Samuel] eventually spread all over Israel . . . it seems that his prophetic office did not yet influence political matters."[27] Tsumura's comment serves to further support the current observation that the voice of the prophet has a different purpose than the voice of the priest. Unlike the voice of the priest, the prophetic voice moves beyond directing ceremonial laws and rituals of the tabernacle but brings the exact words of the Lord that would reach, resonate with, and move an entire nation. This observation does not escape Eslinger when reading 3:11. He says, "Yahweh's mention of the location, 'in Israel,' of the thing he is going to do, and the statement that it will make all its auditors' ears buzz, seems to indicate an event of national significance."[28]

When positioning themselves as political prophets, perhaps Hispanic ministers should consider whether their words—warnings, commands, and even rhetoric—are reflective of a message directing church polity or of a message affecting policy of a much broader societal landscape. There is no debate: "Samuel the priest, God's minister, would become Samuel the prophet, God's spokesman."[29] God set him apart

26 Eslinger, *Kingship of God in Crisis*, 255–56.

27 Tsumura, *The First Book of Samuel*, 185.

28 Eslinger, *Kingship of God in Crisis*, 151–52.

29 Youngblood, "1 & 2 Samuel," 591.

not to be a minster before the Lord but to be a prophet before men: "He had served God as a child in the temple, but now he serves all Israel as a prophet."[30] The noticeable shift in purpose is something of which today's Hispanic ministers may need continual awareness and reminding.

The Nation Prophet's Message and Tone

A second biblical observation of Samuel's prophetic role to the nation comes from the same early passage in the first book of Samuel, and it concerns the subject and delivery of the prophetic message. In 3:11–14 the Lord gave Samuel a message that appeared not only hard for him to cope with but was equally difficult for him to deliver. Samuel was called to speak a prophetic word concerning the priesthood that would forthwith affect his spiritual teacher Eli and Eli's sons. "The content of his first prophetic message was disclosed to him—the divine judgment on Eli's house" for the sins of his sons and his refusal to rebuke their wickedness.[31] Samuel had heard God's message, and Jensen reminds us that "hearing God's word requires Samuel to speak uncomfortable truth to others."[32]

Postured with an undeniable prophetic call and armed with an unambiguously damning message, the Bible does not portray for its readers a brazen and vociferous Samuel. Rather, the audience is confronted with a picture of the prophet Samuel as both reticent and afraid (3:15). Was he fearful of Eli's reaction, the forthcoming judgment of God, or some other reason? The biblical account is not clear. It could simply be, as Jensen supposes, that "these are hard words for an apprentice to bring to his teacher."[33] What is clear is that Eli requested with "an oath of imprecation" for Samuel to divulge the unadulterated message of the Lord (3:17), and Samuel obediently submitted to the request of his teacher (3:18).[34] Samuel, though confirmed as a "prophet" of the Lord—a title that the Bible often demonstrates as commanding

30 Tsumura, *The First Book of Samuel*, 184.

31 Rust, "The First and Second Books of Samuel," 87.

32 Jensen, *1 & 2 Samuel, Belief*, 39.

33 Jensen, *1 & 2 Samuel, Belief*, 39.

34 Youngblood, "1 & 2 Samuel," 592.

attention if not submission, responded as one in submission. If fear initially kept Samuel from sharing the vision with Eli, humility now urged the prophet to deliver the vision to its intended audience.

The fact that "Samuel told [Eli] everything and hid nothing from him" (3:18, NASB) suggests just that; he told Eli "everything" and communicated to him word for word God's message. The message concerning the house of Eli was not altered in any way, and Samuel did not attempt to make it more palatable for his aging and soon-to-be vanquished master. He communicated the truth, the whole truth, and nothing but the truth, and as suggested from the preceding verses, he did so in humility. In Samuel's first instance of delivering a prophetic word, he rose not as a spiritual superior but bowed as a spiritual son who humbly submitted to his spiritual father and master, the one to whom the prophecy was directed.

There is a principle here that should not escape Hispanic ministers who are geared for political prophetic activism to the nation: the prophet of God speaks the pure and unadulterated truth, doing so in humility and in service to those for whom the message is intended. C. F. Keil and F. Delitzsch confirm that Samuel delivered an "unreserved and candid communication of the terribly solemn word of God" and "with regard to [Eli], whom [Samuel] certainly venerated with filial affection, not only as high priest, but also as his own parental guardian."[35] In Samuel's case, "Eli's reaction is both devout and submissive" and "Eli resigns himself to divine sovereignty."[36] Whether today's political prophets receive the same or a similar response from their national audience is irrelevant. The prophetic pattern that the Bible offers of Samuel speaking truth in humility is a compelling model and one arguably in line with what the analogy of faith would reveal concerning Christian character. It is the kind of character that "proved [Samuel] to be a man possessing the courage and the power to proclaim the word of the Lord without fear to the people of Israel."[37]

---

35 C. F. Keil and F. Delitzsch, *Biblical Commentary on the Books of Samuel*, 6th ed., Biblical Commentary on the Old Testament (Grand Rapids, MI: Eerdmans, 1968), 51.

36 Youngblood, "1 & 2 Samuel," 592.

37 Keil and Delitzsch, *Biblical Commentary on the Books of Samuel*, 51.

The Nation Prophet's Audience

A third foundational biblical observation on which Hispanic ministers can build an understanding of the prophet's role is derived from what is gathered about Samuel's early national and political influence in Israel. Following Samuel's prophecy, the Bible informs its readers that the Lord "let none of [Samuel's] words fall to the ground" (3:19, NIV), which, according to Youngblood, communicates that "[the Lord] made sure that everything Samuel said with divine authorization came true."[38] In particular, the judgment upon the house of Eli is witnessed in the following chapter. Tsumura notes, "After this first experience as a prophet of the Lord, Samuel kept growing, preparing to become a mature prophet both physically and spiritually," and as Samuel grew, all Israel from the north to the south (e.g. "from Dan to Beersheba") confirmed him as the Lord's prophet and "the word of Samuel came to all Israel" (3:19–4:1, NASB).[39]

Samuel was a nation prophet. "Samuel, the local seer," Ackroyd writes, "has come to be understood as a prophet to the whole people."[40] Israel was a theocracy, and Samuel was the Lord's prophet to the nation and Israel's judge all the days of his life (7:3–17). According to Peter D. Miscall, "The prophet can be distinguished from the judge in several ways, most importantly through the fact the prophet will speak, in the name of the Lord, *a word* which the Lord has spoken to him."[41] As prophet and as judge, then, the Bible depicts a man who "was seen to be the central character in Israel's history."[42] It is arguably fair to say that his national and political influence was unmatched by any other Israelite. However, a major shift occurred that would challenge the political institution of Israel and Samuel's prophetic influence in the nation. The moment Samuel's capacity and his sons' competency to judge Israel faltered (8:1–4), the elders of Israel clamored for a king (8:4–5).

38 Youngblood, "1 & 2 Samuel," 592.

39 Tsumura, *The First Book of Samuel*, 182–83.

40 Ackroyd, *The First Book of Samuel*, 45.

41 Peter D. Miscall, *1 Samuel: A Literary Reading*, Indiana Studies in Biblical Literature (Bloomington: Indiana University Press, 1986), 45.

42 Ackroyd, *The First Book of Samuel*, 45.

The biblical account reveals that Samuel was displeased with their request (8:6). Miscall suggests one reason for his displeasure was that "Samuel deeply resents the people's demand that he exercise his authority to demote or even remove himself by appointing another leader, a king, especially one who will govern or judge . . . the people as he has been doing."[43] Tsumura argues that Samuel may have even interpreted their petition as "a rejection of the God-given institution of judgeship."[44] Perhaps Samuel did take their request for a king as a personal offense to himself or against Israel's political institutions, or maybe he already knew what God would make plainly clear when he said, "They have not rejected you [Samuel], but they have rejected Me from being King over them" (8:7, NASB). By the end of the passage, in Jensen's words, "God [was] also willing, for the sake of relationship, to live with Israel's demand."[45]

Much attention can and should be given to the weightiness of Israel's sin; however, what should not be lost in the discussion are the incidental and subsidiary consequences of their request that would greatly shape Samuel's role as a prophet to Israel. Eslinger is correct in saying that their request amounts to a "calling for an end to the theocratic system" and to "make Israel a state like any other pagan nation," but what does this truly mean for Israel?[46] Tsumura explains that the establishment of a monarchy meant that rule and authority passed from the Lord's congregation and assembly of elders and judges to the king. "Therefore," he says, "the request for a king would mean *a fundamental change in the socio-political structure* and a major transformation in Israel's life and religion."[47] The people of Israel completely restructured Israel's social and political life, even after Samuel advised and warned them of the various changes that would be brought to bear on their military, children, crops, livestock, and homes (8:11–20). Each of these spheres would now be decided and arranged through the mind and hands of a single individual, the king of Israel.

---

43 Miscall, *1 Samuel*, 47.

44 Tsumura, *The First Book of Samuel*, 250.

45 Jensen, *1 & 2 Samuel, Belief*, 62.

46 Eslinger, *Kingship of God in Crisis*, 255–56.

47 Tsumura, *The First Book of Samuel*, 248, emphasis mine.

God, however, is still God whether a judge or king ruled Israel, and God would expect the king and the people of Israel to continue their pursuit of righteousness by walking in the Lord's way and ultimately submitting to God's word. Though the nation demanded a king so they could be "like all the nations" (8:5, NASB), Eslinger notices that the biblical language and narrative reminds its readers that "Yahweh still controls Israel politics even in the matter of kings," and that "Israel is Yahweh's people." This is confirmed by the fact that the Lord set "the procedure of the king" and used Samuel to deliver those procedures (8:9). The king became an official designate of the Lord and so only because the Lord's prophet Samuel conferred it upon him. Eslinger presents it this way:

> Yahweh tells Samuel that he is to anoint Saul as *[king]*. The act of anointing itself indicates that Samuel is in a position of authority. The fact that Samuel is commissioned by Yahweh to invest Saul with the commission of *[king]* reveals the lines of authority. The theocratic structure remains, as ever, God over mediator over Israel, or in this case, over Saul the *[king]*.[48]

Samuel was no longer the priest who would have seen it as his task to approach God on behalf of the king, but now his assignment was to approach the king on behalf of God in order that the Lord's word would continue to be before the Lord's people. Samuel's prophetic ministry bade him to speak the word of the Lord directly to the one individual in Israel, King Saul, who influenced the course of the entire nation. Throughout his lifetime, the prophet conferred with kings before battle (15:1), rebuked their disobedience (13:13; 15:10–23), pronounced judgment (15:26, 33), and anointed future kings (16:13).

Hispanic ministers should consider the foundational concept that the prophet's voice speaks directly to those sociopolitical institutions, if not individuals, that influence the policy, life, and ideology of a nation. Just as the Lord used the prophet Samuel to ensure that the word of the Lord was before the king in order that the ways of the Lord would influence the nation, today's prophets must be intentional in engaging and finding access with those institutions that influence the course

48 Eslinger, *Kingship of God in Crisis*, 281; see also 303–5.

of the nation in order that the nation may be influenced in a manner consistent with the Lord's word and commands. Eslinger observes that "it is Samuel's goal to make an obedient theocratic servant out of Saul" and that "the order of dominance has been unquestionably established: Samuel commands and Saul obeys."[49] Regardless of whether today's prophets' task in influencing national leaders may be more difficult than ever, especially in a secular culture and climate much more hostile toward Christian evangelical influence, it remains the prophets' job to remind the nation's leaders that a sovereign God exists, one to whom all kings and presidents are subject.

Discussion

An observation of the call and early-life ministry of *el profeta* Samuel offers to Hispanic ministers additional and greater understanding of foundational concepts related to prophetic political engagement, and a perfunctory meditation on the concepts by ministers may offer a sense of the ways the principles play themselves out in practice. First, for those who sense a prophetic calling, it would be important to recognize the specific ministry and the distinct purpose into which he or she is entering. Is it a purpose distinct from priestly, pastoral, or evangelist duties? The biblical account of Samuel suggests it is. The most marginalized and impoverished communities are often replete with churches on every corner, and the prophetic ministry of Samuel encourages today's Hispanic ministers and churches serving disenfranchised communities to evaluate if what the community members need is another midweek Bible-study or an empathetic advocate down at city hall? Why? Because *el profeta* is someone who speaks to people on behalf of God. The Lord must have ministers who preach behind a pulpit at church and those who also will raise their voices behind a podium in the marketplace, those who deliver an exegesis of Scripture in Sunday school and those who deliver speeches and lectures in state universities. What Samuel's prophetic ministry reveals is that the words of the prophet, unlike the priest's, are purposed to affect policy on a societal level.

---

49 Eslinger, *Kingship of God in Crisis*, 315–16.

Second, Hispanic ministers called to prophetic activism should consider the nature of the prophetic message and tone. In a culture that has become accustomed to fake news and political correctness, and unlike the tenor of many political critics and pundits, Samuel's prophetic example promotes impartial truth-telling shared in such a way that clearly conveys to the hearers the prophet's spirit of humility and service. If sin prowls, prophets utter the Holy Word; if prejudice lurks, they point to the hammer of justice; if slavery ensnares, they call for the bells of freedom; and if violence stirs, they sing a song of peace, of course, in a way devoid of arrogance and haughtiness. *El profeta* Samuel heartens today's Hispanic ministers never to hide or compromise the Lord's message, but to deliver words that are pure and true and convey a humble submission to both God and fellow people.

Lastly, current and would-be prophets should be mindful of the audience through which the Lord's message might best permeate the ethos of a nation. In *Faith in the Halls of Power*, Michael Lindsay reveals how Christian evangelicals have been active in influencing four major spheres in America: the academy, arts and entertainment, corporate America, and politics.[50] The prophetic model of Samuel is a foundational one that portrays a God-mandated engagement with culture-shaping spheres and agenda-setting institutions and individuals. The Lord is eager to use his prophets to whisper in the ears of those who lead cities, states, and the nation, to remind the nation and its leaders of their mutual submission to the only Lord and King, and to place before the nation the Lord's righteous laws and statutes so that the policy, life, and ideology of a nation would come to reflect the kingdom culture revealed in God's Word. Hispanic ministers seeking to emulate Samuel's prophetic work understand that God is raising them up to speak into sociopolitical and culture-shaping institutions of the nation.

Further Understanding the Prophet Samuel

Have Hispanic ministers in America today reached a complete understanding or even come to a consensus on what it means to be a *profeta*

50 D. Michael Lindsay, *Faith in the Halls of Power: How Evangelicals Joined the American Elite* (Oxford: Oxford University Press, 2007).

to the nation? No, but perhaps the examination of Samuel's call and early-life ministry has brought them one step closer. What is needed are additional observations of those counted as the major prophets (Isaiah, Jeremiah, Ezekiel, and Daniel) and the minor prophets (Hosea, Joel, Amos, Obadiah, Jonah, Micah, Nahum, Habakkuk, Zephaniah, Haggai, Zechariah, and Malachi) of the Bible followed by the comparison and synthesis of major concepts that arise. In the biblical account of Samuel, readers witness kings of Israel who were receptive to and in large part submissive to the prophet's role. Does the prophet's purpose, message, and tone change in any instances when kings resist and reject the legitimacy of the prophet? Additionally, in what way does the understanding of the political *profeta* change when one considers how King Saul himself prophesied and even the Israelites asked themselves, "Is Saul also among the prophets?" (10:10–12).

Furthermore, a consensus on the political prophet's role can be complicated when one considers the New Testament narratives and epistles. During the prophet Samuel's life, Israel was by and large a sovereign state. How might one's comprehension of the prophet's role change when one takes into account that the New Testament era began with the people of God and the city of Jerusalem in complete subjugation to a foreign power? Individuals occupying prophetic roles, such as John the Baptist and Jesus, wielded little to no formal political influence, so Roman rulers were under no moral or religious compulsion to pay the prophets any mind. Samuel's ministry appeared in the form of a political advisor, but do John the Baptist's and Jesus's prophetic ministry take on a similar message and tone with the rulers of their time? Also, the role of the prophet could take on new and different meanings whether one is examining Luke's narrative recording of glossolalia, Paul's didactic teaching of the gifts of the Spirit, or John's oeuvre of apocalyptic visions.

Lastly, Samuel's life and ministry deserve another look if one is to garner greater understanding of the role of the political *profeta* to the nation, particularly in one regard. An attempt at the demarcation between Samuel the priest and Samuel the prophet has already been made, and rightly so, for the roles are commonly regarded as ministry callings and functions of ministry. However, additional consideration must been given to what ways the roles of prophet and judge may be demarcated or linked together in Samuel's life. Miscall perhaps raises the point of inquiry best:

> We come to 1 Samuel 8 with at least three possible pictures of Samuel—the prophet, the judge, and a combination of the two. . . . Both involve declaring a word that must be listened to and obeyed; the prophet's word is explicitly from the Lord and spoken in the Lord's name. However, the texts analyzed, in both Deuteronomy and 1 Samuel, and my analysis do not permit a clear demarcation of two different leaders or offices that can be separately defined. There can be prophets, there can be judges, and there can be characters who act as both prophet and judge (and perhaps as other officials).[51]

Perhaps Christians feel America is in circumstances similar to the situation into which Samuel was born, where the word from the Lord seemed rare and visions were infrequent (3:1), particularly in politics. If such is the case, now is time for the Lord's prophets to rise. As Hispanic evangelicals continue their efforts in prophetic political activism, they will in time assemble a clearer understanding of their role and responsibilities as political *profetas* to the nation. Hopefully, through their understanding they will be transformed into the personage of a prophet who reflects the biblical depiction of God's intended purpose for the prophets, a message and tone in line with Christian comportment, and a desire to touch the soul of a nation.

---

51 Miscall, *1 Samuel*, 46.

7

Profetas on the Border

CÉSAR M. DURÁN

AS A LATINO PASTOR and scholar with extensive experience of doing ministry on the border, I have much to say about how the Latino church functions on the United States–Mexico border.[1] In this chapter, I will outline its challenges and suggest an effective evangelistic action in the twenty-first century. The United States–Mexico border has a very interesting history, which in some ways influences the interaction and style of life along the entire border. It is also important to describe the meaning of what the border is from a practical and face-to-face perspective, emphasizing the greatness of this emerging culture along the southern border of the United States. This new culture on the border gives rise to some social characteristics that are unique and a little bit different from the social characteristics of other areas of the United States. In some ways, these social characteristics of the border influence the Christian church and the life of each of its members—who they are and how they live. Somehow the present situation of the border and of the Christian church does not look at all pleasant. Even so, it is very important to keep our eyes on the Lord of the church, because the future and the challenges of the frontier church can only be overcome with the guidance and favor of God.

---

1 In addition to his upbringing and ministerial life in Mexico, Rev. César M. Durán served as senior pastor of First United Methodist Church in Laredo, Texas.

Historical Background

When we talk about the border, we are referring to the existing borderline that separates the United States from Mexico. This borderline that divides Mexico and the United States in one area is a wall and in another area is a river. Obviously, in both countries, in some areas an interaction and connection beyond the borderline and barriers exist. There are mountainous areas, desert, rivers, beautiful landscapes full of sea, border ports with small towns, and large cities, where there is a great interaction among all the residents and visitors of both sides.

This borderline was established after many years of struggles and conflicts between the two countries. A simple look at the historical background helps us to understand the great differences that we now experience on both sides of the border. Because America was discovered by European imperialists, each European country planted a seed that today continues producing as intentionally transmitted from the beginning. As a result of this European influence, on the one hand we have the imperialist perspective of the United States and on the other hand we have the weeping and suffering of Latin Americans as a result of the slavery and oppression experienced under Spanish imperialism. According to Justo González, "the Catholic Reformation . . . used the inquisition as one of its tools."[2] Initially used for the repression of Jews and Moors, the Spanish Inquisition was used also to dominate the natives of America. The problem is that in America this oppression was worse. Today, we cannot deny that these circumstances of the past continue influencing the lives of the residents in this border area.

The pope and the kings of Spain made it possible to sponsor the voyages of Christopher Columbus to reach the Indies and recover the investments made. Unfortunately, this is how Columbus, without wanting to, discovered this land that we know as the American continent. In this context, mainly the Spanish for centuries plundered the natural riches of this newly conquered land. The Spaniards also oppressed, enslaved, dominated, and forcibly imposed their law and religion on each of the continent's Indigenous tribes. Generations and generations were

---

2 Justo González, *The Story of Christianity*, vol. 2 (New York: HarperCollins, 2010), 12.

born, lived, grew, and died enslaved to the desires and whims of Spanish imperialism. When the independence of the oppressive yoke was achieved, the main damage had already been done; a perspective and mentality of oppression and conformism had been created, a damned heritage carried by the great majority of Latin American peoples.

After the Spaniards, the British also felt the need to expand their horizons and sent their first settlers to the American continent. This is how the thirteen colonies were formed, which is the origin of the United States. Religious and social life gave rise to new ideas of freedom, power, and liberty, developing a new mentality: "By liberty, or freedom, its frequent substitute, and by power, Asbury described a new order of reality, a new dominion, a new society."[3] These Europeans, guided by their imperialist mentality, little by little expanded their boundaries until achieving all the immense territory that today is the United States of America. A great part of this territory, mainly the central, south, and west parts, were lands that belonged to Mexico—lands that had been dominated and exploited by the Spaniards—and therefore could not be conserved as part of Mexico because of the mentality of oppression and conformism. I will not provide a historical explanation of everything that happened between both Mexico and the United States; this is a brief description of how the geographical boundaries we have today were established.

These geographical boundaries established since the beginning of the nineteenth century marked the life on both sides of the border. The Mexican side was growing as dreams of greatness arose, gradually materializing in a slow way. Little by little, Mexico was awakening to the vision of a better life. On the American side, that dream of greatness and imperialist perspective gradually developed the culture of progress and growth that is what we identify today as the Anglo-Saxon culture. Struggles between these two cultures developed, and both cultures were overcome by the emergence of a new culture, the product of the mix of both. This new bicultural perspective is described in different ways in each area along the border: in one area it is the culture of the *pochos*, in another it is the "Tex-Mex," and in others it is the "*Chicano* power" or

3 Russell E. Richey, Kenneth E. Rowe, and Jean Miller Schmidt, *American Methodism: A Compact History* (Nashville: Abingdon Press, 2012), 11.

the "Latino power." What the Latinos "do is pick and choose from each culture whatever can be beneficial. . . . It is precisely this picking and choosing that gives birth to new cultural and social patterns created by migrants."[4] This is the new culture of the Latinos.

The "Border"

It is impossible to describe the border church without really knowing what the border means. The word *border* means geographical boundaries between countries, but it implies so much more. The border is home to many dreams of greatness that were conceived in the hearts of many men and women after having lived in oppression and poverty. The border represents the birth of a new culture, a new way of seeing and feeling life from a bicultural perspective. It is impossible to understand the magnitude of this lifestyle until you have had the opportunity to feel it through contact with the people despite the discomfort that it can cause.

When we speak of geographical boundaries, we refer to the boundaries previously established by human beings in order to separate two geographical places, either to separate two pieces of land from different owners, or the territories of some states or countries. In this case, when speaking of the border church here in the United States, these geographic boundaries are related to the established boundaries that separate Mexico from the United States. These border boundaries are overcome in many ways by men and women who have the dream of reaching beyond the barriers found in front of them. In this case, these borderlines, geographically speaking, have been marked for centuries through various ways, highlighting the mountains and valleys, rivers, and deserts that separate both countries, and mainly the walls and fences built for the sole purpose of dividing these two great nations.

It should be emphasized that these geographical boundaries only have the purpose of dividing two great peoples who through the centuries have been united by the same blood. We cannot fail to mention the death that these geographical boundaries have caused—thousands who died in the desert in their attempt to cross those boundaries and

4 Ada María Isasi-Diaz, *La Lucha Continues: Mujerista Theology* (Maryknoll, NY: Orbis Books, 2004), 61.

reach the American dream. We cannot forget all the women, men, and children who drowned in their attempt to cross the Rio Bravo, or Rio Grande, as many know it. The point is that these borderlines become a barrier, visibly shown through the walls and fences, but they mean a division much greater than we can imagine. These boundaries create ethnocentrism, prejudice, and racism: "When ethnocentrism is confused with either prejudice or racism or both, it is very difficult to discuss racial, ethnic, cultural, or different issues. Attacking, being defensive, not listening, and overgeneralizing often surface."[5] All this is produced by the geographical division.

In addition, the word *border* means dreams of greatness. This new meaning of the word arises due to the great devastation and limitations that are experienced in all Latin American countries. Many people begin to fantasize about a better life, or they begin to hear from friends, relatives, or neighbors who went to the north to have a better life. All these stories somehow influence the formation of many dreams, dreams of greatness, which many call the *American dream*. This American dream is seen as new opportunities for life and as the desires of a better life, where everything is not ideal and rosy, but at least it is a life in which one has the opportunity to live in a dignified way, humanly speaking.

The vast majority of border ports become the gateway to this new life. Crossing the geographical boundaries, in whatever way, is the opportunity to realize those dreams of greatness and is the opportunity to have a better life. Precisely because of this, borders become attractive places for people with scarce resources, who do everything humanly possible to live in those places, even though it is on the Mexican side. From the perspective of the Central Americans, or Mexicans from the south of the country, the northern Mexican border is viewed as a means to a better life. Obviously, once the Central Americans or Mexicans from the south live there, a way to cross the river or the desert or the wall is sought in order to realize their dream of greatness, their American dream. However, for many, this dream becomes the nightmare of

---

5 Lucia Ann McSpadden, *Meeting God at the Boundaries: Cross-Cultural-Cross-Racial Clergy Appointments* (Nashville: General Board of Higher Education and Ministry, 2006), 25.

the Latin American because he or she could not cross into the American side or because he or she died on the attempt.

The word *border* also means the emergence of a new culture, but this depends on one's perspective. For many, instead of being the birth of a new culture, it is the disintegration and loss of values and culture that were received from their own parents or the customs of the land where they were born. For those who were not born in this border area, it is difficult to see this as the emergence of a new culture, but as the place where they lost those roots that connected them with their ancestors. At the end, they assimilated into the new culture. For those who were born on the Mexican side of the border or came to live on it from a very young age, or who were born on the border, the truth is that for them the border is a new culture where they feel sheltered and embraced, and where they develop new lines of communication, since "communication always occurs in the context of numerous psychological and social factors."[6]

This border, on the one hand, separates the cultures of both countries—countries with very different languages, economies, and cultures—but on the other hand, it gives rise to a new culture where a new language, a new way of surviving and marketing, a new way of being arise. It is lived from a bicultural perspective, where many are called *pochos* and where a mixture of English and Spanish, the language of "Tex-Mex," is spoken by the *Chicano*. This refers to the Latino who has lived on the southern side of the border, can navigate the Anglo-Saxon world, and has the power to live in a culture that is richer and more diverse than others. Precisely because of this, it is important to describe the border as the place where a new culture is created or emerges, a mixture of Latin American culture and Anglo-Saxon culture. Without a doubt, the life of the border clearly shows us how God moves in the midst of diversity, and this "diversity is not an accident of

6 Juan Martínez and Mark Branson, *Iglesias, Culturas y Liderazgo: Una Teología Práctica para Congregaciones y Etnias* (Miami: Editorial Vida, 2013), 227. My translation from the original Spanish: "La Comunicación siempre ocurre en el contexto de numeroso factores psicológicos y sociales."

creation but a reflection of divine intent."[7] This is the diversity you will see along the border.

Social Characteristics

When considering the border church, it is important to look at the distinctive social aspects of the border strip, because these aspects are somehow elements of the social life of the congregants or members of the church of Jesus Christ here on the border. Undoubtedly, the main social characteristic is the mixture of cultures in which we live. This opens up other problems of social origin such as immigration, smuggling, and poverty in this border area.

I have already spoken of the emergence of a new culture—a mixture of both cultures—of *pochos*, of *Chicanos*, of "Tex-Mex." Only one who lives on the border knows what it means to be bicultural and live on both sides of the border. It is important to know what this mixture culture is as well as the cultures existing on each side. This is one of the main characteristics of the border strip.

Living in both cultures means moving in both languages, English and Spanish. It also means being able to coexist with people of all races, colors, and languages, and understanding the problems caused by the financial system of the border. When a person is bicultural, he or she has the skills to interact between different generations of Latinos, because each generation of Latinos has its own characteristics that are developed through the dynamics of bicultural border life. In the United States, most of the Latinos who live on the border, citizens or not, "are often bilingual, bicultural, and biracial; it is important to have some personal insight into our process of forming an ethnic identity . . . based on what is truly our heritage and on the choices we make to align ourselves with that heritage in the United States."[8] Because in the end, we are living here in the United States.

---

7 José David Rodríguez and Loida I. Martell-Otero, *Teología en Conjunto: A Collaborative Hispanic Protestant Theology* (Louisville, KY: Westminster John Knox Press, 1997), 60.

8 Orlando Crespo, *Being Latino in Christ: Finding Wholeness in Your Ethnic Identity* (Downers Grove, IL: InterVarsity Press, 2003), 40.

Immigration

One of the most important social characteristics of the border is immigration. When we talk about immigration, we are talking about immigration that is legal and illegal, documented or undocumented. The border is a point of attraction for people who want to live a better life. Living in the border strip, even on the Mexican side, allows immigrants to have a better life than they had in their places of origin, in addition to living with the hope that at their first opportunity they can emigrate to the American side.

This immigration to the United States, legal and illegal, with documents or without documents, creates a series of economic and social problems. Many cities and border communities grow quickly based on their sources of work that attract migrants, but once the work has been completed, the migrant community disappears and the community returns once again to its previous condition. Work is the main motivation of the migrants. Another detail to highlight is illegal immigration, without documents, which happens across all borders. It is necessary to talk about illegal immigration "because it is very difficult to enter legally."[9] Many people, despite surveillance, enter the country and get a social security number, which they use to restart their lives on this side of the border. This illegal immigration becomes a headache for the border authorities and the immigration authorities, but it also becomes a strong arm of the economy in this border area. "Most illegals are workers . . . serve in low-paying jobs" and in those places where Americans do not want to go.[10]

Another social characteristic of the border is the illegal trade of human smuggling. This illegal trade in the border area mainly consists of the illegal crossing of human beings. People from all over the world are introduced to the United States by the *pateros* (the people who ferry the immigrants) in an illegal manner for large sums of money. It is important to understand how it ends: in many cases, exploiting and prostituting men, women, and children. Nor can we overlook the

---

9 Laura K. Egendorf, ed., *Illegal Immigration: An Opposing Viewpoints Guide* (Farmington Hill, MI: Greenhaven Press/Thompson Gale, 2007), 62.

10 Stephen Currie, *Issues in Immigration* (San Diego: Lucent Books, 2000), 61.

tragic deaths of those smuggled illegally. In the same way, many types of drugs and weapons are introduced. The latter is another commodity that has left major disasters on the border, because they are used by drug cartels to create a sinister environment. Money laundering is perhaps the most profitable trade in the border strip, and many hotels, restaurants, and other small businesses are used for this.

These types of illegal businesses are known within the community, but few dare to denounce them. The reality is that the vast majority of the population benefits from this type of illegal trade. They are sources of employment. The rich and poor live on contraband. Obviously, the consequences of this are also experienced in the border area, since prostitution, the use of drugs, clandestine businesses, deaths, and so on openly occur in many places. It is impossible to describe everything that is contraband in the social life of the border. But this gives us an idea of the environment that prevails.

With all kinds of illegal businesses practiced in the border area, you might think that it is a very rich area, but the reality is the opposite. What prevails on the border strip is poverty. A lot of these people are immigrants looking for a better life, and they find it on the border. However, although these people are living a better life, it is only better compared to the life they lived in their place of origin. Demographically, in the United States, the border is one of the poorest regions. Many people request government social assistance, better known as welfare.

As it happens in all capitalist and imperialist places, a few rich people benefit by all the legal and illegal businesses that exist, and the great majority of the poor people are exploited, only receiving what is necessary to continue subsisting in their poverty. That is why in these areas the big business chains stand out, and the manufacturing factories that pay very low wages for labor receive great profits in their international businesses. These are the legal businesses that predominate in the border area.

Characteristics of the Border Church

Since we have briefly described what the border area is and its main social characteristics, we can get into what the life of the Christian church is in the context of the border. Many may say that they are the same characteristics of the church in other areas of the world or of the country. However, what the border influences is much more than we can imagine in the internal life of the church on the border strip.

The mission of the church of Jesus Christ does not change because it is a frontier church. *The Book of Discipline of The United Methodist Church* says, "The Mission of the Church is to make disciples of Jesus Christ for the transformation of the world."[11] Personally, I believe that God created us to adore and praise him in any place, any time, and in any circumstance that we are living. Furthermore, as a church we must edify one another as brothers and sisters in Christ Jesus, and the reason we exist as a church is the call to reach the lost. This call to evangelization and to reach those who are far from the path of God is, I think, more complicated on the American side of the border than the Mexican side. It is complicated, because, unfortunately, in the US borderlands people are so far from God. What makes evangelism more difficult for the church is that border crossers are made dependent on social services provided by the United States. At least those who live in Mexico do not live at the expense of the government!

Something that bears emphasis is the religiosity in which the people of the border live. The people on both sides of the border are very religious and devout, which is evident either because on one side they suffer from scarcity and persecution or, on this side of the border, because of what they do to appease their consciences. In spite of not being constant in their attendance and participation in local congregations, what we should highlight is the spirituality of all these people. At the same time, two hallmarks of this border church are apparent: its puritanism and its religious fanaticism.

This spirituality of the people on the border is not exclusive of a certain social group or religious affiliation. The practices of Catholicism are well known, but there is also great diversity in the evangelical churches, mainly in the Pentecostals or neo-Pentecostals, which have no religious association. We cannot put aside the large number of churches that are still living under the coverage of the denominations. Along with this religious diversity, the existing divisionism between

11 The United Methodist Church, *The Book of Discipline of The United Methodist Church* (Nashville: The United Methodist Publishing House, 2016), 93.

each of the groups stands out, as if they each think they have an exclusive heaven for their own congregants. Another characteristic in this religious diversity is the strong influence of the charismatic movement with an exclusive retouching in each of these religious groups, even within Catholicism, highlighting the meetings of worship with a more contemporary posture. The Charismatic phenomenon stands out in the vast majority of congregations and denominations, but this does not apply to all.

Churches Living in Self-Compassion

Here, somehow, we must remember some of the social characteristics of the border since its predominant economic situation is reflected in some way within the border church. Just as easy money is earned, it is spent in the same way. The church strives to help people live a comfortable life in which the congregants are not in need of the most essential things. The vast majority of congregations have in their facilities the most necessary means to carry out their worship with freedom. This shows the comfortable life that is lived as a church, despite the minimum wages earned in the few honest jobs in the border area. This forces many of the people with limited resources to live with the social help and benefits offered by the government, which ends up influencing the attitude of people who have a steady and well-paying job. This disproportionate economic resourcing creates a numbed social consciousness and a brake in motion toward the fulfilling of the evangelistic responsibilities of each congregation, resulting in congregations defaulting to a life of relaxation and complacency.

Secular Border Churches

Secular border churches, that is, churches with little spiritual life, often discriminate against the poor and marginalized of society. Social action is the main goal of American Christians "from one extreme to the other."[12] Although churches around the United States are oriented to social action, the border church, for the most part, has a very

12 Ronald J. Sider, Philip N. Olson, and Heidi Rolland Unruh, *Churches That Make a Difference: Reaching Your Community with Good News and Good Works* (Grand Rapids, MI: Baker, 2005), 99.

secularized approach to religious practices within their places of worship, all for the desire to leave behind the old religiosity product of a retrograde and decontextualized mentality. This results in congregations leading a double life. That is to say, the congregation has a certain life within the church but lives in a very different way outside the church. It is a church that attacks the lifestyles of its congregants, but it does not attack them directly as long as they continue to contribute financially. It is a church that attacks the liberal practices of society and politics but that internally does such liberal practices in order to maintain the status quo within society. It is a church that attacks politics but that somehow lives at the expense of the interests of politics and politicians, just as drug traffickers have their hands inside the denominations. In this sense, the frontier church is a church that lives within a world of contradictions, because it takes the position of saying one thing, when in reality its practice and way of living are very different from what was preached.

Present and Future Challenges

Looking to the future is very interesting, because as a border church the challenges of the present seem very difficult to achieve. From a pastoral point of view, it is going to be worse if we do not soon look forward and visualize how the church should be if we want to wake up from this spiritual lethargy that we are living as the border church. I still believe that the church belongs to Jesus Christ and that we are in the hands of God, despite the lifestyle that we live as a church of Jesus Christ here in the border area.

Border Churches Need Social Participation

As a church of Jesus Christ we have one foot inside the church and another in the world that surrounds us. This does not mean that we are fulfilling our evangelizing task before the community that surrounds us; on the contrary, everything indicates that we are turning our backs on those people who live without God, without Christ, and without hope. The many needs around the border church indicate that it is suffering myopia. We only see what is inside our four walls, and we forget the poor, the needy, the orphan, the widow, the homeless, and the immigrant—people who in number are the great majority of the population in this border area. Today we need to be a church that participates more in society; we need to leave our own comfort and go where the poor, homeless, immigrants, and needy are. As congregations we have to embrace and integrate all the people of the community; we have to create links, coalitions, community conversations, and a connection with the community's needs.[13] We need to model the gospel of peace that we preach a lot in the churches but that we practice less than we should. Maybe we will always have the poor around us, but that should help us to show a more human side of life, more in keeping with the heart of Jesus himself. The poor are the people who followed Jesus unconditionally. Undoubtedly, one of the biggest challenges in the future of the church is to more visibly participate in society and bring the image of Jesus outside the walls of the church. Enough with inwardly focused Puritanism!

Border Churches Need a Balanced Christian Life

There must be more coherence between what we preach and what we practice, between what we say and what we do, and between what we teach and live. Without a doubt, the frontier church must have a better balance between the spirituality that is presumed and the practical life that we developed beyond our very noses. We live with such an exaggerated focus on the spiritual, on the divine, on the celestial, that we forget the human condition in which we humans live and die. We forget that we are flesh and blood and that as human beings we need to feel loved, accepted, and embraced by those who are in our midst. Richard L. Hamm rails against a church that denies the pain of human experience expressed in the Good Friday tradition: "These spiritualities want to skip Good Friday and move directly to Easter."[14] Undoubtedly, today, the border church has a great need to live and manifest that love of God in a more practical and humane way, not only toward the needy people of the community, but also toward the very people

13 Nancy Tatom Ammerman, *Congregation and Community* (New Brunswick, NJ: Rutgers University Press, 2001), 360–61.

14 Richard L. Hamm, *Recreating the Church: Leadership for the Postmodern Age* (St. Louis: Chalice Press, 2007), 82.

who are within our congregations. It takes much less spirituality and more love of neighbor. When are we are going to stop putting on that mask of piety and extend a hand to the needy while transmitting in that greeting an embrace of the purity and integrity of the heart that seeks a greeting and a sincere embrace in a reciprocal way? Enough of hypocrisy!

Border Churches Need Religious Unity

Here I am referring to joint work, unity, and ecumenism. In the border strip, the influence of the Mexican church is great; the community lives a very active religious life, whether Catholic or Protestant. Some say that there are two major religious groups, Catholics and evangelicals, but this is a half-truth. Unfortunately, Catholicism is more divided today than in past decades. People practice Catholicism differently according to their place of origin: those who call themselves Catholic but never go to church, those who keep the festivities and traditions of the church, those who are unconditionally loyal to the pope, those who are liberal and focused more on social work, and those charismatics who appear more evangelical.

A Divided Church

Evangelical churches are more divided than Catholic churches. Some churches are mainly influenced by conservative currents. Other churches are more Pentecostal-like or without denomination, including the neo-Pentecostals. And other churches are still emerging. All this speaks of the division of the twenty-first-century church of the border strip. Fifty years ago, we were scandalized by the term *ecumenism* and we demonized it, but personally, I believe that one of the things the church in this border area needs most is to seek a little bit more unity beyond the denominational and philosophical barriers. The apostle Paul "asked individuals to refresh their memory of what they had received and what was expected of them. He did not describe a perfect community."[15] What we need today is not a perfect church, but a church serving God and the community in togetherness. We live in a world in crisis, dying

15 Gil Rendle and Alice Mann, *Holy Conversations: Strategic Planning as a Spiritual Practice for Congregations* (Durham, NC: The Alban Institute, 2003), 18.

in disbelief and ignorance, and on the border the devil manifests in different ways such as smuggling and other illegal activities. Ecumenism, in its simple meaning of seeking unity, is the solution to many problems of the church. Enough with divisionism!

Border Churches Need Advanced Technology

Unfortunately, we have lived a bad concept of what humility is, and we have made legalism our main weapon to counteract the darkness. Along with that bad concept of humility, we have let boasting blind us to the modern times in which we live as a church. As a church, we have closed ourselves to the outside world; we have paid the consequences. Outside there is a modern world that we know very little about. We are losing a new generation, and we do not seem to mind losing them. We are left with the music of centuries ago, antiquated forms of worship, and we turned our backs on everything that involved more modern and advanced technology. Before, the high price of technology was the pretext, but today we are at least forty years behind in technology. We need more presence in electronic media, in the use of social networks, and in the computational and cybernetic world. We need to know how to reach the new generations through technology and in this way expand the path toward a more modern era. Enough of outdated religious practices!

Conclusion

This church of the border has many challenges; we are an alive church that is moving all the time, and we need to learn more about the movement of God in the rest of the country. At the same time, there are many things that are part of us as the church of the border, such as the mix of languages and cultures, that we must keep. We are still walking, and we have to let God lead us in this process. *¡Si se puede con el favor de Dios!*

8

Profetas with a Latin American Mission

VINICIUS COUTO

TERTULLIAN (155–220 AD), a leading patristic theologian, once asked what Jerusalem has to do with Athens. For him, there was some tension between religion and philosophy. Today, in the Brazilian Christian religious sphere, we could describe the passive behavior of many Christians, paraphrasing Tertullian's question as follows: "What does Christianity have to do with Brasília?"[1] The passivity of many Christians regarding public issues is a negative phenomenon because it proliferates social injustice and often ends up conniving with the nation's structural sins. What should be the attitude of the church toward the challenges of society? Should it create alternative structures in a kind of post-modern structural monasticism? Should it adhere to everything culture does and sacralize secular public practices? Should it live faith only in the religious and liturgical environment and live paradoxically when in society? Should it force society to live up to its values, Christianizing culture? I believe none of these alternatives are plausible. Therefore, I understand that the best way to position ourselves in relation to current public challenges is in a transformational vision.[2]

---

1 Brasília is the capital and political headquarters of Brazil.

2 Vinicius Couto is an ordained minister of the Church of the Nazarene in Brazil. He is a PhD student in religious sciences at the Methodist University of São Paulo and a member of the research group RIMAGO (a visual arts group) and has received a CAPES scholarship. He has a master's in theology from the Baptist

To be transformational is to put into practice the prophetic mission of the church and to denounce the socioeconomic and religious ills we see every day. It is not to be silent, but to act consciously; not militantly, but legitimately. Thus, to bring more relevant reflections and notes on this theme, this chapter will address the prophetic mission of the church in a contextual way. One model that I find interesting and will use here as a methodological basis to guide our praxis is an adaptation of five questions. They are grounded first in four questions that Richard Middleton and Brian Walsh have established as important for building a worldview: (1) Where am I? (2) Who am I? (3) What is wrong? and (4) What is the solution?[3] The last question comes from the reflections of Anglican N. T. Wright, who, besides agreeing with the previous questions, added one more: What time is it?[4]

From these five questions I will show the need to strengthen our identity as Christians and our identity within some branch of the great tradition of Christianity; after all, we are not isolated in Christianity. Next, I will cover how we need to know our geographic context better. The place where we are is very important for us to understand our culture and to map our prophetic action more effectively. The next step is to contextualize our age. We are Christians, we use the Bible, and we are part of some tradition, but our time is different from the times of the sacred writers and the icons of our theological roots. Therefore, we need to open our minds to the challenges of the twenty-first century in

---

College of Paraná, postgraduate studies in history of theology from FaeteSF and in science of religion from the Cândido Mendes University, and graduated with a bachelor's degree in business administration from the Castelo Branco University and in theology from the Brazilian Nazarene College. He is the editor of the *Bona Conscientia* journal (a periodical specializing in Arminian and Wesleyan theology), a founding member of NEW (Núcleo de Estudos Wesleyanos), the coordinator of the specialization course in Wesleyan-Arminian theology and social transformation at the Brazilian Nazarene Theological Seminary, and professor in various institutions. He is the author and translator of various books of Arminian and Wesleyan theology.

3 Brian Walsh and Richard Middleton, *The Transforming Vision: Shaping a Christian World View* (Downers Grove, IL: InterVarsity Press, 1984), 35.

4 N. T. Wright, *Jesus and the Victory of God: Christian Origins and the Question of God* (London: SPCK, 1996), 446.

mature dialogue with our sources of authority. Finally, after mapping our identity and our geographical and chronological contexts, I will discuss some of the main problems we experience in our reality and propose practical ideas so that our prophetic mission can be a prophetic reality.

Who We Are (Part 1): Reaffirming Our Christian Identity and Our Prophetic Role

In the early twentieth century, sociologist Max Weber was interested in analyzing why Protestants were more economically advantaged than many Catholics in the European context of their day. One of his conclusions was drawn from Luther's theology of work. For the German reformer, the vocation is beyond the religious order, since the priesthood of believers is universal, which implies that Christians can fulfill their vocation even in professional settings. Instead of working for a boss, they work for God and therefore should perform their duties to the glory of God. The behavior that would glorify God should be of care and honesty. Such behavior, in the Weberian view, favored capitalism because it encouraged workers to produce the maximum and perform the service with quality. The result was increased industrial productivity and, in some cases, employee promotion through performance. Thus, the spirit of capitalism would be profit (a cultural necessity that preceded even capitalism itself), which in Protestantism is not a sin because it is the result of personal work that dignifies the human being. The accumulation of profit, therefore, is the result of merit earned through personal effort.[5]

The contemporary Christian reality also has some questions that raise concerns. How do poor people donate large sums to neo-Pentecostal denominations? How do people with undergraduate and postgraduate education from higher social backgrounds also make their donations to the same denominations without questioning their inconsistent biblical interpretation? It may be possible to identify some answers in the way neo-Pentecostalism fits perfectly into postmodernism and late capitalism. According to Stephen Hicks, postmodernism

5 Max Weber, *A ética protestante e o espírito do capitalismo* (São Paulo: Companhia das Letras, 2004), 41–84.

has four characteristics: (1) the weakening of truth, (2) immediateness, (3) consumerism, and (4) pretermit submission.[6] Without entering into the theological or religious question of such points and not even in a value judgment analysis, it is possible to understand why neo-Pentecostalism has grown exponentially in the last three decades in Brazil in all social classes.

This new Pentecostalism undermines the evangelical and Protestant notion of truth in the sense that it has no commitment to the exegesis of biblical texts. Neo-Pentecostal services are prepared from a utilitarian, existentialist, and anthropocentric perspective. Divine power must be demonstrated to the faithful; the suggestion is that such an extraordinary virtue has the ability to break all kinds of evil and bring financial prosperity to those attending neo-Pentecostal service meetings. Such suggestions are made with "themes [that] always involve some impossibility and [that] carry an impactful and sensational title, such as the *Impossible Causes Campaign, service with 318 Pastors* etc."[7] In such campaigns, biblical texts are used without any fidelity to the original meaning (either hermeneutically or exegetically). The methodology of biblical interpretation transcends Origen's (184–253 AD) proposition of allegory, which at least aimed at linking biblical symbols to Christ. The type of neo-Pentecostal allegory centralizes wealth and the accumulation of goods.

The immediacy is a consequence of the culture of consumerism. The type of capitalism practiced today is a wild model, called by Fredric Jameson "late capitalism."[8] This culture gained strength in the Western world, especially after World War I, when a consumerist culture was established as a solution to postwar restructuring. One of the initiatives has been the construction of shopping centers since 1916, encouraging popular consumerism; another initiative was the Marshall Plan, which

6 Stephen Hicks and Ronald Craig, *Explicando o Pós-modernismo: Ceticismo e socialismo—de Rousseau a Foucault* (São Paulo: Callis, 2011), 11–17.

7 Vinicius Couto, "A liturgia nos cultos pentecostais e neopentecostais," in *Culto cristão: Origens, desenvolvimento e desafios contemporâneos* (São Paulo: Reflexão, 2016), 181.

8 Fredric Jameson, *Postmodernism, or, The Cultural Logic of Late Capitalism* (Durham, NC: Duke University Press, 1991).

helped establish capitalism in Europe by strengthening the same system in the United States. The two characteristics can be clearly seen in the neo-Pentecostal service, whose songs and homilies focus on the human being and his or her current needs (e.g., employment, health, money, home, car). For Carlos Caldas, the church is resignified in this new theology as an "agency of the supernatural, which in a very utilitarian way can be manipulated to solve the problems of the congregation."[9] Therefore, it is common to "see in the Neo-Pentecostal service people witnessing about miraculous healings, extraordinary jobs, the acquisition of houses and other monumental possessions," as well as "people who were in the gutter but who mysteriously had the opportunity to have a financial life booming better."[10] Caldas comments that in the neo-Pentecostal denominations, the testimony is an "impressive account of how someone, after attending such a church and carefully following all the instructions given to him, went from misery to wealth."[11]

While divinity can bestow the desires of the postmodern heart in its breadth—that is, houses, cars, jewelry, electronics, and so on—such acquisitions need not go through a very long waiting period. They can be received very quickly. The health of the human being also enters this discussion. Rather than health insurance and expensive medical consultations, which are often nearly impossible for a poorer population, divine healing is available at the very moment a person uses faith. Rather than waiting many days (or years) for a release from the Unified Health System,[12] the prayer of faith can cure any kind of illness instantly. If consumerism is filled by the divinity that gives "all

9 Carlos Caldas, *Fundamentos da Teologia da Igreja* (São Paulo: Mundo Cristão, 2007), 45.

10 Couto, "A liturgia nos cultos pentecostais e neopentecostais," 179.

11 Caldas, *Fundamentos da Teologia da Igreja*, 46.

12 In Brazil there are two ways to manage health plans: one public and the other private. The public plan, called the Unified Health System, is managed by the government and is free for the entire population. The private plan is run by several companies that charge high monthly fees to cover medical care, exams, surgeries, and so on. The problem with the public plan is that Brazil has a very large population (over 200 million), so consultations, examinations, and surgeries are not of good quality. It often takes too long to schedule an appointment, and in some cases people die waiting for an appointment.

things" liberally, immediacy is filled with the instantaneousness of faith when properly performed.[13] The proper form of the exercise of the neo-Pentecostal faith is not in the conditionality of obedience or in some penitential form, but in disregarding the supreme authority, that is, God himself. Rather than pleading for his eternal goodness and other attributes such as his grace and mercy, the believer should require from God the rights that were supposedly granted to human beings. The idea of requiring came from the exponent Kenneth E. Hagin, one of the parents of the neo-Pentecostalism movement. In his analysis of John 14:13, 14, Hagin taught that a Christian should not ask God to keep his promises. Instead, the proper exercise of faith is in demanding from God such compliments:

> The word "ask" also means "demand." "Whatever you demand in My Name, I [Jesus] will do it." An example of this is recorded in the 3rd chapter of Acts with Peter and John at the gate called Beautiful. We have already discussed that Peter knew he had something to give when he said to the crippled man, "Silver and gold have I none, but what I have I give thee." Then Peter said, "In the Name of Jesus Christ of Nazareth, rise up and walk." He asked, or demanded, that the man get up and walk in the Name of Jesus.[14]

Postures of respectability, contrition, humility, recognition of divine sovereignty, glory, and supremacy are converted into an act of demanding. In Hagin's neo-Pentecostal theological scheme, the landlord (God) assumes the position of human servitude. Thus, the divinity, once held sovereign in classical theologies, becomes hostage to its

13 There is a misconception in Brazil based on Jesus's Sermon on the Mount (Matthew 6–7) that if one seeks first the kingdom of God and his righteousness, all things will be added. "All things" suggests a very wide range of things, and neo-Pentecostalism uses this device to say that people who were bankrupt went into a very high estate condition, having imported motorboats, yachts, mansions, and cars, among other things. By contrast, the New Testament text says that Jesus had committed himself to "all these things" rather than "all things" (cf. Matt 6:33). "All these things," in the immediate context, refers to the basic necessities of life, represented by food, drink, and clothing.

14 Kenneth E. Hagin, *The Name of Jesus* (Tulsa, OK: Faith Library Publications, 1979), 74.

promises, obliged to be subservient to the statements and demands of its human masters. Given these approaches, it is easier to understand why Luiz Felipe Pondé stated that Latin American theologies (liberation theology and integral mission theology) chose the poor but the poor instead chose neo-Pentecostalism.[15] Since the desire of the Latin American poor is to have a better life, it is more comfortable and contextualizing to personal needs to adhere to the neo-Pentecostal ufanist or self-aggrandizing message than to a more philosophical theology, which teaches the need for the empowerment of social classes and the struggle for structural changes. After all, the world teaches to consume; the media does consumerist and immediate marketing; technology works with the production of programmed obsolescence; having is better than being; if it is to be, let it be on a material level and not on character. And so neo-Pentecostalism caters to both the rich and the poor: the rich become anesthetized, and the poor have their heads filled with ideas on becoming rich on the way.[16]

But is this the kind of Christianity we should adopt? The answer is an echoing and resounding *no*! The biblical attitude toward social ills is not a symbiosis between Christians and corruption, but a denunciation of such practices. In the Sermon on the Mount Jesus said that "blessed are those who hunger and thirst for righteousness, for they will be filled" (Matt 5:6, NIV). The word *righteousness* there is δικαιοσύνην (*dikaiosynēn*), whose meaning has to do with correct integrity; virtue; and purity of life, thought, feeling, and action (*orthopathy* and orthopraxis). Jesus also said that blessed are those who hunger (πεινῶντες [*peinōntes*]) and thirst (διψῶντες [*dipsōntes*]). Hunger, in that context, has to do with being truly hungry, having need, being very poor. It is a metaphor about longing, about seeking with impetuous desire. Thirst, in turn, has to do with suffering from thirst. Figuratively, it has to do with those who feel a painful need for water.

At the end of the Beatitudes, Jesus compares his followers with two elements: salt (ἅλας [*halas*]) and light (φῶς [*phōs*]). Salt is a symbol of lasting agreement because it protects food from decay and preserves

15 Luiz Felipe Pondé, *Para Entender o Catolicismo Hoje* (São Paulo: Benvirá, 2011), 92.

16 Robinson Cavalcanti, *A Igreja, o País e o Mundo: Desafios a uma fé engajada* (Viçosa: Ultimato, 2000), 121.

it without change. Light, in turn, derives from an archaic *phao* form, which means "to shine or make manifest, especially by emitting rays." In this talk of Jesus, light is used as a metaphor for good works: "let your light shine before others, that they may see your good deeds and glorify your Father in heaven" (Matt 5:16, NIV). Jesus's speech thus demonstrates that Christians need to live with an engaged, practical, transformational faith. Our actions speak louder than words thrown to the wind, so the church must resume its Christian identity and fulfill its prophetic mission before society. Prophetic mission is the task of denouncing the sin of the authorities (religious or political) who are seduced by the thirst for power and money and the spiritual, social, and moral decay of the people. The prophet is the one who points the finger and represents the Creator on earth. It is the Christian's task not to be silent before the ills, corruptions, and sinfulness of the situation in which he or she is inserted. It must be a nuisance to those who delight in injustice. The finger that touches the open wound must be applied wisely, always aiming for it to close. The prophetic role of the church is not to be confused with a pessimistic and murmuring worldview that is always complaining about everything and only serves to find faults. The prophetic role must aim at transformation, otherwise it will be nothing more than an accuser that adds to Satan's efforts in his kingdom of opposition to the Creator. Because of this, Cheryl Sanders's threefold view of the prophetic mission of the church is interesting, embracing accountability, compassion, and empathy.[17]

Scripture shows the need for *accountability* by saying that "whoever oppresses the poor shows contempt for their Maker, but whoever is kind to the needy honors God" (Prov 14:31, NIV). Taking advantage of the underprivileged is a sin that needs to be reported. God said, "Do not deny justice to your poor people in their lawsuits" (Exod 23:6). Men like Elijah, Micaiah, and John the Baptist denounced the injustices and atrocities of various natures (e.g., spiritual, moral, social) of the authorities of their time.

Scripture also demonstrates that *compassion* is needed: "It is a sin to despise one's neighbor, but blessed is the one who is kind to the needy"

17 Cheryl J. Sanders, *Ministry at the Margins: The Prophetic Mission of Women, Youth, and the Poor* (Eugene, OR: Wipf & Stock, 1997), 19–40.

(Prov 14:21, NIV). "To look after orphans and widows in their distress and to keep oneself from being polluted by the world" is regarded by James as characteristics of true religion (James 1:27, NIV). Daniel, instrumentalized by God, told King Nebuchadnezzar that he should put an end to his "sins by doing what is right, and your wickedness by being kind to the oppressed" (Dan 4:27, NIV). In the context of Israelite law, God warned that there should be no injustice and compassion among people: "If you lend money to one of my people among you who is needy, do not treat it like a business deal; charge no interest. If you take your neighbor's cloak as a pledge, return it by sunset, because that cloak is the only covering your neighbor has. What else can they sleep in? When they cry out to me, I will hear, for I am compassionate" (Exod 22:25–27, NIV). When we worry about these issues, people outside the gospel world see transformational behavior and glorify our heavenly Father (Matt 5:16).

Empathy, in turn, is nothing more than putting oneself in another's shoes, that is, identifying oneself intellectually or affectionately with an idea or person. Jesus said, "In everything, do to others what you would have them do to you" (Matt 7:12, NIV). Many injustices occur a priori because of the sinful depravity that the human race inherited from Adam. But in the second instance, injustices occur because many people do not take this counsel of Jesus into account. As an example, we may mention rulers (and even religious leaders) who enjoy luxury lodgings, vacations in places that can be considered wonders of the world, and exorbitant wages, without putting themselves in the shoes of the poor, often homeless and sometimes without anything to eat. Empathy also can be shown in the way we deal with people from different cultures. God warned the Israelites, "Do not oppress a foreigner; you yourselves know how it feels to be foreigners, because you were foreigners in Egypt" (Exod 23:9, NIV). Empathy for the different is part of the concept of hospitality in the ancient Eastern world. The Greek word for hospitality is φιλοξενια (*philoxenia*) and is a junction of two other Greek words, namely φίλος (*phílos*, which means "friend" or "friendly") and ξένος (*xenos*, which means "strange" or "foreign"). Φιλοξενια therefore means kindness to strangers and foreigners, and showing an attitude of integration toward people of different culture. It is not specifically about receiving and welcoming immigrants or people from another nation, but also people from different cultural backgrounds, treating them with respect, love, affection, and humanity.

Who We Are (Part 2): The Importance of Our Tradition

First, we need to assume our Christian identity. Knowing who we are and what our role is makes all the difference. We know that Christianity is very fragmented, but we are also sure that the neo-Pentecostal worldview is not aligned with the Scriptures. We are not isolated in the midst of Christianity. Scripture is our primary source in authoritative terms, but we are also informed by our traditions and identity legacies. Still in this prophetic function, I would like to expose some of this relevance in the Wesleyan tradition of which I am part. John Wesley (1703–1791) was a British Anglican clergyman who sought to reconcile orthodoxy and orthopraxis, that is, the doctrines that his denomination professed (the formal faith) with the required practice of such beliefs (the works). The England of his day faced various social difficulties, and Wesley set out to engage in the issues of his time to bring about social transformation. In this way he engaged in the search for better conditions for the imprisoned, seeking prison reform; he acted openly against the slave system; he wanted the inclusion of the poorest in Anglican parishes.[18] He also visited hospitals, poor houses, and prisons thinking about the restoration of the individual. He taught his listeners how to better manage financial resources; he explained the ecological responsibility that Christians have. He was concerned with health and public

18 Many seats were bought by the rich at this time, so that the poor were excluded from the Anglican liturgy and would have to attend service meetings outside and, more rarely, at the back of the parish hall. For more information see Carolyn Nystrom, *The Wesleys: Amazing Love* (Downers Grove, IL: InterVarsity Press, 2002), 29; R. A. Soloway, *Prelates and People: Ecclesiastical Social Thought in England, 1783–1852* (London: Routledge, 2007), 444.

health issues, and he was inclusive of women in leadership[19] in the services of Methodist societies,[20] among many other things.[21]

Wesley explained that "Christianity is essentially a social religion; and that to turn it into a solitary religion is indeed to destroy it."[22] By calling Christianity a social religion, Wesley meant that it "would not subsist at all, without society," that is, "without living and conversing with other men."[23] A social religion does not admit to "lonely saints," meaning people who live in isolation from society in order to seek monastic sanctification. This is not possible because even holiness is social. He asked, "Will any man affirm that a solitary Christian [. . .] can be a merciful man, that is, one that takes every opportunity of doing all good to all men?"[24] How can one be light (do good works) living in isolation from society? Such good works are works of righteousness and lead to practical and social holiness. A Christian cannot turn a blind eye to social ills and injustices, even if such injustices were legal. An example of this is the criticism raised against people who wanted to justify slavery:

19 Women were moved from a condition of expectant clients to valued workers who not only performed behind-the-scenes services (e.g., cleansing, prayer), but began to contribute more directly to discipleship in the Church of England.

20 Methodist societies were small groups that met several times a week to study the Bible; visit hospitals, poor houses, and prisons; and partake of the sacrament of the Lord's Supper (Eucharist). Wesley pioneered allowing women to teach in these groups and to exercise leadership over other women. These Methodist groups emerged in 1729 at Oxford University, where Wesley studied. He and his friends earned the nickname Methodist because of the strong discipline with which they practiced their methods of visiting the needy and studying the Bible.

21 To understand John Wesley better, read the biographies by Richard P. Heitzenrater, *Wesley and the People Called Methodist* (Nashville: Abingdon Press, 2013); Matthieu Lelièvre, *John Wesley: His Life and His Work* (London: Wesleyan Conference Office, 1871); Timothy J. Crutcher, *John Wesley: His Life and Thought* (Kansas City: Beacon Hill Press, 2015); Kenneth J. Collins, *A Real Christian: The Life of John Wesley* (Nashville: Abingdon Press, 1999); and Kenneth J. Collins, *John Wesley: A Theological Journey* (Nashville: Abingdon Press, 2003).

22 John Wesley, *The Works of the Rev. John Wesley* (London: Thomas Cordeux, 1811), 7:378.

23 Wesley, *The Works of the Rev. John Wesley*, 7:378.

24 Wesley, *The Works of the Rev. John Wesley*, 7:379.

> The grand plea is "They are authorized by law." But can human law change the nature of things? Can it turn darkness light or evil into good? By no means. Notwithstanding ten thousand laws, right is right, and wrong is wrong still. There must still remain an essential difference between justice and injustice, cruelty and mercy. So that I still ask, Who can reconcile this treatment of the Negroes, first and last, with either mercy or justice?[25]

Wesley clearly emphasizes the fact that justice needs to be central, even if it goes against current laws. Thus, the law must be changed to suit righteousness, justice. Although patriotic, "Wesley's practical theology . . . forced him to place his own patriotism under the judgment of what God is doing for the world."[26] An example of this can be seen in the sermon "The Mystery of Iniquity," when Wesley exposed the misbehavior of English "Christians" who were acting in the region of India in service to the British crown. Rather than bearing good testimony among Hindus, instead by killing them they "desolated whole countries, and clogged the rivers with dead bodies." Therefore, he commented on the coexistence of the two ethnic groups and asked reflexively: "There are Christians and heathens too. Which have more justice, mercy, and truth? The Christians or the heathens? Which are more corrupt, infernal, devilish in tempers and practice? The English or the Indians?"[27]

Change, however, should not only be legislative, but should occur in other spheres, in this case economic and labor. González explains this by saying that there were people who wanted to justify slavery "for economic reasons, because without it industry and trade would suffer."[28] Wesley, however, argued that it is "better no trade, than trade procured by villainy. It is far better to have no wealth, than to gain wealth at the expense of virtue. Better is honest poverty, than all the riches bought by the tears, and sweat, and blood of our fellow-creatures."[29]

---

25 Wesley, *The Works of the Rev. John Wesley*, 16:454.

26 Justo González, *Juan Wesley: Desafíos para nuestro siglo* (Buenos Aires: Cátedra Carnahan, 2003), 55.

27 Wesley, *The Works of the Rev. John Wesley*, 9:218.

28 González, *Juan Wesley*, 53.

29 Wesley, *The Works of the Rev. John Wesley*, 16:459.

Wesley understood that "rich" are not exactly people who have heaps of gold and silver, but people who "[possess] more than the necessaries and conveniences of life," that is, those who have "food and raiment sufficient for himself and his family and something over."[30] He based this concept on the way the apostle Paul spoke of the importance of the Christian community being content to possess the basic necessities of food and clothing, for those who desire to enrich themselves fall into various negative situations and sink into ruin and perdition (1 Tim 6:8–10). Wesley explained that the Pauline counsel was not against illicit enrichment but against one's own desire for enrichment, that is, to accumulate possessions that transcend the necessary and the convenient, whose effort is destined to live superfluously.[31]

One should not think from these excerpts that the British theologian was opposed to rich people or wealth per se. In fact, according to him, it is not impossible for a Christian to be rich. He admitted that the miraculous work of Christ can make someone rich and that this person can use resources responsibly and for the glory of God, if he or she has "the mind that was in Christ and walk as Christ walked."[32] Wesley believed that their concern revolved around the fact that the wealth of the rich (large houses, furniture, cars, clothes, and various luxury items) is "an almost irresistible tendency to make him think himself a better man, than those who have not these advantages."[33] In fact, the problem for Wesley is not wealth itself, but misuse of it, for as the apostle Paul said, "the love of money is a root of all kinds of evil" (1 Tim 6:10, NIV). Money therefore can be used to do good or bad things. It depends on how it is administered. According to Wesley, the use of money "is full as applicable to the best, as to the worst uses. It is of unspeakable service to all civilized nations, in all the common affairs of life."[34] If money is well spent, there is "food for the hungry, drink for the thirsty, raiment for the naked. It gives to the traveller and the

30 Wesley, *The Works of the Rev. John Wesley*, 10:363. See the sermon "On Riches."

31 Wesley, *The Works of the Rev. John Wesley*, 10:104–5. See the sermon "The Danger of Riches."

32 Wesley, *The Works of the Rev. John Wesley*, 10:364. See the sermon "On Riches."

33 Wesley, *The Works of the Rev. John Wesley*, 10:364. See the sermon "On Riches," 369.

34 Wesley, *The Works of the Rev. John Wesley*, 8:382. See the sermon "The Use of Money."

stranger where to lay his head."[35] Through it, "we may supply the place of an husband to the widow, and of a father to the fatherless. We may be a defence for the oppressed, a mean of health to the sick, of ease to them that are in pain; it may be as eyes to the blind, as feet to the lame; yea, a lifter up from the gates of death."[36]

After reading these placements it becomes easier to understand Wesley's concerns about the dangers of wealth. Instead of using it selfishly and wickedly, it should be for the needy. This option for the poor was a hallmark of Methodism, so much so that M. Douglas Meeks claimed that the "Methodist revival began between, with, for, and through the poor."[37] Thus, it is noteworthy that Wesley's real concern was social rectitude, a just economy, and the balanced use of human and material resources. One way to balance it all was proposed in his sermon "The Use of Money," in which Wesley recorded the following advice: "Gain all you can, save all you can and give all you can."[38]

"Gain all you can" involves lawful actions but not necessarily at any cost. Thus, "the worker may strive to obtain his financial and material resources, but this should be done modestly, as overworking could be detrimental to health."[39] According to the Anglican clergyman, "We ought to gain all we can gain, . . . But this it is certain we ought not to do; we ought not to gain money at the expense of life; nor, (which is in effect the same thing), at the expense of our health."[40] Thus, unhealthy works, "as those which imply the dealing much with arsenic, or other equally hurtful minerals; or the breathing an air tainted with steams of melting lead, which must at length destroy the firmest constitution,"[41] must be avoided, as well as those "which require many hours to be spent in writing; especially if a person write sitting, and lean upon his

35 Wesley, *The Works of the Rev. John Wesley*, 8:382. See the sermon "The Use of Money."

36 Wesley, *The Works of the Rev. John Wesley*, 8:382. See the sermon "The Use of Money."

37 M. Douglas Meeks, *Economia global & economia de Deus* (São Bernardo do Campo: Editeo, 2001), 42.

38 Wesley, *The Works of the Rev. John Wesley*, 8:383, 387, 390. See the sermon "The Use of Money."

39 Vinicius Couto, *Fé x Obras: Ortodoxia e ortopraxia na teologia de John Wesley* (São Paulo: Reflexão, 2018), 130.

40 Wesley, *The Works of the Rev. John Wesley*, 8:383. See the sermon "The Use of Money."

41 Wesley, *The Works of the Rev. John Wesley*, 8:383. See the sermon "The Use of Money."

stomach, or remain long in an uneasy posture."[42] Earning as much as you can, in Wesleyan thinking, therefore does not follow the flow of market society. Work activities need to be carefully analyzed, sifting through reason and experience. If the conclusion of this analytical inquiry "shows to be destructive of health or strength, that we may not submit to [this job]," because "life is more valuable than meat, and the body than raiment."[43] Another line that goes against market society is in his teaching that if Christians are "already engaged in such an employ, we should exchange it as soon as possible, for some, which, if it lessen our gain, will, however, not lessen our health."[44]

According to Couto, "this was because in Wesley's thinking, health was something that was part of the Christian stewardship of the gift of life. The human being needs to take care of the body, the mind," and therefore "of the health, because they are God's gifts so that the human being can live on this earth and live with the people around."[45] Thus, "to stop caring for these elements is to stop worrying about the stewardship of the body, that is, the temple of the Holy Spirit."[46] In this sense, Wesley stated that God charged people with diverse talents: "Such is bodily strength: such are health, a pleasing person, an agreeable address; such are learning and knowledge in their various degrees, with all the other advantages of education."[47] The care of these divine gifts should be performed in a responsible stewardship, since "thy Lord will farther enquire, 'Hast thou been a wise and faithful Steward, with regard to the talents of a mixt nature which I lent thee? Didst thou employ thy health and strength, not in folly or sin?' "[48]

How we could realize that "gain all you can" is not advice to do anything at any price? If, on the one hand, the worker should not harm him- or herself, then, on the other, he or she should not hurt his or her

42 Wesley, *The Works of the Rev. John Wesley*, 8:383. See the sermon "The Use of Money."

43 Wesley, *The Works of the Rev. John Wesley*, 8:383. See the sermon "The Use of Money."

44 Wesley, *The Works of the Rev. John Wesley*, 8:383. See the sermon "The Use of Money."

45 Couto, *Fé x Obras*, 131.

46 Couto, *Fé x Obras*, 131.

47 Wesley, *The Works of the Rev. John Wesley*, 8:289. See the sermon "The Good Steward."

48 Wesley, *The Works of the Rev. John Wesley*, 8:298.

neighbor. "Hurting" in this case may concern two situations. The first is that we cannot "gain [as much as we can] by hurting our neighbour in his body."[49] This principle involves not subjecting people to unworthy and unhealthy work, as well as selling "anything [to the people] which tends to impair health. Such is, eminently, all that liquid fire, commonly called drams or spirituous liquors."[50] The second implication of not "hurting" concerns expertism, fraud, and any kind of situation that generates dishonest profit. Commercial transactions need to follow a path called, in business management, a *win-win relationship*, that is, a form of negotiation in which both parties benefit from a fair price that does not give the trader financial loss and is not costly for whoever is buying the product. In addition to the buy–sell relationship, the win-win relationship also takes into account productivity and effectiveness, and maximizes the use of human, material, and financial resources; ergonomic working conditions; wages and benefits; professional progress; cost savings; and so on.[51] According to Wesley,

> We cannot, consistent with brotherly love, sell our goods below the market price; we cannot study to ruin our neighbour's trade, in order to advance our own; much less can we entice away or receive any of his servants or workmen whom he has need of. None can gain by swallowing up his neighbour's subtance, without gaining the damnation of hell![52]

"Save all you can" is the other Wesleyan maxim. However, it is not about saving money in the bank or practicing capital accumulation. Rather than having a bank account full of money, González explains that Wesley's proposal was to use financial resources wisely and not spend on superfluous things.[53] Such "idle expenses" came from "the desire of the flesh, the desire of the eye, or the pride of life," which

49 Wesley, *The Works of the Rev. John Wesley*, 8:385. See the sermon "The Use of Money."

50 Wesley, *The Works of the Rev. John Wesley*, 8:385. See the sermon "The Use of Money."

51 Idalberto Chiavenato, *Gestão de pessoas* (Rio de Janeiro: Elsevier, 2008), 5.

52 Wesley, *The Works of the Rev. John Wesley*, 8:385. See the sermon "The Use of Money."

53 González, *Juan Wesley*, 56.

Wesley compared with "elegant epicurism."[54] In another sermon, Wesley criticized this unbridled and irresponsible pursuit of the pleasure of luxury living as disgusting. According to him,

> Is there a character more despicable than even that of a liar? Perhaps there is; even that of an epicure. And are we not a generation of epicures? Is not our belly our god? Are not eating and drinking our chief delight, our highest happiness? Is it not the main study (I fear, the only study) of many honourable men to enlarge the pleasure of tasting? When was luxury (not in food only, but in dress, furniture, equipage) carried to such an height in Great Britain ever since it was a nation? We have lately extended the British empire almost over the globe. We have carried our laurels into Africa, into Asia, into the burning and the frozen climes of America. And what have we brought thence? All the elegance of vice which either the eastern or western world could afford.[55]

Wesley considered this unruly use of financial resources as one of the causes of poverty. The lack of work also corroborated this situation. This poverty, however, is not caused by laziness but by the comfort and indifference of the rich.[56] For this reason, Wesley criticized the superfluous use of money, along with the unbridled desire for enrichment, as the root causes that made income distribution increasingly unequal. In his letter "Thoughts on the present scarcity of provisions," Wesley asked the question, "Why are oats so dear?" The answer, according to him, is "because there are four times as many horses kept to speak within compass for coaches and chaises in particular as were a few years ago."[57]

---

54 Wesley, *The Works of the Rev. John Wesley*, 8:387, 388. See the sermon "The Use of Money." Epicureanism was a philosophical system created by Epicuro de Samos that advocated the pursuit of immediate pleasure. The apostle Paul seems to have ironically criticized this kind of behavior when he said, "Let us eat and drink, for tomorrow we die" (1 Cor 15:32, NIV).

55 John Wesley, *The Works of the Rev. John Wesley* (New York: J. Emory & B. Waugh, 1831), 1:519. See the sermon "National Sins and Miseries."

56 Frederico A. Meléndez, *Ética y economia: El legado de Juan Wesley a la iglesia en América Latina* (Buenos Aires: Kairós Ediciones, 2006), 77.

57 John Wesley, *The Works of the Rev. John Wesley* (New York: J. Emory & B. Waugh, 1835), 6:276.

The price increase was made to maintain the farmers' high standard because "unless therefore four times the oats grew now that grew then they cannot be at the same price."[58] The high mortality rate among the poor was associated with poor diet, which, as one eighteenth-century journal explained, "the poor have been obliged to feed on" and caused people's immune systems to collapse, rendering them susceptible to numerous diseases, such as various types of flu and very high fevers, among others.[59] In this way, the luxury of the rich caused the principle of "gain all you can" to be broken by seeking gain at the expense of the physical integrity of many people who would not be able to feed themselves with dignity.

Another phenomenon that corroborated the rise in prices was the industrial monopoly: "Why are pork poultry and eggs so dear? Because of the monopolizing of farms; perhaps as mischievous a monopoly as was ever introduced into these kingdoms."[60] The nonintervention of the state in this monopoly practice meant that "the land which was some years ago divided between ten or twenty little farmers, and enabled them comfortably to provide for their families, is now generally engrossed by one great farmer."[61] In a win-lose business management model, the landowner reduced the cost of production by exploiting the cheap labor of the employees and retained most of the profits by selling the products for the price it wanted, since there was no competition. For this reason, Wesley explained that the cause of all this inequality was the unbridled desire for enrichment that was motivated by the willingness of entrepreneurs to live in "luxury," that is, in extravagance.[62] As Marquardt attested, "personal striving for increasing wealth and social injustice are two sides of the same coin."[63] In addition to the poorer class having a hard time buying food that was sold at high prices, England still levied

58 Wesley, *The Works of the Rev. John Wesley*, 6:276.

59 Wesley D. Tracy, "Economic Policies and Judicial Oppression as Formative Influences on the Theology of John Wesley," *Wesleyan Theological Journal* 27 (1992): 44.

60 Wesley, *The Works of the Rev. John Wesley*, 6:276.

61 Wesley, *The Works of the Rev. John Wesley*, 6:276.

62 Wesley, *The Works of the Rev. John Wesley*, 6:276.

63 Manfred Marquardt, *John Wesley's Social Ethics: Praxis and Principles* (Nashville: Abingdon Press, 1992), 38.

high taxes on its citizens. The reason for such taxation came from the rulers' mismanagement, which included high wages, unnecessary positions, and corruption. So, Wesley pointed out that one way to improve this tax burden on the population was by "abolishing all useless pensions, . . . especially those ridiculous ones given to some hundreds of idle men as governors of forts or castles which forts have answered no end for above these hundred years unless to shelter jackdaws and crows."[64]

What does "save all you can" ultimately mean? It means using resources responsibly, taking care to "provide things needful for yourself," that is, "food to eat, raiment to put on, whatever nature moderately requires, for preserving the body in health and strength" and these same things "for your wife, your children, your servants, or any others, who pertain to your household."[65] Following this, one should then "give as much as he can," beginning with the household of the faith and, with opportunity, to all other human beings.[66] While Lutheranism and Calvinism put more emphasis on the dignity of labor, which values the "spirit of capitalism," the Wesleyan ethic represents an exception to the Protestant ethic of its time, as described by Marquardt.[67] This was because "while politically [Wesley] was conservative, his economic views were deeply intertwined with his ethical, pastoral, and theological vision of holiness," as "the faith that works through love."[68]

Where We Are and What Time It Is: Achieving Our Prophetic Role from Our Geographical and Chronological Context

TO TAKE EFFECTIVE PROPHETIC action, we need to contextualize our home and our time. In this case, I am writing as a Brazilian who is part of a Latin American culture and living in the twenty-first century. Admittedly, the Scriptures are the sources of authoritative faith and

64 Wesley, *The Works of the Rev. John Wesley*, 6:278. See the tract "Thoughts on the Present Scarcity of Provisions."

65 Wesley, *The Works of the Rev. John Wesley*, 8:391. See the sermon "The Use of Money."

66 Wesley, *The Works of the Rev. John Wesley*, 8:391. See the sermon "The Use of Money."

67 Marquardt, *John Wesley's Social Ethics*, 43.

68 Meléndez, *Ética y economia*, 91.

practice for my life as a Christian. But how can narratives of people who lived in Palestine, North Africa, and even regions of Europe two millennia earlier really be relevant today in a highly secularized society? This is our great challenge: just as the ancient prophet said, "Thus saith the Lord," we must use prophecy (i.e., Scripture) and point to our societies today and say what the Lord says. We cannot be silent in the face of such widespread ill health and chaos. The Brazilian challenges regarding social issues do not differ much with regard to the rest of Latin America. We may differ in the cultural field (customs and language), but we are identical in public affairs. Perhaps the fact that Latin America was colonized by Spanish and Portuguese Europeans, whose extractive and Eurocentric similarity were preponderant roles in contact with our lands, is a bit of what we have in common. The Spanish arrived in America in 1492, and the Portuguese arrived in Brazil in 1500. Their arrival here was for the sake of progress, that is, the progress of their respective crowns. The relationship of the colonizers with the colonies was merely capitalist and extractivist, the process of independence as well as industrialization in Latin America was slow due to the profits that could be raised in the new world, and the European crowns did not want to lose this source of wealth. However, this colonial management has left very negative marks on Latin American nations.

One of the biggest current problems in Brazil (and elsewhere in Latin America) is corruption. The term *corruption* is controversial because of its breadth of meaning. However, the present chapter is dealing with corruption in the sense of embezzlement of public money, the illicit enrichment of politicians, their high wages at odds with that of the national population, and the lack of concern for better income distribution that brings dignity and humaneness to the population. In this sense, corruption in Brazil has occurred since its colonial period and, obviously, is not limited to just this nation; it is a global problem. Lucas Rocha Furtado noted that in the early years "after the discovery of Brazilian ground, the most common fraud in the young colony was related to the smuggling of goods. Gold smuggling, which was practiced even by clerics, occurred on a large scale."[69] Hence, for example, the Brazil-

69 Lucas Rocha Furtado, "As raízes da corrupção: Estudos de caos e lições para o futuro" (PhD diss., Universidad de Salamanca, 2012), 2.

ian slang "saint of the hollow stick" was born, because many people hid precious stones inside Catholic images. Illicit enrichment in Brazil, as it turned out, is not recent. In the colonial period this often occurred. Sérgio Habib explained that "such was the eagerness with which people came here to get rich" that they were attracted by the fame of abundance of the new colony.[70] Many saw not an opportunity to work and earn a prosperous life from worthy and honest labor, but to accumulate illicit goods. In 1682, during the reign of Dom Pedro II (1667–1706), the Company of Commerce of Maranhão was created. The purpose of this company was to promote sugar agromanufacturing as well as the cultivation of cotton to producers in the region. However, the corruption in this venture was vexing. Wilson Martins reported that "the company was far from functioning properly: the weights and measures they used were counterfeit; the edible farms exposed for sale, of the worst quality, and even corrupt."[71] They practiced overpricing so that everything was "insufficient to supply the market, and at prices higher than taxed," and "the governor himself was in the hands of the patron."[72]

Transparency International provides an annual ranking of the most corrupt countries in the world. In its 2017 report of 180 countries, Brazil ranked 96th least corrupt and 84th most corrupt.[73] The 2018 report showed Brazil in the position of 105th most corrupt.[74] It would not be wrong to conclude, therefore, that Brazil's history of corruption has generated a negative image of the political system in the minds of Brazilians. In the language of the cognitive science of religion, this negative image is nothing more than a "mental representation." When a Brazilian hears the words *politics* and *politician*, usually the first thing that comes to mind is corruption. Although data are lacking to

70 Sérgio Habib, *Brasil: Quinhentos anos de corrupção—Enfoque sócio-histórico-jurídico-penal* (Porto Alegre, Brazil: Sergio Antônio Fabris Editor, 1994), 3.

71 Wilson Martins, *A História da Inteligência Brasileira* (Ponta Grossa, Brazil: UEPG, 2010), 1:250.

72 Martins, *A História da Inteligência Brasileira*, 1:250.

73 Report data can be viewed at "Corruption Perceptions Index 2017," Transparency International, February 21, 2018, www.transparency.org/news/feature/corruption_perceptions_index_2017.

74 "Corruption Perceptions Index," Transparency International, accessed February 10, 2022, www.transparency.org/cpi2018.

substantiate such mental representation, "it is possible that proximity to corrupt acts, at a minimum, enhances resignation, forming a mass of individuals conformed to their manifestation in society."[75]

Country	Position	Country	Position
Venezuela	168	Peru	105
Haiti	161	El Salvador	105
Nicaragua	152	Brazil	105
Guatemala	144	Colombia	99
Mexico	138	Panama	93
Paraguay	132	Guiana	93
Honduras	132	Argentina	85
Bolivia	132	Trinidad and Tobago	78
Dominican Republic	129	Suriname	73
Ecuador	114	Cuba	61

Table 1: Most corrupt Latin American countries.[76]

In addition to the problem of corruption, Latin America is experiencing a very acute crisis of social inequality, a type of social Darwinism, a natural market selection of social classes that "believes that it is the duty of the economically qualified to drive the economically disqualified from business and to drive them to economic extinction."[77] The market has no feelings and does not deal with employees as human beings, but as numbers that make up an organization's fixed cost and that in times of economic crisis will need to be crossed out to maintain

75 Robert Bonifácio and Ednaldo Ribeiro, "Corrupção e participação política no Brasil: Diagnósticos e consequências," *Revista Brasileira de Ciência Política*, Brasília 20 (maio–agosto de 2016): 36.

76 "Corruption Perceptions Index," Transparency International, accessed February 10, 2022, www.transparency.org/cpi2018.

77 Meeks, *Economia global & economia de Deus*, 10.

the same standard of profitability. The market is not concerned with how many children a parent needs to support. Therefore, the invisible hand, explains Estela Fernandéz Nadal, "is opaque and naturalized" because "life and death seem to be arbitrarily distributed by nature itself."[78] Ladislau Dowbor presents three basic challenges for this contemporary economic system: (1) environmental dynamics, (2) rising inequality, and (3) the sterilization of financial resources.[79]

The first case concerns the challenge of using natural resources. Human needs are endless and insatiable. However, natural resources are limited. Many raw materials come from nonrenewable sources, and this compromises not only the production of tangible goods, but the entire ecosystem as well. The world population in 1900 was approximately 1.5 billion people, and it currently exceeds 7.2 billion. The problem with this is that the population has been growing bigger and bigger, and "everyone [is] wanting to consume more, each corporation [is] wanting to extract and sell more, and [the technologies] are getting more and more powerful to extend the process."[80]

Social inequality is the second problem raised by Dowbor. Poor income distribution, however, is not due to global poverty, but to the accumulation of wealth in a tiny population minority. There is no objective reason for the social dramas that the world lives on. With the world GDP around US $80 trillion, the average per capita product is US $11,000. This represents $3,600 per month per family of four. This is also the case in Brazil, which is exactly the world average in terms of income. The gigantic misery of billions of people should not happen, except that "no frame of reference has emerged to guide policies and practices"; the system is ungoverned—or, rather, badly governed—and no changes are on the horizon.[81]

---

78 Estela Fernandéz Nadal, "Prólogo," in Franz Josef Hinkelammert, *La vida o el capital: El grito del sujeto vivo y corporal frente a la ley del mercado* (Buenos Aires: CLACSO, 2017), 25.

79 Ladislau Dowbor, *A era do capital improdutivo: Por que oito famílias têm mais riqueza do que a metade da população do mundo?* (São Paulo: Autonomia Literária, 2017), 17–38.

80 Dowbor, *A era do capital improdutivo*, 18–19.

81 Dowbor, *A era do capital improdutivo*, 22.

Meeks also pointed out this problem. According to him, one of the worst consequences of market society is the "widening gulf between rich and poor," so that "less than 1% [of US citizens] own more than 40% of [the nation's] wealth."[82] That is why Dowbor claimed that "inequality has reached obscene levels," since "eight individuals own more wealth than half the world's population, while 800 million people starve."[83]

Finally, the sterilization of financial resources is a problem. According to Dowbor, this problem is not in the lack of money, but in "its appropriation by financial corporations that use them [the sterilization of financial resources] to speculate rather than invest," since "the financial system began to use and drain the productive system instead of streamlining it."[84] This also testifies to the ideas of Meeks, who explained that with the end of the Cold War, no one nation holds world economic power, because corporations have succeeded in overcoming such ethnic control.[85]

What Are the Problems and What Are the Solutions?: Theory and Practices in Our Prophetic Mission

Are there then any solutions to these dilemmas of corruption and social inequality? It is hard to know. However, this does not mean that it is impossible to conjecture in this regard. It might be possible that more socioeconomic balance would be achieved if the sacrifice was made from top to bottom, that is, if (paraphrasing Wesley) the rich sacrificed themselves "gaining all they could, saving all they could, and giving all they could." That would be a kind of socioeconomic propitiation. The propitiatory analogy would work as follows: capitalism is a deity in this case, and two social classes, rich and poor, are the believers who follow and depend on this "god." Present in all theistic[86] religions is the concept

82 Meeks, *Economia global & economia de Deus*, 10.

83 Dowbor, *A era do capital improdutivo*, 22.

84 Dowbor, *A era do capital improdutivo*, 32.

85 Meeks, *Economia global & economia de Deus*, 10.

86 Theism is the belief in the existence of some deity(s). Theism can be *mono*, that is, believing in only one deity; *poly*, when there are countless (from two to millions) of deities; or *heno*, with a supreme and sovereign deity to whom other gods

of propitiation, the idea that a sacrifice softens the wrath of divinity. In today's Brazilian economic system the rich sacrifice the poor (through low wages, exploitation, bad working conditions, etc.) to obtain the favor (wealth) of the "god" capitalism. Maintaining a focus on the propitiation of the poor is tantamount to saying that in the "religion of Capital, the only salvation consists in the intensification of the system, in capitalist expansion, in the accumulation of more and more commodities; but this 'remedy' results only in the aggravation of despair."[87]

The way the rich sacrifice the poor is fierce, without respite or mercy. Such an attitude can be empirically evidenced in the way some rich people deal with market trading. Some cities in the interior of the state of São Paulo have condominiums and houses valued at more than US $5 million. These cities are considered dormitory cities, that is, a place where these rich people rest for some long weekends. They do not live there because they work in large centers, but at some time of the year they travel to rest. In addition to the millionaire property, it is not uncommon for such rich people to have in their personal property very expensive imported cars, some even standing in the condominium.[88] In order to maintain such a property, they need to hire property caretakers (e.g., housekeepers and cleaning people) and in specific cases hire sporadic labor for specific repairs. It is not uncommon for bricklayers who budget for contract work to receive bargaining counterproposals to cut costs and minimize the ultimate value of the service. But why is such an attitude characteristic of this market society? Because to obtain the favor (enrichment) of the "god" capitalism, one must sacrifice the poor.

Is the solution to this problem an equitable division of goods and total state intervention? The answer may lie in other questions: Would it be fair that professions with greater responsibility had the same financial return as others with lower responsibility? Should a doctor

---

subordinate (e.g., the Greek mythology in which Zeus was the supreme deity and subordinate to him were several others such as Eros, Hades, and Hermes).

87 Michael Löwi, "Capitalism as Religion: Walter Benjamin and Max Weber," *Historical Materialism* 17, no. 1 (January 2009): 68.

88 Bruno Ribeiro, "Paulistanos trocam a capital por condomínios no interior," *Folha de S.Paulo*, March 29, 2011, www1.folha.uol.com.br/saopaulo/895183-paulistanos-trocam-a-capital-por-condominios-no-interior-ouca.shtml.

who is responsible for the lives of humans have the same salary as a car mechanic? Is the responsibility for a mechanical part that can be changed in case of damage the same as organs and systems of the human body? Is the degree of knowledge required in medical study compatible with the degree of knowledge that a sweeper needs to have? Faced with such reflections, it is possible to conjecture that this does not bring equity and justice. On the other hand, other questions also need to be asked: Is an economy that does not charge the rich for effective proportional taxation legitimate? Is an economic system that does not care about generational wealth gaps fair?[89] Should one be responsible for one's own entrepreneurial effort to attain the gifts of the capitalist deity? Reality itself is in charge of demonstrating that this system, despite operating throughout the world for over three centuries, cannot promote social justice.

In this case, a dialectic of the two systems (capitalism and socialism) could be interesting. For Meeks, "solving human problems requires both self-giving and the exchange of goods."[90] If self-giving happened, surely the story could be different. However, expecting this to be done with self-sacrifice and in a conscious and charitable manner will make the act unfeasible. While the suggestion of self-giving is important, one must also bear in mind that society, from a theological point of view, is not intrinsically good. Augustine, based on texts of the apostle Paul, debated with the monk Pelagius, arguing that the human being is inherently born spiritually dead, that is, evil and alienated from God. Therefore, to expect widespread awareness of human beings would be utopia, as "the unregenerate human being tends to be right in his own eyes" and "thinks that sin is just killing, stealing, tampering, using

89 "Late capitalism" encourages the majority of wealth always to be concentrated in the hands of a tiny minority. As much as the speech of many is in favor of individual creativity, entrepreneurship, and opportunity, it must also be recognized that a certain group of people (the richest) outweigh the most disadvantaged. This picture can be illustrated as a 400-meter track race where a group of 100 athletes are competing. The start, however, is not the same. Only two people leave from 350 meters. Five leave from 200 meters. The rest leave from the starting point, that is, 400 meters. No need to think long and hard to tell which ones will arrive first at the finish line.

90 Meeks, *Economia global & economia de Deus*, 46.

drugs or committing crimes that they are viewed by society as something more immoral."[91] This Augustinian thought was called "original sin" and, for Wesley, was a primary doctrine of Christianity, so that those who denied it could be considered pagans.[92] In this way, Wesley understood that human sinfulness caused the attachment to money to hinder the true practice of loving God and one's neighbor. Riches could even facilitate atheism because of a false sense of independence and autonomy. Wesley believed that "from the love of God, and from no other fountain, true humility likewise flows."[93] Love of money, therefore, is "a hinderance to the loving our neighbour as ourselves; that is, to the loving all mankind as Christ loved us," and a corrupt nature prevents human beings from having a "disinterested good-will" toward the next, so that such pseudo-love is selectively addressed to those in the same social circle and to those with the same opinion.[94]

Not even Methodist societies were exempt from such social and spiritual evil. Wesley criticized ministers who knew his threefold principle about the use of money but who in practice despised such guidelines: "Many of your brethren, beloved of God, have not food to eat; they have not raiment to put on; they have not a place where to lay their head. And why are they thus distressed?" Wesley, the Anglican clergyman, asked and then replied, "Because you impiously, unjustly, and cruelly detain from them what your Master and theirs lodges in your hands on purpose to supply their wants."[95]

Protestantism dealt with the problem of human sinfulness under the nomenclature of "total depravity," an idea that the completeness of the human being was affected by the Adamic fall, rendering him

91 Vinicius Couto, *Em favor do arminianismo-wesleyano: Um estudo bíblico, teológico e exegético de sua relevância na contemporaneidade* (São Paulo: Reflexão, 2016), 174.

92 "Is man by nature filled with all manner of evil? Is he void of all good? Is he wholly fallen? Is his soul totally corrupted? Or, to come back to the text, is 'every imagination of the thoughts of his heart only evil continually'? Allow this, and you are so far a Christian. Deny it, and you are but an Heathen still." Wesley, *The Works of the Rev. John Wesley*, 7:290. See the sermon "On Original Sin."

93 Wesley, *The Works of the Rev. John Wesley*, 10:325. See the sermon "On Riches."

94 Wesley, *The Works of the Rev. John Wesley*, 10:325. See the sermon "On Riches."

95 Wesley, *The Works of the Rev. John Wesley*, 10:415. See the sermon "Causes of Inefficacy of Christianity."

evil in all anthropological faculties (material and immaterial, in body, soul, and spirit). That is why Meeks acknowledged that "it is possible for this society not to be outraged when many of its children no longer have access to what is needed to live," because "institutions in our society" are threatened "by amnesia and anesthesia."[96] Recently, the famous Notre-Dame Cathedral, located in Paris, was damaged by a devastating fire. According to the BBC (British Broadcasting Corporation) virtual newspaper, many people, "from billionaires to ordinary people," have pledged to donate to the restoration of this historical and cultural heritage. On April 15, 2019, "750 million euros [about R$3.3 billion] had been raised in the first ten days after the collapse of the main needle and the ceiling of the cathedral."[97] The amount collected is interesting, and the timing of this is impressive. Why have these same people never come together with the same amount of money to help poor regions around the world? Such a situation merely demonstrates that expecting a collective consciousness is utopian and unworkable. Therefore, there must be some degree of intervention by regulatory bodies.

In Brazil, social security laws favor some classes, such as the military, magistrates, and politicians. While the average retiring population cannot keep up with the economy, because the readjustments are never even proportional to inflation, the retirement ceiling is extremely different among the classes. Wesley's questioning of unnecessary benefits meets this question. According to him, one way to help improve the British economy at his time was by "abolishing all useless pensions, . . . especially those ridiculous ones given to some hundreds of idle men as governors of forts or castles which forts have answered no end for above these hundred years unless to shelter jackdaws and crows."[98] Remember that in the Old Testament, a law on harvests involving social justice was instituted (cf. Lev 19:9; 23:22; Ruth 2). H. Ray Dunning explained that according to this Mosaic law, "landowners were not to glean their

96 Meeks, *Economia global & economia de Deus*, 13.

97 Alice Cuddy and Bruno Boelpaep, "Estão doando dinheiro demais para reconstruir Notre-Dame?" *BBC News Brasil*, April 25, 2019, www.bbc.com/portuguese/internacional-48050826.

98 Wesley, *The Works of the Rev. John Wesley*, 6:278. See the tract "Thoughts on the Present Scarcity of Provisions."

fields and were to leave the corners unharvested so that the poor could glean the grain freely," because "it supplied the poor with both sustenance and the dignity of work in gathering their own harvest."[99] Dennis F. Kinlaw also explored this Israelite norm by adding that this law was about the unfolding of divine grace and benevolence; since God had given his children generosity, it was extremely "appropriate that they should remember the poor and the stranger."[100] Patrick Miller Jr. made the following note:

> The crucial question that remains for us as for Israel: What should we do with the land God gives? From the Christian perspective—and in the light of Deuteronomy—we are called to see that the enjoyment of the land and the use of its benefits are made available to all who dwell in it. What that means in terms of economic program and land use must be determined in very specific contexts, but because God has given the good gift we shall see that it is available to all. Because some—by God's blessing—shall benefit greatly from this gift, it is imperative that we see that provision for enjoyment of the land and its produce is made for the poor and the weak and the left out.[101]

Miller's initial question seems to have some answer in Wesley's commentary on Leviticus 23:22. According to the Anglican cleric, God "would press this duty upon every person who hath an harvest to reap, that none might plead exemption from it."[102] Although the immediate context of Leviticus 23 pertains to the worship of God, Wesley explained that the Creator "makes a kind of excursion to repeat a former law of providing for the poor, to shew that our devotion to God is little esteemed by him if it be not accompanied with acts of charity

---

99 H. Ray Dunning, *Reflecting the Divine Image: Christian Ethics in Wesleyan Perspectives* (Eugene, OR: Wipf & Stock, 2003), 112.

100 Dennis F. Kinlaw, "The Book of Leviticus," in *Beacon Bible Commentary*, vol. 1, ed. George Herbert Livingstone et al. (Kansas City, MO: Beacon Hill Press, 1969), 381.

101 Patrick Miller Jr., "The Gift of the Land," *Interpretation: A Journal of Bible and Theology* 23, no. 4 (1969): 464.

102 John Wesley, *Wesley's Notes on the Bible: The Old Testament: Genesis–Ruth* (Ingersoll, ON: Devoted Publishing, 2017), 165.

to men."[103] Wesley further pointed out that after God established the social justice law concerning the portion that should be bestowed on the poor, the Creator signed "I am the Lord your God" (initially at Lev 19:10, but repeated at 23:22), that is, he who "gave you all these things with a reservation of my right in them, and with a charge of giving part of them to the poor."[104]

On the basis of inherent human evil, therefore, it would be impossible to expect Israelite society to consciously think of those most in need. The more someone can win, the better life is for this person. The hegemonic relationship of the human race, affected by the lapsary (fall from grace) effects of Eden, is a win-lose relationship. Therefore, divine law established that "the right to harvest is not a voluntary act of charity of the rich toward the poor, but the right of the poor to livelihoods."[105] Stricter, more proportionate laws regarding social classes can help balance the economic status quo. But the difficulty is also in the fact that rulers are generally in a privileged socioeconomic position, and laws, rather than serving the common good, are designed to privilege those very rulers. Societies can (and should) come together and demand that change happen. The Pharaoh who ruled Egypt in the days leading up to the birth of Moses feared exactly this kind of union. The countless Hebrews who were subject to slavery could unite at any moment and reverse their social roles. Therefore, the attitude of the ruler was to increase the workload and slow the population growth of the Hebrews through the murder of male babies. To paraphrase Martin Luther King Jr., which is worse: the imposing cry of the wicked or the silence of the oppressed?[106] This silence is a metaphor for passivity and therefore destructive permissiveness. The opposite, however, does not require a guerrilla stance of resorting to weapons and creating social upheavals. Wesley's stance can serve as an example. He became politically

103 Wesley, *Wesley's Notes on the Bible*, 165.

104 Wesley, *Wesley's Notes on the Bible*, 160.

105 Meeks, *Economia global & economia de Deus*, 31.

106 Martin Luther King Jr., *I Have a Dream: The Quotations of Martin Luther King Jr.* (New York: Grosset & Dunlap, 1968), 6.

involved in the abolitionist cause as he spoke in the pulpit.[107] His legacy remained in early Methodism, so much so that almost a year after his death, one of his leading preachers, Samuel Bradburn, wrote *An Address to the People Called Methodists; Concerning the Wickedness of Encouraging Slavery* in the hopes of inspiring Methodists to support the boycott of products (e.g., sugar and gin) from slave labor.[108] This movement began in 1791 when the Quaker William Fox published the pamphlet *Address to the People of Great Britain on the Utility of Refraining from the Use of West India Sugar and Rum* in London against the purchase of sugar produced by enslaved people.[109]

Final Considerations

There is a tendency within Brazilian Christianity to think that faith and politics are antagonistic issues. However, to discuss economics, social justice, labor, and the result of this equation, it is indispensable to analyze the economic and political structures. Passivity in these matters only helps the authorities to continue to enjoy dizzying power at the expense of the people's efforts. Passivity leads to permissiveness, and thus the community status quo never changes for the better, only for some specific structures that relate to a privileged minority. Based on this background, I have shown in this chapter that from a religious point of view, the evangelical group that aligns with the

107 There is an excellent article in Portuguese on this subject: Helmut Renders, "O envolvimento de John Wesley (1703–1791) na causa abolicionista: De experiências pessoais, via a criação de uma rede de contestadores/as até uma ação política orquestrada," *Revista Caminhando* 18, no. 1 (January/June 2013): 107–22. Renders has also published *John Wesley e a luta abolicionista* (São Paulo: ASTE, 2019). This is a great book because he analyzes the abolition not in a hagiographic perspective, that is, talking about Wesley as a saint leader. In this book, Renders makes a great exposition of Wesley's involvement but recognizes the leadership of other people in abolition movement.

108 David N. Hempton, "Wesley in Context," in *The Cambridge companion to John Wesley*, ed. Randy Maddox and Jason E. Vickers (Cambridge: Cambridge University Press, 2010), 72.

109 Harry Dickinson, "Public Opinion and the Abolition of the Slave Trade," *Revue Française de Civilisation Britannique* 15, no. 1 (2008): 133.

current type of capitalism, that appears "late" and "savage," is precisely neo-Pentecostalism. However, the proposal found here differs in many respects, as it stems from eighteenth-century British evangelicalism, from the Wesleyan tradition. It is not a question of seeking anachronistic answers in a movement that has been going on for centuries, but of revisiting the ideas proposed by John Wesley with the intention of contextualizing them for the present century.

That said, it is possible to see that Wesley's ideas about economic, political, labor, and social justice discussions have an interface with today. Wesleyanism has always proposed a *via media* in various subjects. Therefore, since this essay concludes that both the extremes of savage capitalism and those of socialism are harmful, a dialectical view that brings a kind of moderate capitalism is possible. Rather than abandoning capitalism altogether, it may be interesting to sacrifice the rich in the socioeconomic process so that there is a fairer opportunity for the social classes below in the social pyramid, with the aim of bringing them closer and reducing the striking difference in income distribution. The measures to make this happen, however, involve nontotalitarian state intervention and more active participation of the population in civics, thus exercising a real democratic role and legitimate prophetic action. The proposal of this essay, however, is not to think, in a romantic way, that this is the solution for all socioeconomic ills, but to understand that it can be a legitimate way to a more just and balanced society.

Profetas in the White House

DANIEL F. FLORES

THE WHITE HOUSE IS at once the most accessible and the least responsive venue for Hispanic leaders to deliver the counsel of God. The Trump administration gave more access to evangelical Hispanic leaders than any administration before him, though it may be argued that his motives were political. Hispanic evangelical leaders may have privately counseled President Trump on sensitive issues, but the evidence of his administration suggests he likely was not persuaded. Moved by their religious convictions to support him as a pro-life president, these evangelical Christian leaders grudgingly overlooked his obvious moral failings. Some may have benefited personally from these close encounters with the most powerful man in the world. However, they also continue to suffer bitter criticism and painful ostracization by other Hispanic Protestant and evangelical leaders who opposed Trump as a deceptive anti-Christ figure harmful to the church and the nation. It is not my intention to persuade my readers to take sides or to judge those who have enjoyed privileged access to the White House. Rather, the purpose of this chapter is to offer a historical perspective on the phenomenon that made it possible for the first Hispanic Christian leaders to enter the unlikely role as prophets to the White House.[1]

1 Portions of this chapter were previously presented by the author in "The Joseph Dilemma: Spiritual Advisors and the Burden of Political Access" (paper,

The Faith of Presidents

The adage is true that it is lonely at the top. On May 26, 1899, President McKinley signed a personal note to himself that he later tucked into his letter book: "My belief embraces the Divinity of Christ and a recognition of Christianity as the mightiest factor in the world's civilization." This confession of faith, minimal as it was, was written not to estrange himself from Methodism, but to affirm that his personalized faith still resided in the Methodist communion.[2] Some presidents have found it inconvenient to maintain relationships with their respective pastors. Instead, they have relied on other clergypersons to act as their spiritual advisors. Candidates for this role are typically high-profile religious leaders whom they feel they can trust with their innermost secrets or they find a public association with them politically advantageous. Clergy have accepted these rare high-level invitations for entirely different reasons. Perhaps the noblest reason is to fulfill the role of Joseph, who, apart from his famous technicolor dream-coat, was celebrated for his rise to a high position to advocate for his suffering people. Those who have been ushered into this covenant with the president have done so with the understanding that they have no official capacity on the Cabinet, yet equivalent fidelity is expected. Furthermore, like all appointed officials, they serve at the pleasure of the commander in chief.

Since the first president was inaugurated, clergy members have endeavored to present their brand of spiritual counsel to the White House. Almost without exception, a select number of clergypersons have been granted the privilege of being the confidant of presidents. It is important to note that Methodist bishops and pastors played an important role in nearly every administration beginning with Francis Asbury, the first Methodist bishop, who lobbied George Washington, to Joshua DuBois, a cradle AME and a Pentecostal who was dubbed the "President's Pastor" to Barack Obama. The Trump administration is one notable exception. The religious leaders who have enjoyed favorable access were, by and large, either political surrogates or endorsing

---

Fourteenth Oxford Institute of Methodist Theological Studies, Pembroke College, August 18, 2018).

2 Margaret Leech, *In the Days of McKinley* (New York: Harper & Brothers, 1959), 462.

personalities during the 2016 presidential campaign. While the formal Evangelical Advisory Board ended after the campaign, remnants of the board continued to provide the administration with what journalist Noah Weiland calls "a constellation of religious figures to lend its platform gravitas among evangelicals."[3] Their access to the White House enabled them to build professional rapport with the president and vice president. When hot-button issues arose, they served as a convenient focus group representing evangelical interests. In the public eye, they were expected to offer ethical and moral advice on issues of national and global importance. For those spiritual advisors who have served in more intimate and sensitive situations, they functioned as chaplains offering pastoral counsel and a steady hand during times of great stress.

Chaplains and the Three Branches of Power

Presidents from Franklin Delano Roosevelt to Donald J. Trump have taken their retreats at Camp David, the former Naval Support Facility Thurmont. While they are in residence, they may attend chapel services conducted by navy chaplains. However, presidential stays at Camp David are so infrequent that no lasting pastoral relationship is ever possible. Even so, navy chaplains, unlike civilian pastors, are subject to frequent assignment rotations.

Whenever presidents enter a public or government hall to deliver an address, they are traditionally announced as "The President of the United States" followed by a standing ovation and, where appropriate, a brass band rendition of "Hail to the Chief." No set protocols exist for invocations for a presidential address outside of inaugural ceremonies. Typically, this involves public prayers, Scripture readings, and taking the oath of office on a family Bible or two. The only exceptions to swearing on a Bible were Theodore Roosevelt, John Quincy Adams, Franklin Pierce, and Lyndon B. Johnson. It is interesting to note that Johnson swore on a Roman Missal on Air Force One. Even though clergy are frequently present at public addresses, the executive

3 Noah Weiland, "Evangelicals, Having Backed Trump, Find White House 'Front Door Is Open,'" *New York Times*, February 7, 2018, www.nytimes.com/2018/02/07/us/politics/trump-evangelicals-national-prayer-breakfast.html.

branch does not appoint chaplains to read Scripture, lead in prayer, or deliver sermons. In the White House, however, it is not unusual to see clergy in and out of the Oval Office. Even though they are without an official appointment, clergypersons are normally the least conspicuous actors in the White House. Only one clergyperson, Billy Graham, has ever achieved the honorific designation of "chaplain to the White House." The fact that no constitutional provision was made for a presidential chaplain has not deterred the parade of clergy up 1600 Pennsylvania Avenue.

Seventeenth-century colonist Roger Williams may have had the separation of church and state in mind when he went off to settle Rhode Island. American colonists were not keen to live under a theocracy, neither were they interested in separating faith from politics. The motto of the US Army Chaplain Corps is *Pro Deo et Patria*, or "For God and Country." It is noteworthy that the founding fathers gave attention to the primacy of God over the state. Thomas Jefferson's concept of separating church and state was possibly inspired by reading the classic Greek author Xenophon, who chronicled the political exploits of Cyrus the Great. This is significant because Cyrus is credited as the ancient champion of multiculturalism and religious tolerance.[4] The First Amendment clearly states that there would be no establishment of religion in the United States. Before World War II, this Establishment Clause was ignored by judges as irrelevant to constitutional debates. After the war, when the US Supreme Court turned to it for guidance on religious issues, "the justices found the words of the clause devoid of any meaning that could be found in the Framers' intentions, historical experience, or judicial precedent."[5] What is clear is that the role of religion was not entirely removed from government proceedings.

The first appearance of spiritual advisors can be traced to the founding fathers. On September 7, 1774, the Continental Congress

4 Neil MacGregor, "2600 Years of History in One Object," TED Talk, July 2011, www.ted.com/talks/neil_macgregor_2600_years_of_history_in_one_object.

5 William M. Wiecek, "The Stone and Vinson Courts (1941–1953): Transition and Transformation," in *The United States Supreme Court: The Pursuit of Justice*, ed. Christopher Tomlins (Boston: Houghton Mifflin, 2005), 258.

commenced with a prayer offered by Reverend Jacob Duché, a local Philadelphia rector. This was a good start for religion to play a role in forming the character of the new nation, or so it seemed. Unfortunately, Duché displayed Tory sympathies, and he eventually defected from the rebels to the British.[6] Benjamin Franklin, not widely known as a person of faith, was instrumental in institutionalizing the practice of soliciting prayer for the state. Reverend William Linn was elected the first chaplain of the House.[7] The first convening of the US Senate, held in New York City on April 6, 1789, included an agenda item to identify a candidate for a chaplain. The Right Reverend Samuel Provost, the Episcopal bishop of New York, was appointed the first Senate chaplain on April 25, 1789.[8] The most famous Senate chaplain was Dr. Peter Marshall, a Scottish immigrant and pastor of the New York Avenue Presbyterian Church. In 1947, he accepted the appointment as the fifty-seventh chaplain of the United States Senate.[9]

The Supreme Court, though derived philosophically from Judeo-Christian principles of jurisprudence, has never appointed chaplains to serve the justices. Perhaps the unfortunate episode of the Salem Witch Trials convinced the founding fathers not to let religion have dominion over the court system. President Washington's qualifications for justices were not only legal knowledge, but support for the Constitution,

---

6 James P. Moore, *One Nation Under God: The History of Prayer in America* (New York: Doubleday, 2005), 56–60.

7 Office of the Chaplain, United States House of Representatives, accessed March 9, 2022, https://chaplain.house.gov/chaplaincy/history.html.

8 "Office of the Senate Chaplain," United States Senate, accessed March 9, 2022, https://www.senate.gov/reference/office/chaplain.htm.

9 Catherine Marshall, his widow, wrote his biography, *A Man Called Peter* (New York: McGraw Hill, 1951). The book was so popular that it was made into a movie by the same title in 1955. Catherine Marshall remained a popular writer, going on to write twenty-one inspirational books and novels. The first African American Senate chaplain, the sixty-second chaplain, was Rear Admiral Barry C. Black, and he started July 7, 2003 (www.senate.gov/reference/common/person/barry_black.htm). The first female House chaplain, the sixty-first chaplain, was Rear Admiral Margaret Grun Kibben, who started January 3, 2021 (https://chaplain.house.gov/chaplaincy/index.html). To date, there have been no Hispanic clergy appointed to either the Senate or the House.

geographic diversity, "character, training, health, and public renown." Of the highest importance was their participation in the Revolution.[10] The terms *character* and *public renown* may suggest a religious background. However, religious affiliation was not a marker of a good candidate for federal service. Although chaplains were never appointed to the Supreme Court, the Crier still opens the sessions with a chant ending with an invocation that at least mentions God:

> The Honorable, the Chief Justice and the Associate Justices of the Supreme Court of the United States. Oyez! Oyez! Oyez! All persons having business before the Honorable, the Supreme Court of the United States, are admonished to draw near and give their attention, for the Court is now sitting. God save the United States and this Honorable Court![11]

Since the Supreme Court has the most important role in setting a legal precedent for the nation, it should not be surprising that candidate Trump used the selection of conservative justices as a talking point in his campaign rallies. To the delight of his supporters, two such opportunities came in rapid succession. The untimely death of Justice Antonin Scalia and the early retirement of Justice Anthony Kennedy were magnanimous gifts to the Trump administration, whose evangelical supporters interpreted a much-anticipated opportunity to restore "constitutionalists" to the Supreme Court in opposition to a subjective "living, breathing" constitutional philosophy associated with liberals.[12] The death of Justice Ruth Bader Ginsberg likely sealed the fate of the Supreme Court for generations to come.

---

10 Maeva Marcus, "The Earliest Years (1790–1801): Laying Foundations," in *The United States Supreme Court: The Pursuit of Justice*, ed. Christopher Tomlins (Boston: Houghton Mifflin, 2005), 28.

11 "The Court and Its Procedures," Supreme Court of the United States, accessed February 11, 2022, www.supremecourt.gov/about/procedures.aspx.

12 Penny Nance, quoted by Erik Rosales, "Trump to Get 2nd High Court Pick: Supreme Court Justice Anthony Kennedy Retiring," CBN News, June 27, 2018, www1.cbn.com/cbnnews/politics/2018/june/supreme-court-justice-anthony-kennedy-retiring-trump-to-get-2nd-high-court-pick.

Lobbyists, Chaplains, and Focus Groups

There are at least three major categories of spiritual advisors to US presidents. First are the lobbyists. The lobbyists seek audiences with presidents to discuss issues that concern their communities or national policy closely related to their faith-based worldviews. Second, there are those spiritual advisors whose primary role is a chaplain and who are dedicated to the spiritual well-being of the president. He or she may listen to concerns, pray, administer sacraments, and—if necessary—grant absolution. Third, some spiritual advisors are a type of hybrid between the first two. They may not always meet with the president, but they function more as members of *focus groups*. Typically, this third category is a board or council consisting of religious leaders handpicked by someone close to the president such as an advisor (e.g., the chaplain). Once appointed, members of this group assemble only when their input is needed by the White House. These categories will be easily recognizable in the following snapshots of American religious history.

Presidents and Religious Advisors

George Washington

John Wesley, the founder of Methodism, concerned with the growing tensions between Britain and the American colonies, sent Francis Asbury and Thomas Coke as superintendents to the Methodist diaspora. John Wigger says that Asbury had little taste for politics and Coke was a dyed-in-the-wool Tory. Asbury sent a gift of Methodist prayer books and a collection of sermons for the Washington family to mark their initial meeting at Mount Vernon. Remarkably, neither Asbury nor Coke would have had much to say to any politician let alone the new president of the former colonies. Even so, a Methodist delegation consisting of Asbury, Coke, John Dickins, and Thomas Morrell arranged a meeting with President-Elect George Washington in New York. In their collective promise of intercession, they prayed God would "fill up your important station to his glory, the good of his church, the happiness and prosperity of the United States, and the welfare of mankind."[13] It is notable that Bishop Richard Allen, founder of the African Methodist Episcopal Church, may have been the first African American leader to meet a sitting president because of his contract for chimney sweeping Washington's Philadelphia home. Though we may speculate slavery would have made a lively topic, we have no record of any such meeting.[14] The right to petition is guaranteed by the First Amendment to the Constitution, and the Methodist delegation that petitioned Washington wanted him to address the evil of slavery. Unfortunately, Washington dismissed the Methodist lobbyists without making any promises. Washington endeavored to set a precedent so that the United States of America would be committed to free expression for all religions but no special treatment for any one religion.

In Washington's time, other religious groups also sent messages of support to the new president-elect. Washington responded with official letters to the United Baptist Churches in Virginia; the Hebrew Congregation in Newport, Rhode Island; and the New Church in Baltimore. In this body of correspondence, he thanked them for their support and restated a national commitment to protect their religious rights and defend against threats of persecution.[15]

Abraham Lincoln

It is well known that President Abraham Lincoln, though pious in his way, did not claim membership in any one denominational affiliation. While in residency at the White House, he attended the New York Avenue Presbyterian Church, where Phineas D. Gurley was pastor.[16] When his son Willie died unexpectedly, Lincoln was counseled by Gurley that his son was indeed in heaven. Lincoln reported that he experienced a process of "crystallization," though he was neither

---

13 John Wigger, *American Saint: Francis Asbury and the Methodists* (Oxford: Oxford University Press, 2009), 181.

14 Richard S. Newman, *Freedom's Prophet: Bishop Richard Allen, the AME Church, and the Black Founding Fathers* (New York: NYU Press, 2008), 140.

15 George Washington, *George Washington: Writings* (New York: Library Classics of the United States, 1997), 738–39, 766–67, 833–34.

16 William Warren Sweet, "Bishop Matthew Simpson and the Funeral of Abraham Lincoln," *Journal of the Illinois State Historical Society* 7, no. 1 (April 1914): 62, www.jstor.org/stable/10.2307/40193943.

converted nor moved to join a Christian denomination. Lincoln found more comfort in the fatalistic words of Shakespeare's *Hamlet*:

> There's a divinity that shapes our ends,
> Rough-hew them how we will.[17]

The Civil War made spiritual advisement a hazardous duty since both sides of the slavery issue were eagerly represented by visiting clergy. In the case of Abraham Lincoln, lobbyists from both sides of the slavery–abolition debate often contradicted each other so that their influence was difficult to gauge. Lincoln had little patience for their penchant for citing Scripture while claiming a divine mandate to communicate God's will to him. He did believe in the words of the Bible, and he sought divine guidance. Addressing visitors who claimed God was on their side, Lincoln quipped, "I hope it will not be irreverent for me to say, that if it is probable that God would reveal his will to others, on a point so connected with my duty, it might be supposed he would reveal it directly to me. And if I can learn what it is . . . I will do it!"[18]

It is difficult to say how much influence Gurley had on Lincoln's policies. In the Lincoln funeral sermon, Gurley remarked on Lincoln's grasp of faith and history. The entire sermon, published in the *New York Times* on April 20, 1865, gives evidence of a view of history consistent with the Calvinism of Gurley's Presbyterianism.

> He [God] gave him a calm and abiding confidence in the overruling providence of God and in the ultimate triumph of truth and righteousness through the power and the blessing of God. This confidence strengthened him in all his hours of anxiety and toil and inspired him with calm and cheering hope when others were inclining to despondency and gloom. Never shall I forget the emphasis and the deep emotion with which he said in this very room, to a company of clergymen and others, who called to pay him their respects in the darkest days of our civil

17 David Herbert Donald, *Lincoln* (New York: Simon & Schuster, 1995), 336–37.

18 William K. Klingaman, *Abraham Lincoln and the Road to Emancipation, 1861–1865* (New York: Viking, 2001), 179.

conflict: "Gentlemen, my hope of success in this great and terrible struggle rests on that immutable foundation, the justice and goodness of God."[19]

Methodist historians are quick to note that the very influential bishop Matthew Simpson was also a personal friend of President Lincoln as well as of several other presidents. Simpson was frequently summoned to the White House to discuss matters of state with the president. As editor of the *Christian Advocate*, his comprehension of the nation's political climate was very valuable to President Lincoln.[20] In this sense, Simpson served as a representative of the Methodist focus group while also lending true Christian fellowship to the commander in chief. Although Gurley preached the funeral sermon, it was Simpson who gave the eulogy. His preaching eloquence had contributed much to the success of the 1864 campaign. His delivery at the burial ceremony was no disappointment. In it, Simpson extolled the fallen leader as an exemplar and martyr whose character was consistent with "Honest Abe" mythology. The tender words were crafted to elicit patriotism, which likely would have pleased the dutiful president whom he served as friend and advisor:

> Abraham Lincoln was a good man. He was known as an honest, temperate, forgiving man, a just man, a man of noble heart, in every way. Certainly, if there ever was a man who illustrated some of the principles of pure religion, that man was our departed President. His example urges the country to trust in God and do right.[21]

William McKinley

President McKinley was well known as a faithful Methodist throughout his life. It is a strange twist of fate that a Roman Catholic archbishop should interrupt the sequence of Protestant spiritual advisors,

19 Phineas D. Gurley, "Abraham Lincoln's White House Funeral Sermon for Abraham Lincoln," accessed February 11, 2022, www.abrahamlincolnonline.org/lincoln/speeches/gurley.htm.

20 George R. Crooks, *The Life of Bishop Matthew Simpson of the Methodist Episcopal Church* (New York: Harper & Brothers, 1890), 368, 369.

21 Sweet, "Bishop Matthew Simpson and the Funeral of Abraham Lincoln," 71.

especially when one considers the difficulties the Irish Catholics faced in predominantly Protestant America. However, it was just that climate that created the opening for Archbishop John Ireland. During McKinley's campaign for the presidency, supporters of the Christian fundamentalist William Jennings Bryan spread falsehoods that McKinley was a crypto-Catholic and that his children were attending Catholic catechism. (Bryan did not know that the McKinley children were actually deceased at the time of his accusation.) McKinley, known for his gentle and charitable spirit, said nothing to suppress the rumors. Rather, his campaign was able to use the opportunity to reach out to Catholic voters for a narrow-margin victory. This did not escape the attention of Bishop Ireland. McKinley, finding himself in need of a confessor, established a long friendship with Ireland that extended to the president's deathbed.

While residing at the White House, McKinley attended Metropolitan Methodist Episcopal Church. Though he enjoyed worship and Sunday school, he disliked the undue attention given to him by gushing preachers and gawking churchgoers. On one occasion he publicly announced his decision to no longer frequent the church. Unwilling to specify his reason for the abrupt cessation of attendance, a local newspaper journalist suggested that it was due to his dull Methodist pastor: "Scoffers will suspect that the President stays away from church because, under the pretense of finding his pastor an indiscreet and intemperate person, he really finds him a bore."[22] McKinley kept good relations with the Methodist pastors of Metropolitan MEC. In the first term, he worked closely with Cardinal Ireland and other Catholic leaders. He appointed a Catholic as attorney general and later named him as a Supreme Court justice. In the second term, he relied less on the advice of clergy, including Methodists and Catholics.

It is hard to discount the prophetic role that religious lobbyists played in speaking truth to power during McKinley's administration. General James F. Rusling reported on an alleged interview that occurred on November 21, 1899, with McKinley and a delegation of the General Missionary Committee of the Methodist Episcopal Church that

---

22 "The President's Pastor," *New York Times (1857–1922)*, December 3, 1897, https://www.nytimes.com/1897/12/03/archives/the-presidents-pastor.html.

included Bishop Thomas Bowman, Bishop John F. Hurst, Dr. Samuel F. Upham, Dr. John M. Buckley, and Rusling. The Methodist clergy were concerned about the outcome of the seized territories after the Spanish–American War. McKinley's vision of expanding the American empire into the Far East was probably influenced by the Methodist delegation, though his mind was made up before they arrived. They presented their concerns and turned to leave the president's office when he stopped them: "Hold a moment longer! Not quite yet, gentlemen! Before you go I would like to say just a word about the Philippine business."[23] McKinley openly confessed that his fears were relieved after much time in prayer. In a bizarre testimony that combined imperialism and religious fervor, McKinley claimed the United States had a divine mandate to take control of the islands and their people.

> I walked the floor of the White House night after night until midnight; and I am not ashamed to tell you, gentlemen, that I went down on my knees and prayed Almighty God for light and guidance more than one night. And one night late it came to me this way—I don't know how it was, but it came: (1) That we could not give them back to Spain—that would be cowardly and dishonorable; (2) that we could not turn them over to France and Germany—our commercial rivals in the Orient—that would be bad business and discreditable; (3) that we could not leave them to themselves—they were unfit for self-government—and they would soon have anarchy and misrule over there worse than Spain's was; and (4) that there was nothing left for us to do but to take them all, and to educate the Filipinos, and uplift and civilize and Christianize them, and by God's grace do the very best we could by them, as our fellow men for whom Christ also died.[24]

Harry S. Truman

It is a given that running for president takes more than a war chest full of big money. It also takes high confidence in one's personal success and

---

23 General James Rusling, "Interview with President William McKinley," *The Christian Advocate* 22, no. 1 (January 22, 1903): 17, quoted in Charles S. Olcott, *William McKinley*, vol. 2 (Boston: Hougton Mifflin Company, 1916), 109–11.

24 Rusling, "Interview with President William McKinley."

a sense of destiny. In Christian parlance, we might say that a candidate for office should feel called to service. This was certainly the case with Harry S. Truman, a devout Baptist, who interpreted his presidency as a divine calling. He was unprepared for the approach of young Billy Graham, who aspired to become the confidant of the president. Despite some minor political missteps, Billy Graham would do more to define the role of a chaplain than anyone before or after him. Thanks to the promotional efforts of newspaper magnate William Randolph Hearst, the young Billy Graham rose from relative obscurity to national prominence. In his first attempt to take on the role of a presidential spiritual advisor, he was rebuffed by Truman, who accused him of being a publicity seeker.[25] An avid Bible scholar and a Baptist, Truman came to believe that by taking the lead in supporting the post–World War II establishment of the state of Israel he was fulfilling the role of the biblical Persian benefactor who funded the return of exiles to Jerusalem. In November 1953, while on a visit to the Jewish Theological Seminary in New York, he was introduced as "the man who helped create the state of Israel." As the story goes, Truman responded by proclaiming, "I am Cyrus. I am Cyrus!"[26]

John F. Kennedy and Lyndon B. Johnson

John F. Kennedy and Lyndon B. Johnson were so intertwined they need to be considered together. Before we can consider Kennedy, we must discuss the religious giants Norman Vincent Peale, Billy Graham, and Martin Luther King Jr. Norman Vincent Peale began his ministry as an ordained Methodist pastor. In 1932, he transferred his credentials to the Dutch Reformed Church to accept a call to the pastorate of the historic Marble Collegiate Church in New York City. He held this position for fifty-two years. Blessed with a fine preaching voice and an approachable teaching style, Peale rose to national prominence on his syndicated radio show *Live with Confidence*. He was best known for his best-selling inspirational book *The Power of Positive Thinking*

25 William Martin, *A Prophet with Honor: The Billy Graham Story* (Grand Rapids, MI: Zondervan, 1991, 2018), 136.

26 Paul Charles Merkley, "I AM Cyrus," *Christian History & Biography* 99 (Summer 2008): 30–32.

(1952), which at one time was second in sales only to the Bible. In 1935, his wife, Ruth Stafford Peale, formed a partnership with Frank Gannett, a Unitarian, philanthropist, and newspaper magnate, and with Branch Rickey, a fellow Ohio Wesleyan alumnus, a Methodist, and the general manager of the Brooklyn Dodgers. Together, they published *Guideposts* magazine.[27] Peale's criticism of FDR's New Deal and subsequent positive influence on President Dwight D. Eisenhower may have given him too much confidence in politics. His involvement in the Nixon–Kennedy campaign nearly ended his career. It is worth noting that Eisenhower had no church affiliation before his presidency. At the insistence of Graham, he joined a church. He was baptized as an adult and received as a member of the Presbyterian Church. During his term, Eisenhower is credited for adding the phrase "under God" to the Pledge of Allegiance.

Norman Vincent Peale was an avid supporter of presidential candidate Richard M. Nixon. In the 1960 presidential campaign, Peale allied himself with Billy Graham, who, on August 18, 1960, hosted a meeting of twenty-five ministers in Montreux, Switzerland, to strategize how they might block the election of John F. Kennedy. Peale was the guest of honor. On September 7, 150 Protestant ministers met in Washington, DC, and signed a statement opposing Kennedy on the grounds of his Catholic faith. The newly formed National Conference of Citizens for Religious Freedom shocked America with anti-Catholic rhetoric that closely resembled the smear tactics of the 1928 presidential campaign that pitted Herbert C. Hoover against Alfred E. Smith, a Roman Catholic. At the heart of their demagoguery was the question of whether a good Catholic would have a stronger allegiance to the United States or Rome on matters of state. Peale's brief association as their spokesperson added to their clout but also drew intense ire from other religious leaders. Reinhold Niebuhr, a fellow Reformed minister and professor of ethics at Union Theological Seminary, publicly chastised Peale for leading the anti-Catholic cabal. Union Theological Seminary president John C. Bennett and radio host Rabbi Maurice N.

---

27 "10 Things to Know about Norman Vincent Peale," *Guideposts*, accessed February 11, 2022, www.guideposts.org/better-living/positive-living/positive-thinking/10-things-to-know-about-norman-vincent-peale.

Eisendrath, aghast at this blatant religious bigotry, rebuked him, citing the constitutional rule prohibiting a religious test for office.[28] Even First Lady Eleanor Roosevelt could not keep her silence:

> It is a long time since I sat in my office and read the scurrilous literature that came into the Democratic headquarters of Alfred E. Smith's campaign. Nothing quite so bad is reaching me now. . . . To tell a man he cannot run for any office in this country because he belongs to a certain religion or is a member of another race—even though he is required to fulfill all the obligations of citizenship, including fighting and dying for his country—is completely illogical and unconstitutional.[29]

Meanwhile, Graham had quietly and shrewdly distanced himself from Peale and the anti-Catholics. Remarkably, he dodged the bullet. In the eleventh hour, when it was clear that the ballots were favoring Kennedy, Graham offered his prayerful support to President-Elect Kennedy. Dr. Peale was fired by the same committee that appointed him their spokesperson. Humiliated by public outcries against his anti-Catholicism, Peale threatened to resign from Marble Collegiate Church. However, he was convinced to remain as senior pastor until his retirement in 1984.

On June 13, 1957, Dr. Martin Luther King Jr. arranged a meeting with vice president Richard Nixon to discuss racial problems in the American South. King tried persuading Nixon to make a personal visit, but the vice president graciously declined.[30] The cool reception was a foreshadowing of Nixon's later reticence to show support for the struggle for civil rights. In due course, King was arrested and sentenced to four months of hard labor in Reidsville State Prison in Georgia for the charge of trespassing, which was ruled a violation of probation for a traffic ticket. John Kennedy, acting on the advice of Morris Abrams,

---

28 Peter Steinfels, "Beliefs," *New York Times*, October 31, 1992, 10, www.nytimes.com/1992/10//31/us/beliefs-627392.html.

29 Eleanor Roosevelt, "Excerpt, My Day," The Eleanor Roosevelt Papers, September 21, 1960, www2.gwu.edu/~erpapers/mep/displaydoc.cfm?docid=jfk60.

30 David Levering Lewis, *King: A Biography* (Chicago: University of Illinois Press, 2013), 129.

an Atlanta attorney, and Harris Wofford, his minority affairs special advisor, telephoned King's wife, Coretta, to assure her of his support. This strategic move blindsided President Eisenhower, who had contemplated intervening on behalf of King but delayed at the counsel of his vice president and then presidential candidate Richard Nixon. Robert Kennedy managed to get King out on bail. That gesture did not go unnoticed by the Black community. Rev. Martin Luther King Sr., a Baptist minister, registered Republican, and influential supporter of Nixon, made a 180-degree turn to support Kennedy. "I've got a suitcase of votes," he shouted, "and I'm going to take them to Mr. Kennedy and dump them in his lap." Wofford made sure of this by distributing two million copies of a pamphlet criticizing Nixon and extolling Kennedy's "heart."[31]

Despite the definitive role African Americans played in Kennedy's victory, King himself remained at arm's length from President Kennedy. Robert Kennedy, now the attorney general, instructed the FBI to wiretap King.[32] Since the new administration was disinclined to move expeditiously on civil rights, King was unable to find success as a lobbyist. His assassination elevated him from prophet to martyr, a status that far exceeded that of Billy Graham.

A discussion about spiritual advisors to Kennedy and Johnson is a study in stark, politically charged contrasts. Kennedy, the Roman Catholic outlier, received only the lukewarm support of Billy Graham after winning the presidential election. Theirs was a marriage of convenience, though without evidence of consummation. Johnson, on the other hand, sought opportunities to spend time with Graham. The unfortunate trauma of tragedy in Dallas created space for the Texas-born president, a committed member of Disciples of Christ, to collaborate with a nationally recognized evangelist with middle-of-the-road conservative politics. Together, they worked for the healing of the nation through the Gospel Campaigns and the Great Society, which included the Civil Rights Act of 1964. By supporting Johnson, Graham more than made up for his cold relationship with Kennedy.

---

31 Lewis, *King*, 129.

32 Lewis, *King*, 257.

Richard M. Nixon

In 1962, Richard M. Nixon moved to New York and attended Marble Collegiate Church. His friendship with Norman Vincent Peale was genuine, and it lasted beyond Watergate. But Peale had a much smaller public role to play after the Nixon–Kennedy election. Graham was another story. When Nixon first eyed the presidency, Graham had rallied behind him almost in protest to the Roman Catholic candidate John F. Kennedy. The anti-Catholic coalition's failure to defeat Kennedy did not deter Graham from maintaining a close relationship with Nixon in the background. When Nixon finally managed to get control of the White House, Graham's association vaulted Nixon to a more favorable position with evangelical voters. On June 8, 1969, the *New York Times Magazine* profiled Graham in an article titled "The Closest Thing to a White House Chaplain." When Graham delivered the prayer at Nixon's inauguration, he became "the *de facto* Presidential chaplain," the content of which bordered "on being a political treatise."[33]

Graham had great affection for Nixon as a fellow Christian and political leader. However, as William Martin has demonstrated, Nixon used Graham to bring in the votes. The release of the Watergate tape transcripts exposed this sad fact along with Nixon's moral turpitude. Graham recalled this painful moment in his autobiography:

> I did not have to distance myself from Watergate; I wasn't close to it in the first place. The President had not confided in me about his mounting troubles, and after the full story eventually broke, he all but blocked my access to him during the rest of his presidency. As I have said, I wanted to believe the best about him for as long as I could. When the worst came out, it was nearly unbearable for me.[34]

Tapes later emerged that suggested Graham's complicity with Nixon's antisemitism. This nearly destroyed Graham's reputation with the

---

33 Edward B. Fiske, "The Closest Thing to a White House Chaplain," *New York Times Magazine*, June 8, 1969, https://archive.nytimes.com/www.nytimes.com/books/97/07/06/reviews/graham-magazine.html.

34 Billy Graham, *Just As I Am: The Autobiography of Billy Graham* (New York: HarperCollins, 1997), 458.

Jewish community. Stinging from this painful episode, the president's chaplain resolved never to become involved with partisan politics again. Graham befriended eleven sitting presidents: Dwight D. Eisenhower, John F. Kennedy, Lyndon B. Johnson, Richard M. Nixon, Gerald R. Ford, Jimmy Carter, Ronald W. Reagan, George H. W. Bush, William J. Clinton, George W. Bush, and Barack H. Obama.

Ronald W. Reagan

Ronald W. Reagan felt a divine calling to seek the office of president, though his humility may have caused him to doubt.[35] Throughout his presidency, he took the threat of godless communism very seriously. He quickly became known to the Kremlin for his strong evangelical faith. Though he was hospitable to lobbyists and grateful for Graham's friendship, he preferred to meditate and pray alone with God. Quoting Edmund Morris, Paul Kengor states that Reagan relied on "silent colloquies with God, usually at an open window."[36]

When one considers Reagan's strong personal faith, it is curious that he was plagued by spurious claims that he made presidential decisions based on astrology. However, it was Nancy Reagan who fell under the spell of astrologer Joan Quigley, who preyed on her fears of a presidential assassination. The president himself sought to end the controversy when he responded to a reporter who sarcastically asked whether he would continue to let astrology guide his daily schedule. Reagan's rejoinder was rapid and pointed: "I can't because I never did."[37]

William "Bill" Jefferson Clinton

While William "Bill" Jefferson Clinton resided in the White House, United Methodist Elder Philip Wogaman was the family's spiritual advisor. At the time, Wogaman was professor of Christian ethics at Wesley Theological Seminary and senior pastor of the historic Foundry

---

35 Paul Kengor, *God and Ronald Reagan: A Spiritual Life* (New York: HarperCollins, 2004), 152.

36 Paul Kengor, "Ronald Reagan's Faith and Attack on Soviet Communism," in *Religion and the American Presidency*, ed. M. J. Whitney (New York: Palgrave Macmillan, 2007), 178.

37 Kengor, *God and Ronald Reagan*, 192.

United Methodist Church in Washington, DC. Among the most serious of personal struggles they faced was the impeachment proceedings related to Clinton's affair with intern Monica Lewinsky. In his book *From the Eye of the Storm: A Pastor to the President Speaks Out*, Wogaman said much about his role in providing counsel to the family. Conversely, the person closest to Hillary Rodham Clinton, Dr. Donald Jones, refrained from making any statement of record. Although Jones was not publicly known as a spiritual advisor to President Clinton, he played an important role from behind the scenes. Dr. Jones was a longtime friend of Hillary, having served as her youth pastor in Illinois, and he continued to influence her during her sojourn at Wellesley College. Correspondence between Jones and the collegiate Hillary Rodham reveals her interest in politics. Jones encouraged her exploration of the tension between faith and social action. Her crossing over from middle-of-the-road conservative Christianity to neo-orthodoxy was complete when she embraced the social justice teachings of Paul Tillich and Reinhold Niebuhr.

Jones went on to become a popular ethics professor at United Methodist–related Drew University. A frequent guest at the White House, his reassuring presence was greatly appreciated during the impeachment proceedings. Jones protected the privacy of the Clinton family even after he passed away. The surviving family members declined to give interviews regarding interactions with Hillary Clinton.[38] It is notable that Reverend Bill Shillady, a pastor to Secretary Hillary Clinton, attempted to publish a book of devotions titled *Strong for a Moment Like This: Daily Devotions of Hillary Clinton*. However, it was recalled after an investigation at Abingdon Press revealed portions of the book were plagiarized from a blog.[39]

---

38 "Informational Memo Regarding Media Requests about Don Jones/Hillary Clinton," May 4, 2015, Drew University Archives.

39 Julie Zauzmer, "Book by Hillary Clinton's Pastor Will Be Pulled from Shelves Due to Extensive Plagiarism," *Washington Post*, September 5, 2017, www.washingtonpost.com/news/acts-of-faith/wp/2017/09/05/book-by-hillary-clintons-pastor-will-be-pulled-from-shelves-due-to-extensive-plagiarism/?noredirect=on&utm_term=.1c2ad8650c86.

Barack H. Obama

During the 2008 primaries, President Barack H. Obama was forced to distance himself from his pastor Dr. Jeremiah Wright Jr. of Trinity United Church of Christ for widely publicized controversial "anti-patriotic" comments.[40] President Obama appointed Reverend Joshua DuBois, the son of an AME pastor and self-described Pentecostal, to lead the White House's Office of Faith-Based and Neighborhood Partnerships. *Time* magazine called DuBois the "pastor-in-chief." In this role, he assembled a multifaith and multicultural committee of pastors, rabbis, priests, and other religious leaders. President Obama's overt efforts to support faith-based organizations did little to counteract the pervasive rumors that he was a fifth-column Muslim agent. Pastors such as Bishop T. D. Jakes, Reverend Adam Hamilton, and Bishop Vashti McKenzie worked very closely with Obama on national strategies. Finding themselves in the public eye, they were criticized and forced to defend the claim that President Obama was a true believer in Jesus Christ. It is interesting to note the president's pastoral presence during the eulogy for victims of the tragic Bible class shooting at Emanuel AME Church in Charleston, South Carolina. President Obama, with AME bishop Vashti McKenzie at his right hand, spontaneously led the mourners in the singing of "Amazing Grace."[41]

Donald John Trump

Donald John Trump may have had his first real encounter with a national religious influencer when, as a child, he attended Marble Collegiate Church, where Dr. Norman Vincent Peale was senior pastor. Later, he would return to Peale's church two more times for life-altering events: first, in 1977 to marry his first wife, Ivana Marie, and second, in 1999 to bury his father, Fred Trump. Lessons learned about the power of positive thinking may have had a positive effect on Trump

40 Carl A. Grant and Shelby J. Grant, *The Moment: Barack Obama, Jeremiah Wright, and the Firestorm at Trinity United Church of Christ* (Lanham, MD: Rowman & Littlefield, 2013).

41 NPR. "Watch: President Obama Sings 'Amazing Grace' in Eulogy," NPR, June 26, 2015, www.npr.org/sections/itsallpolitics/2015/06/26/417839374/watch-president-obamas-eulogy-at-emanuel-ame-church.

when about six decades later and against all odds he won the 2016 presidential election. While taking his victory lap, President-Elect Trump announced that longtime friend Reverend Paula White would transition into the role of presidential spiritual advisor. White assembled her group of advisors, evangelical and charismatic leaders, who also served as Trump surrogates during the 2016 campaign.[42] It was not long before public criticism of the White House policies challenged the optics of these unofficial spiritual advisors. Political pundits and religious leaders questioned the silence or open support the other pastors gave regarding the president's controversial language and actions.

President Trump's spiritual advisors, operating under the leadership of White, came under fire from outsiders for their apparent reticence to speak out over Trump's divisive manner of speech and apparent insensitivity to those most vulnerable in society. Reverend A. R. Bernard resigned in protest to President Trump's equivocation over white nationalists who clashed violently with peaceful protestors in Charlottesville, Virginia. Bernard posted his explanation on Twitter:

> In a social and political climate such as ours, it often takes a gathering of unlikely individuals to shape the future of our nation on issues of faith and inner-city initiatives. I was willing to be one of those unlikely individuals, and that is why I agreed to serve on the President's Evangelical Advisory Board. However, it became obvious that there was a deepening conflict in values between myself and the administration. I quietly stepped away from my involvement with the Board several months ago, and submitted my letter of formal resignation as of Tues, Aug. 15, 2017. I am always grateful and honored by any opportunity to serve my country. Pastor A. R. Bernard.[43]

---

42 With few exceptions, the same political surrogates also participated in the 2020 presidential campaign.

43 Alfonso R. Bernard, "In a social and political climate such as ours, it often takes a gathering of unlikely individuals to shape the future of our nation on issues of faith and inner-city initiatives," Twitter, August 18, 207, 4:44 p.m., https://twitter.com/arbernard/status/898661983146397700?lang=en.

Crossing over from an advisor to a prophet is not a common occurrence. Bernard's resignation was a gradual process that began once he recognized the motive behind the Evangelical Advisory Board: "There was nothing hidden. [Trump] wanted that voting bloc. He wanted their votes. . . . It was transactional. He wanted to do whatever he thought would get those votes."[44]

In an unrelated but telling incident, the House chaplain Rev. Patrick J. Conroy, a Jesuit, was forced by Speaker Paul Ryan to resign after Conroy prayed that the legislators would "guarantee that there are not winners or losers under the new tax laws, but benefits balanced and shared by all Americans." Shortly afterward Ryan said, "Padre, you just got to stay out of politics," and the chaplain was forced to resign, but other members of the House pressured Ryan to hire him back.[45] This is an interesting reversal of roles where the chaplain historically has served as the prophetic conscience of the government.

Partisan Evangelical Advisors

For some unknown reason, Billy Graham was launched into the public eye by newspaper magnate William Randolph Hearst, who sent a telegram to his editors saying, "Puff Graham."[46] Graham never knew the reason for his promotion to the national spotlight. However, he threw himself into the dual honorific roles as chaplain to presidents and America's pastor. His capacity to fulfill this calling faithfully with relatively little controversy earned him the right to become the *sui generis* evangelical prophet of the twentieth century. He continued to work with presidents for many years to come. However, his title as "chaplain to presidents" abruptly ended after Watergate, when Graham, severely burned by Nixon's duplicity, resolved to stay out of partisan politics.

44 Weiland, "Evangelicals, Having Backed Trump."

45 Martin Marty, "Prayer Rattles Speaker Ryan, but House Chaplain Gets to Stay in Politics," Religion News Service, June 5, 2018, https://religionnews.com/2018/05/07/prayer-rattles-speaker-ryan-but-house-chaplain-gets-to-stay-in-politics/.

46 Francis Fitzgerald, *The Evangelicals: The Struggle to Shape America* (New York: Simon & Schuster, 2017), 175.

In a career start paralleling that of Billy Graham, lesser-known Hispanic evangelical leader Samuel Rodriguez has risen to national prominence in a short period. Reminiscent of William Randolph Hearst's "puff Graham" situation, Rodriguez caught the attention of media moguls Roma Downey and husband Mark Burnett, who decided to groom him. The couple has to their credits several movies and successful TV shows including *The Bible* miniseries, *Survivor*, *The Voice*, *Shark Tank*, and *The Apprentice*. Early in his public debut, Rodriguez described himself as a fusion of Graham and King with "salsa sauce on top."[47] On the surface, this may seem to be laced with irony since Graham refused King's invitations to assist in the civil rights movement.[48] However, Rodriguez understands this disconnect. In his book *The Lamb's Agenda*, he explains how Graham's and King's distinct mission statements merged into his calling: "After watching a Billy Graham crusade and a subsequent special on Dr. King, I felt like my life's mission statement could write itself: reconcile the salvation message preached by Billy Graham with the justice message of Dr. King."[49]

Rodriguez maintains that he is committed to being a nonpartisan spiritual advisor. His now-familiar saying is that he represents "not the agenda of the Donkey or the Elephant, but only the agenda of the Lamb."[50] Rodriguez was identified as a surrogate during the 2016 presidential campaign when he found himself defending Trump against charges of racism. His loyalty was rewarded when he was invited to read Scripture at the 2016 presidential inauguration. He continues to face critiques from other national Latino leaders including Dr. Miguel De La Torre, professor of social ethics and Latino studies at Iliff School of Theology.[51] Rodriguez enjoys success as a megachurch pastor, bestselling author, television personality, and movie producer. From his

47 Samuel Rodriguez, *The Lamb's Agenda: Why Jesus Is Calling You to a Life of Righteousness and Justice* (Nashville: Thomas Nelson, 2013), 96.

48 Fitzgerald, *The Evangelicals*, 205.

49 Rodriguez, *The Lamb's Agenda*, 67.

50 Rodriguez, *The Lamb's Agenda*, 40.

51 Note Miguel De La Torre's sardonic dedication of his book *Decolonizing Christianity: Becoming Badass Believers* (Grand Rapids, MI: Eerdmans, 2021) to Guillermo Maldonado, Samuel Rodriguez, Mario Bramnick, Pasqual Urrabazo, and Ramiro Peña. They are all former evangelical advisors to President Trump.

perspective, he continued to speak truth to power. He considered his role as a presidential advisor as "an assignment from heaven" that did not include giving President Trump a pass for offensive language and policies such as family separations.[52]

It is not clear how many chaplains to the president have publicly spoken truth to power. Graham often did this privately. Jim Wallis, the evangelical leader of the socially conscious organization Sojourners, tweeted in 2018 this thinly veiled barb: "We can't control the words or actions of those in political power or those in religion who have become their chaplains. But we can control what we do."[53] These critiques may be too harsh and lacking in perspective. Rodriguez explained his position in an interview with PBS *NewsHour*'s William Brangham. According to Rodriguez, the reason for their commitment to the President's Evangelical Advisory Board is to influence public policy:

> Evangelicals experienced or felt that, in the past number of years, the past 10 years, issues of religious liberty, issues of advancing their Judeo-Christian value systems stood in a de facto and du jour manner, for that fact, threatened. . . . So, all of a sudden, we have President Donald Trump, and the public policy initiatives as it pertains to faith is much more favorable to the evangelical community indeed.[54]

The Ministry of Reconciliation

Former senator John Danforth made a good case stating that Christians who dabble in politics choose to be either reconcilers or dividers. The problem is that reconcilers are rarely taken seriously, while dividers get all the media attention. The work of reconciling, says Danforth, is

52 Heather Sells, "Trump Faith Advisor Says He's Fulfilling 'Assignment from Heaven,'" CBN News, June 8, 2018, www1.cbn.com/cbnnews/us/2018/June/trump-faith-advisor-says-hes-fufilling-assignment-from-heaven.

53 Sojourners, "We can't control the words or actions of those in political power, or that in religion who have become their chaplains. Be we can control what we do," Twitter, May 10, 2018, 3:30 p.m., http://twitter.com/sojourners?lang=eng%20may.

54 "Evangelicals Keep Faith in Trump to Advance Religious Agenda," PBS *NewsHour*, May 3, 2018, www.pbs.org/newshour/show/evangelicals-keep-faith-in-trump-to-advance-religious-agenda.

boring: "Reconciliation depends on acknowledging that God's truth is greater than our own, that we cannot reduce it to any political platform we create, no matter how committed we are to that platform, and that God's truth is large enough to accommodate the opinions of all kinds of people, even those with whom we strongly disagree."[55]

The role of spiritual advisor to the president probably will never become an official position on the Cabinet. The separation of church and state ensures the possibility of genuine prophetic speech with the moral compass and spiritual power to rebuke government leaders and freely expose injustice. On the other hand, presidential appointments are an important way for citizens to get real-time experience navigating the federal system. Trinidad "Trini" Garza of the Bill Clinton administration[56] and Lisa Treviño Cummins of the George W. Bush administration[57] are two excellent examples of devoted Christian lay leaders who turned their federal service experiences into ministries benefiting their church and the Hispanic community.

The federal government looks dimly on anything that smacks of the establishment of religion. Yet there is a recognition that religion plays an important role in American life inclusive of politics. This harkens back

---

55 John Danforth, *Faith and Politics: How the "Moral Values" Debate Divides America and How to Move Forward Together* (New York: Viking, 2006), 16, 17.

56 Trinidad "Trini" Garza was a longtime active member of a Spanish-speaking United Methodist congregation and active in MARCHA, the Hispanic caucus of the United Methodist Church. He was appointed as a regional deputy director for the Department of Education under the Clinton administration, and he was a well-known leader in the Dallas Hispanic community due to his work with Dallas Independent School District. An early college high school was named in his honor. See www.dallasisd.org/Page/33329.

57 Lisa Treviño Cummins was raised in the Spanish-speaking Assemblies of God church. In 2001, the George W. Bush administration appointed her as associate director of White House Office of Faith-Based and Community Initiatives. She is the founder of Urban Strategies, LLC, a faith-based consulting firm. See https://latinoinheritance.com/authors/. She shares her personal story along with colleague Lorena Garza Gonzalez in *Inheritance: Discovering the Richness of Latino Family and Culture* (Arlington, VA: Urban Strategies, 2012). For more on the origins of the Faith-Based Initiatives program, see Jo Renee Formicola, Mary C. Seegers, and Paul J. Weber, *Faith-Based Initiatives and the Bush Administration: The Good, the Bad, and the Ugly* (Lanham, MD: Rowman & Littlefield, 2003), 116.

to the earliest days of the Republic, where the anti-monarchy phrase "no king but Jesus" clearly placed the divide between politics and religion without completely dismantling either one. The clergy in the late eighteenth century were no less interested in politics than those of the twenty-first. Consequently, they have sought to influence the leadership of the nation either directly by petition or indirectly by supporting or panning candidates for office. Since the Kennedy–Nixon campaign, spiritual advisors have divided themselves between the neo-orthodoxy of Niebuhr and the neo-evangelicalism of Billy Graham. It has been suggested that we might consider updating our understanding of the divide between self-described Red-Letter evangelicals such as Shane Claiborne and Tony Campolo and those further to the right such as Paula White and other evangelical supporters of President Trump. It may be more helpful to think of them as "red" and "blue" evangelicals. This sober observation was recently made at a summit of evangelicals seeking dialogue on the future of their shared tradition.[58]

Shrewd politicians have long understood the potential of religion or religious institutions to curry the favor of the masses. It is difficult to decipher whether politicians are genuine in their public faith or if they are following a Machiavellian game plan, or both. At best, we can exercise our powers of observation to determine who are the players and what are their actions. It has been a mixed bag, with some clergy being an assuring presence for presidents when no one else, even Cabinet members, could provide solace. Others such as McKinley, Nixon, and Reagan, who were genuinely devout according to their testimonies, truly appreciated having a prayer partner or confessor to deal with the burden of national leadership. I believe that the unofficial office of presidential spiritual advisor will continue unless a sharp cultural turn against public religion is codified to the point of eliminating all federally employed chaplains in the House, Senate, military branches, and prisons.

---

58 Emily McFarlan Miller, "Evangelical Leaders Discuss Future of Their Movement in Trump Era," Religion News Service, April 17, 2018, https://religionnews.com/2018/04/17/evangelical-leaders-discuss-future-of-their-movement-in-trump-era/.

The Problem with Clay Feet

The #MeToo movement has awakened the collective American consciousness to the issue of abuse of power and gender inequality. Power brokers in the entertainment industry, politicians, business executives, and, more recently, church leaders have stepped down as their harassment misdeeds have been made public. The striking thing is that this movement did not originate from churches or morality watchdogs. Rather, this was borne of a secular society sick of the pervasive abuse of women and other vulnerable populations. Social media has made us more aware than ever before of the dangers of narcissistic leaders.[59]

A shortlist of epic failures in the Trump White House is instructive for providing a historical perspective on the public's expectations for moral leadership: Jefferson's slaves; Jackson's Trail of Tears; Johnson's war on emancipation; McKinley's religious imperialism; FDR's internment of American citizens of German, Japanese, and Italian descent; Truman's controversial decision to drop atomic bombs on Japan; JFK's secret trysts with a Hollywood starlet; Nixon's Watergate; Clinton's scandalous affair with an intern; and Trump's divisive language, racial slurs, misogynistic conversations, porn-star payoff, and the separation of children from parents seeking asylum. Surprisingly, the only three presidents impeached by authority of the Twenty-Fifth Amendment were Andrew Johnson, Bill Clinton, and Donald J. Trump. None were impeached for moral failure, but for their violation of federal laws. Trump was impeached first for abuse of power and obstruction of justice. He was impeached a second time for incitement of insurrection. None of these four impeachments resulted in a conviction.

It is commonly thought that Nixon was impeached, but this is not true. Nixon held the unhappy distinction of being the only American president to resign from office. Partisan accusations have been leveled at George W. Bush for the invasion of Iraq and at Barack Obama for the Benghazi fiasco. In 2021, Donald Trump was accused of attempting to obstruct Congress from certifying the 2020 presidential election

---

59 For a closer look at the phenomenon of narcissistic religious leaders see Chuck De Groat's *When Narcissism Comes to Church: Healing Your Community from Emotional and Spiritual Abuse* (Downers Grove, IL: InterVarsity Press, 2020).

and for inciting the January 6, 2021, attack on the US Capitol. Despite these moral failings and impeachments, Bill Clinton is still held in high regard in many places. Strange as that seems, a recent Gallup poll may be even more surprising. In a poll on presidential moral leadership, only 63 percent of Republicans believe that moral leadership is very important. This is down from 86 percent under Clinton. Gallup concludes that "Americans believe the president should provide moral leadership for the country. However, Republicans' and Democrats' commitment wavers when moral leadership is a point of concern for their own party's president."[60]

Donald J. Trump's influence and support also remain strong. When the *Access Hollywood* tapes emerged, it appeared that Trump's run for office was over. However, evangelical supporters such as Paula White and James Dobson reported that Trump had since had a conversion experience, thus granting him a clean slate. The disappointing revelation about Michael Cohen's arrangement to pay hush money to adult actress Stormy Daniels did little to tarnish Trump's reputation with his evangelical advisors. Tony Perkins, president of the Family Research Council, said that the evangelical community was granting Trump a mulligan (a golf term meaning a do-over).[61] Rhetoric and behavior following this seem to be the most bothersome to critics of the evangelical advisors. Attorney Rudy Giuliani said that President Trump, his client, could get away with shooting James Comey, though it may risk immediate impeachment. This comment drew on Trump's brazen campaign comment, "I could stand in the middle of Fifth Avenue and shoot somebody, and I wouldn't lose voters."[62]

The reticence of the evangelical advisors to call out President Trump for his much-publicized moral failures and persistent use of

---

60 Jeffrey M. Jones, "Presidential Moral Leadership Less Important to Republicans," Gallup, May 29, 2018, https://news.gallup.com/poll/235022/presidential-moral-leadership-less-important-republicans.aspx.

61 Jennifer Hansler, "Conservative Evangelical Leader: Trump Gets a 'Mulligan' on His Behavior," CNN Politics, January 23, 2018, www.cnn.com/2018/01/23/poliitcs/tony-perkins-trump-affairs-mulligan/index.html.

62 Nikki Schwab, "Giuliani: Trump Couldn't Be Indicted Even if He Shot Comey," *New York Post*, June 3, 2018, https://nypost.com/2018/06/03/giuliani-trump-couldnt-be-indicted-even-if-he-shot-comey/.

divisive language evoked the ire of other evangelicals, liberal mainliners, and Roman Catholics, not to mention Jewish and Muslim Americans. It is important to note that the issue was not to dismiss the advisors' identities as Christian ministers but to call them to prophetic action. Foremost on my mind as a religious historian is the functional role of spiritual advisors in American history. In an op-ed, evangelical historian John Fea dubbed such clergy members "court evangelicals."[63] This pejorative label echoes Baptist activist Will Campbell's depiction of Billy Graham as a "false court prophet" for not confronting Nixon and the Pentagon about the war in Vietnam.[64] In his book *Believe Me: The Evangelical Road to Donald Trump*, Fea takes to task evangelical advisors for not calling out the Trump administration for policies and behavior that clash with Christian values:

> Like the members of the kings' courts during the late Middle Ages and the Renaissance, who sought influence and worldly approval by flattering the monarch rather than prophetically speaking truth to power, Trump's court evangelicals boast about their "unprecedented access" to the White House and exalt the president for his faith-friendly policies.[65]

Not all spiritual advisors provided cover for President Trump. Samuel Rodriguez issued his statement of solidarity with protesters who opposed the Department of Justice's policy of zero tolerance of illegal border crossers and separating of children from parents. In an interview with Jorge Ramos, host of *Al Punto* of Univision, Rodriguez denounced this policy as "anti-Christian" and "anti-American."[66] At the same time, he argued for maintaining access with the Trump administration, basing his decision on Dr. King's teaching that "a bridge is more powerful

---

63 John Fea, "The Evangelical Courtiers Who Kneel before the President's Feet," Religion News Service, May 12, 2017, https://religionnews.com/2017/05/12/the-evangelical-courtiers-who-kneel-before-the-presidents-feet/.

64 Martin, *A Prophet with Honor*, 367.

65 John Fea, *Believe Me: The Evangelical Road to Donald Trump* (Grand Rapids, MI: Eerdmans, 2018).

66 *Al Punto*, "'Basta ya': Este reverendo asegura que 'no podemos estar mudos' ante la separación familiar," featuring Jorge Ramos, aired July 8, 2018, on Univision Noticias, www.youtube.com/watch?v=PBaWIncOL1k.

than a wall." This insider approach is a rare prophetic action by an evangelical advisor. Franklin Graham and Johnnie Moore also criticized the separation policy as inhumane, though they remained committed to Trump's overall leadership.

The Moral Mandate

Hispanic Evangelical spiritual advisor Rev. Gabriel Salguero told me they thought of their role in the Trump White House as akin to that of biblical hero Joseph, who found favor with Pharaoh to save their nation.[67] The prophetic words of Jürgen Moltmann are instructive in distinguishing between service to the God of the patriarchs and the gods of the world: "The God of Abraham, Isaac and Jacob ist [*sic*] not the divine Lord of the Pharaos [*sic*], the Caesars and the slave owners. He is the Father of the humiliated, the saviour [*sic*] of the opressed [*sic*]."[68] In many episodes in American history, Christian leaders met unjust laws with dissent and protest. In the case of African American slavery, resistance against enslavers was the most Christian thing to do: "When the master's will conflicted with God's, slaves faced a choice which was simultaneously an opportunity to assert their own free will and to act virtuously, even heroically, in the context of Christianity, in which disobedience to white authority, no matter the consequence, could seem morally imperative."[69]

We could list several periods in American history when speaking truth to power was considered by Christian leaders as a moral mandate. Such prophets were there to speak against racial segregation, for women's suffrage, against Japanese American internment, against homelessness, against poverty, against gang violence, and so on. Denominational and ecumenical leaders regularly publish a consensus

---

67 Rev. Gabriel Salguero is founder and president of the National Latino Evangelical Coalition (NALEC). Interview with the author, May 5, 2018.

68 Jürgen Moltmann, "The God of Abraham, Isaac and Jacob ist not the divine Lord of the Pharaos, the Caesars and the slave owners. He is the Father of the humiliated, the saviour of the opressed," Twitter, July 1, 2018, 7:08 p.m., https:///twitter.com/moltmannjuergen/status/1013574994943717378.

69 Albert J. Raboteau, *Slave Religion: The "Invisible Institution" in the Antebellum South*, updated ed. (Oxford: Oxford University Press, 1978, 2004), 307.

of social principles and resolutions addressing contemporary social issues. In addition, other leaders speak out publicly on issues of social justice. In 1966, UMC bishop Joel N. Martinez joined an estimated fifteen thousand *huelguistas* in their 400-mile march from the Rio Grande Valley to the Texas State Capitol in Austin to demand just wages and better working conditions for *campesinos*.[70] UMC bishop Minerva Carcaño developed a reputation as a "key religious player" for immigrant rights.[71] AME bishop Vashti Murphy McKenzie used her highly visible public platform to speak prophetically as an advocate for the urban poor.[72] Nondenominational groups may have a harder time determining their theological stance on social issues, because they are not necessarily bound by the same bureaucracy of mainline or denominational evangelicals.

Conclusion

Polarization in this nation has rarely been higher after two controversial presidential elections; two impeachments; the January 6, 2021, insurrectionist attack on Capitol Hill; threats to voting rights; the rise of white supremacy groups; domestic terrorism; Christian nationalism; the fight over gun control and gun violence; the public execution of George Floyd; the private killing of Breonna Taylor; relentless deadly police brutality against African Americans, Latinos, and other people of color; systemic racism; the global pandemic; and the failure to address humanely the tragedy of refugees and unaccompanied minors crossing the border. Our elected officials rely on religious leaders to check their inner moral compass. It is truly an honor for anyone to be called to serve as a spiritual

70 Joel N. Martinez, "Marching Again for Farmworkers to Honor Those That Came before Us," *Austin American-Statesman*, September 26, 2018, https://amp.statesman.com/amp/10015051007.

71 Lilly Fowler, "Methodist Bishop Minerva Carcano on Front Lines of Immigration Battle," *Washington Post*, March 10, 2013, www.washingtonpost.com/national/on-faith/methodist-bishop-minerva-carcano-on-front-lines-of-immigration-battle/2013/03/08/8bd246c2-883b-11e2-b412-2e8596e7c927_story.html.

72 Brooke Obie, "Bishop Vashti McKenzie on the Right Way to Mix Christianity and Politics," *EBONY*, February 26, 2013, www.ebony.com/faith_spirituality/the-spiritual-life-bishop-vashti-mckenzie-405/.

advisor no matter who sits in the White House or, for that matter, Congress. I do not doubt that many such folks use their privileged platforms to speak truth to power. However, there remains a rare class of spiritual advisors whose power is not derived from the principles and powers of this present age. True prophets resist political agendas promoted by political parties and elected officials. They defend the weak and speak out for justice at their own personal risk. Such biblically grounded individuals are driven by the zeal of the Holy Spirit rather than self-interest. Like the biblical prophet Jeremiah, they must speak lest their hearts become burning fire shut up in their bones (Jer 20:9).

Profetas in Leadership

DANIEL E. RUARTE

IT IS AN INTERESTING time to talk about the notion of prophecy, but my intention is not to approach prophecy as a way of predicting the future, but rather as the rise of a prophetic voice (prophetic leader) that has a kind of divine influence over a generation for the good of God, the church, and the people. In this chapter, I will present a theoretical conceptualization of prophetic leadership theory. Several well-known leadership theories exist, such as servant leadership, participative leadership, transformational leadership, the leadership grid, and more.[1] Some of these have been incorporated into educational programs for Christian leaders and even applied at the local church level, but there is no clear definition or understanding of prophetic leadership. This is not the first conversation about a possible theoretical framework; for example, Nik Maheran Muhammad has presented academic research on the possibility of this new construct based on the Abrahamic religions of Christianity, Judaism, and Islam. He believes that prophetic leadership "rests in the tenets of trait theory."[2] This is helpful as we develop a

1 Peter Northouse, *Leadership: Theory and Practice*, 7th ed. (Thousand Oaks, CA: SAGE, 2016).

2 Nik Maheran Muhammad, "Prophetic Leadership Model: Conceptualizing a Prophet's Leadership Behaviour, Leader-Follower Mutuality and Altruism to Decision Making Quality," *European Journal of Interdisciplinary Studies* 1, no. 3 (2015): 93–94.

scholarly conceptualization of prophetic leadership theory, in our case through the lens of the Hispanic movement in the United States.

The Hispanic Leader Prophet

It is no secret that Hispanics are drawn to lead and have a strong voice in the social, political, and religious aspects of our culture. Espinosa, in his extensive work, *Latino Pentecostals in America*, clearly shows that "contrary to popular perception, Latino Pentecostals have been involved in faith-based social, civic, and political action throughout the twentieth century."[3]

Theoretical Definition of Prophetic Leadership

As mentioned before, prophetic leadership theory (see figure 1) is not about predicting the future, but rather the rise of prophetic voices (prophetic leaders), who have a kind of *divine* influence over a generation for the good of God, the church, and the people.

Bruce C. Birch argues that people "long for voices of wisdom and passion to help us find just and equitable paths into the future."[4] This is true in religious, social, and political aspects of human beings. Organizational leadership studies examine the relationship between leaders and followers in scientific ways, with the hopes of finding effective principles that help accomplish their objectives. It always points to the dyadic relationships and leadership dynamics.[5] People want good, just,

Figure 1: Theoretical definition of prophetic leadership (Daniel Ruarte, 2021).

3 Gastón Espinosa, *Latino Pentecostals in America: Faith and Politics in Action* (Cambridge, MA: Harvard University Press, 2014), 322.

4 Bruce C. Birch, "Reclaiming Prophetic Leadership," *Ex Auditu* 22 (2006): 10, 1.

5 Northhouse, *Leadership*, 2016.

and strong leaders who can represent them well, leaders who exercise their influence in multiple directions and become their voices to the world. Samuel Rodriguez rightly states, "Movements stand or fall based on one significant element: leadership. . . . The agenda of the Lamb movement will require many voices and many leaders."[6] We will discuss further Rodriguez in later sections.

Latinos and other underrepresented groups have suffered and many times felt voiceless before the dominant culture and the structures of this nation. Justo González calls for deep self-reflection and historical understanding by the denominational leaders who have not recognized the troubling history of those past generations.[7] It is true, things have not been always great; however, true prophetic leaders go beyond and speak the truth in the right spirit and with a dose of love.

> At the center stands the undeniable fact that we exist because it is the will of God, expressed and sealed by action of the Holy Spirit, that we hear the gospel "each in our own tongue." It was in the power of the Spirit that Hispanics embraced Methodism, and it is by the power of the Holy Spirit that we have survived and even increased in the face of circumstances, policies, and structures that have not always been favorable. It is the Spirit who unites us with other sisters and brothers who do not speak our language or share in our traditions but who also hear and celebrate the same faith, each in their own tongue. And it is the Spirit who repeatedly gives testimony within our spirits, in our own tongue, that we too are beloved children of God.[8]

Helen Doohan attests to this prophetic principle while presenting about the prophet Isaiah's message: "Prophecies convey the delicate balance between *confrontation* and *compassion*, an ideal on this level of

---

6 Samuel Rodriguez, *The Lamb's Agenda: Why Jesus Is Calling You to a Life of Righteousness and Justice* (Nashville: Thomas Nelson, 2013), 119.

7 Justo González, *Each in Our Own Tongue: A History of Hispanics in United Methodism* (Nashville: Abingdon Press, 1991), 19–22.

8 González, *Each in Our Own Tongue*, 38.

leadership."[9] The Hispanic Protestant church in the United States has had a great number of prophetic leaders. We do not have the number of pages needed to include all those who have divinely influenced a generation. I will share about a few Latino leaders who have been prophetic voices to so many and who have crossed ethnic, social, political, and denominational barriers as their influence and message continue to affect this generation and the next.

Hispanic Voices That Shaped Our Present and Future

We have defined prophetic leadership as the rise of prophetic voices (prophetic leaders) that have a kind of divine influence over a generation for the good of God, the church, and the people. These leaders are not about predicting the future but are more focused on influencing the present and the future. In the following section, I will share about five Hispanic leaders who have had a profound impact on me and on society, politics, and religion.

Dr. Justo González

I first heard about Dr. Justo González in a Christian history class at a local Bible institute. His amazing work, *History of Christianity*, was being used as the course textbook. It was the first time I was being introduced to a systematic historical account of my new Christian faith besides the normal references my pastor would make from time to time during a Sunday sermon. I was captivated by the book, and it was great to see a Latino last name as the author since most of the books were Spanish translations of white, Anglo pastors or leaders. I can honestly say that he was a voice to all of us; the students in that small classroom and I were being influenced at that moment in our Christian formation. Dr. González has been a prophetic voice in education, theology, Christian history, and much more. According to Juan Francisco Martínez, González is "probably the most well-known Latino theologian in the United States and Latin America . . . one of the Latino leaders with

---

9 Helen Doohan, "Contrasts in Prophetic Leadership: Isaiah and Jeremiah," *Biblical Theology Bulletin* 13, no. 2 (1983): 42.

strong influence in mainline, evangelical, and Pentecostal circles."[10] He is a well-known author, with influence not only on first-generation Latinos in the United States, but also second, third, and beyond. His writings also have influenced other audiences, including other underrepresented groups and the Anglo-American movements.

Some of his accomplishments and renowned works are listed here.

- Dr. González has written more than one hundred books, the most widely known of which are *The History of Christianity* (volumes 1 and 2) and *A History of Christian Thought* (volumes 1, 2, and 3).
- During the 1990s, he helped start three organizations that continue to address theological education to this day: Hispanic Summer Program (HSP), Hispanic Theological Initiative (HTI), and Asociación para la Educación Teológica Hispana (AETH).[11]
- In 2014, he received the Distinguished Service Medal Award from the Association of Theological Schools (ATS).
- He is an ordained minister, speaker, and theologian in the United Methodist Church.
- Dr. González graduated with an undergraduate degree from the United Seminary in Cuba.
- He graduated from Yale Divinity School with an MA and PhD in historical theology.
- After graduation, he joined the faculty at the Evangelical Seminary of Puerto Rico.
- In 1969, he began teaching full-time at the Candler School of Theology, Emory University in Atlanta, Georgia.
- By 1977, he gave up full-time teaching to serve the needs of the Latino movement in the United States by speaking, writing, presenting, and developing organizations to promote educational opportunities for Hispanics.

---

10 Juan Francisco Martínez, *The Story of Latino Protestants in the United States* (Grand Rapids, MI: Eerdmans, 2018), 229.

11 Martínez, *The Story of Latino Protestants in the United States*, 230.

- Dr. González is respected and known around the world, having given hundreds of lectures in North America, South America, Europe, and Asia.

Recognized by high-caliber leaders as a "key voice in the development of Latino theology . . . his influence has been felt throughout the Latino Protestant world."[12] There is no doubt the life and work of Dr. González have been a prophetic voice of divine influence that continues to speak in classrooms, leadership meetings, and churches around the world.

Dr. Jesse Miranda

If you are in any kind of academic or ecclesiastic circles in the Latino Protestant community of California, you likely know about Jesse Miranda. As I continued my academic journey, I was able to meet great students, faculty, and leaders from multiple denominations and backgrounds. Dr. Miranda's name continued to surface; his voice had made an impact. He had earned the respect of many, and they would tell stories of his work and service for the Latino Protestant church. I remember meeting him for the first time at a conference organized by the Jesse Miranda Center at Vanguard University. It was not long ago, in 2018, that he went on to be with the Lord. I was very surprised by his kindness; he made time to talk to all who came and wanted a few minutes with him. He was a strong visionary leader who worked tirelessly to serve the needs of the Hispanic community. Espinosa believes that the work of Dr. Miranda was fundamental to the Latino movement's involvement in sociopolitical matters, because Dr. Miranda wanted "to unite the Latino evangelical community so that they could speak as a common social and civic voice in national politics."[13]

Some of his accomplishments and renowned works are listed here.

- Dr. Miranda was the founder and president of the National Alliance of Evangelical Ministries (AMEN), which later merged with the National Hispanic Christian Leadership Conference (NHCLC).

---

12 Martínez, *The Story of Latino Protestants in the United States*, 230.

13 Espinosa, *Latino Pentecostals in America*, 343.

- He served as the original executive director of the NHCLC, the nation's largest Hispanic Christian organization.
- He worked with multiple US presidents (Ronald Reagan, George H. W. Bush, Bill Clinton, George W. Bush, and Barack Obama) and was invited to the White House and to participate in various White House task forces, symposiums, or committees.[14]
- Dr. Miranda graduated from Latin American Bible Institute (LABI), a historic Assemblies of God (AG) school of ministry specifically dedicated to developing Hispanic leaders.
- He graduated from Southern California College (now Vanguard University), Talbot Theological Seminary, and Fuller Theological Seminary for his DMin degree.
- He is the author of two books: *The Christian Church in Ministry*, translated into ten languages, and *Liderazgo y Amistad* (Leadership and Friendship).
- Dr. Miranda served as AG pastor, assistant superintendent, and superintendent, and taught at LABI, Fuller, Azusa Pacific University, and Vanguard University.[15]
- Samuel Rodriguez, president of the NHCLC, honored Miranda with the following words: "Jesse served as my spiritual father, mentor and chairman emeritus of the NHCLC. Arguably, there would be no Latino evangelical association today without [him]."[16]
- Dr. Miranda's "organization, founded in 1994, brought together 27 denominations, 70 parachurch agencies, and 22 nationalities across the US, Puerto Rico, Mexico, and Canada."[17]
- The general superintendent of the Assemblies of God said his impact was "immeasurable": "Beyond the enormity of his

14 Espinosa, *Latino Pentecostals in America*, 343.

15 Espinosa, *Latino Pentecostals in America*, 342–43.

16 John W. Kennedy, "Hispanic Patriarch Dies," July 15, 2019, Assemblies of God, https://news.ag.org/news/hispanic-patriarch-dies.

17 Morgan Lee, "Died: Jesse Miranda, Hispanic Evangelicals' Bridge-Builder," *Christianity Today*, July 18, 2019, www.christianitytoday.com/news/2019/july/died-jesse-miranda-hispanic-evangelicals-pentecostals-amen.html.

> influence, he was equally known for his humility and eagerness to serve."[18]

Dr. Miranda also worked on educational endeavors with the Hispanic Theological Association (ATH) and taught at multiple accredited institutions. I believe his life and work have been a prophetic voice of divine influence to a generation. He inspired others to follow in his steps and was able to do something many others have a difficult time achieving: healthy leadership transitions. He worked with Rodriguez and was able to transition his work successfully with AMEN to the new NHCLC. According to Espinosa, "One of the most important outgrowths of Jesse Miranda's ministry is the work of Samuel Rodriguez . . . and the NHCLC."[19] As they celebrated his life and legacy, Rev. Dennis Rivera, director of the AG Office of Hispanic Relations, said, "Jesse Miranda will always be known as a visionary whose greatest joy was to pass the baton and mentor a new generation of Hispanic AG leadership."[20] Leadership transitions are not easy, but prophetic leaders also understand this important need to transfer divine influence and prophetic voice to younger leaders who will continue to build on the work they have started.

Dr. Enrique Zone-Andrews

I have the honor to know Dr. Zone-Andrews at a personal level, because we have collaborated on multiple educational endeavors through Facultad de Teología (FTI), the Hispanic Theological Center he founded at Azusa Pacific University, as part of the adjunct teaching team in the seminary, and with the Hispanic Theological Association. I have also known him as a pastor; while we were in ministry transition my family attended his church in Montebello, California, and we were blessed to be part of that wonderful congregation for about two years. I want to share a story to demonstrate his heart. During the season we were attending his church, my sister got very sick and ended up in the hospital. I was so touched when I saw Dr. Zone-Andrews and his wife show

---

18 Lee, "Died: Jesse Miranda, Hispanic Evangelicals' Bridge-Builder."

19 Espinosa, *Latino Pentecostals in America*, 348.

20 Kennedy, "Hispanic Patriarch Dies."

up at the hospital to pray for my sister and my family. He is such a busy leader, but even so, he did that for us and for other church members too.

He is an educational leader who has given all his life to serving the Hispanic community. Professor Zone-Andrews's major emphasis over the last forty years has been his prophetic voice as a creator of pathways into formal theological education for first- and second-generation Latinos. His influence shaped thousands of students in the last four decades as an educator, and many have gone on to do great things. As an ordained pastor of the International Church of the Foursquare Gospel, he has helped Latinos find access to accredited graduate programs at renowned Christian universities. Graduates from FTI have attended institutions such as Fuller Theological Seminary, Azusa Pacific University, University of Southern California (USC), Vanguard University, Indiana Wesleyan University, Oklahoma Wesleyan University, Biola University, Life Pacific University, Point Loma Nazarene University, and Southern Baptist Theological Seminary, to name a few.

Some of his accomplishments and renowned works are listed here.

- Dr. Zone-Andrews has served as ordained minister, International Church of the Foursquare Gospel, Los Angeles, since 1974.
- From 1998 to 2010, he was the Hispanic regional superintendent, Southern California District, La Crescenta.
- From 1978 to the present, he has served as senior pastor, Beverly Boulevard Foursquare Church, Montebello.
- From 1985 to 1998, Dr. Zone-Andrews was the superintendent of San Gabriel Valley Hispanic Division, Southern California District.
- From 1979 to 1987, he was chaplain to the Montebello Police Department.
- From 1974 to 1979, he was senior pastor, Erwin Street Foursquare Church, Reseda.
- From 1973 to 1974, he was senior pastor, Pico Foursquare Church, Pico Rivera.
- From 1966 to 1971, Dr. Zone-Andrews served as a missionary to Central America.

- He was the president and founder of one of the most successful institutions, FTI.
- He served as the executive director, and later as president, of the Hispanic Theological Association (ATH), formerly known as ATEH.
- Has served at Azusa Pacific University for almost thirty years in multiple capacities: full-time professor, associate dean for Hispanic programs, chair of intercultural programs, and director of Leadership Ministry Development Institute.
- He completed a BA in Bible from Life Pacific University, an MA in theology and MDiv from Azusa Pacific University, an MA in missions from Fuller Theological Seminary, and an EdD in higher education leadership from Pepperdine University.
- He is a member of the Spanish Translation and Editorial Committee, *Biblia de las Américas* (NASV), Lockman Foundation, La Habra.
- Dr. Zone-Andrews is a member of the editorial committee for *Bosquejo de Historia de la Iglesia* by Dr. Justo González (published by AETH).
- He served as the Latino general editor for the Spanish version of the internationally recognized book *Foundations of Pentecostal Theology* (*Fundamentos de Teología Pentecostal*) by Guy P. Duffield and Nathaniel Van Cleave (San Dimas, CA: LIFE Bible College and the Foursquare Church).
- He was elected to the 2000 Academic Hall of Fame, Azusa Pacific University, Haggard School of Theology, Azusa.
- In 1990, he earned a Certificate of Appreciation for Enhancing the Meaning and Goals of Hispanic Youth from the Christian Education Department, Spanish Western Territory, Pentecostal Church of God.
- In 1985, he received the Theological Education Ministry Award from Alianza Ministerial Evangélica, Sur de California, and the Outstanding Hispanic Leadership Award from the International Bible Institute, Los Angeles.
- He is the author of *Diario de un Inmigrante*, published in 2020 by Hispanic Theological Association.

Dr. Zone-Andrews has presided over Asociación Teológica Hispana (ATH, formerly Asosiación Teológica para la Educación Hispana [ATEH]) for the past two decades.[21] The organization is "the first effort at addressing these [Latino Educational] issues" such as access to formal education and the new realities of Hispanic Protestant leaders. In his book *Diario de un Inmigrante*, Dr. Zone-Andrews tells the story of how the organization came about. A Latino coalition of educational leaders from different higher education institutions gathered to talk about the needs of Latinos and to be a voice for those who could not be at the table. It was called on by one of the main accrediting agencies in the United States, the Association of Theological Schools (ATS). According to Zone-Andrews, the first meeting, circa April 19, 1973, was prompted by the doctoral work of Dr. Cecilio Arrastía. It was then that ATS developed an interest in light of the evident need to develop pathways for Hispanic groups into formal education programs that would allow them to obtain the required degrees needed for ordination.[22] He has been a prophetic voice and has exercised divine influence over a generation of leaders. Dr. Zone-Andrews is well known in educational circles as a bridge-builder, and many recognize his leadership.

Rev. Samuel Rodriguez

The first time I met Rodriguez was electrifying. If you have heard him speak you know exactly what I am saying. He is young, he is a great orator, he speaks with passion and eloquence, he makes a convincing point. He inspires and can bridge two generations, the young and the old. He can talk about history, church, politics, and social issues with an intellectual edge but at the same time a vocabulary that anyone can understand. I was young, and I was new to church, to the academy, and even to social and political issues, but when I heard him speak, I just got it! He made it clear, and I was just pumped. I wanted to join his cause. This happened several years ago when he was invited to speak at a conference for Hispanic leaders, with more than 400 senior leaders attending from around the country and the world. During that same

21 Martínez, *The Story of Latino Protestants in the United States*, 259.

22 Enrique Zone-Andrews, *Diario de un Inmigrante: Reflexiones de un líder bicultural* (Montebello, CA: Asociación Teológica Hispana, 2020), 195.

conference, he spoke at the main session with more than 3,000 leaders of my denomination from the United States, key area representatives, missionaries, the board, and the president; everyone was *listening*. He was a prophetic voice and divine influence; he was speaking because I could not, and I was not invited to speak but to listen. His message was powerful, and it was received well.

Drs. Martínez and Espinosa were both quoted in the article "The Latino Reformation," an interview about the impact of the work done by Rodriguez and the National Hispanic Christian Leadership Conference (NHCLC), published in 2013 by a well-known secular news outlet, *Time* magazine. For Martínez, Reverend Rodriguez "is the most prominent spokesperson for Latino Protestants today and considered one of the most influential evangelical leaders in the United States today."[23]

Some of his accomplishments and renowned work are listed here.

- Rodriguez has been an Assemblies of God ordained minister since the age of twenty-three. He serves as senior pastor of New Season Christian Worship Center in Sacramento.[24]
- He earned his master of arts degree in educational leadership from Lehigh University.[25]
- He is currently the president of the National Hispanic Christian Leadership Conference (NHCLC), the world's largest Hispanic Christian organization with more than 42,000 US churches.[26]
- Rodriguez has been on many lists of influencers in America in recognition of his impact throughout religious and Latino communities, including the following:
  — "40 People Who Radically Changed the World," *Charisma Magazine*, 2015
  — "101 Most Influential Leaders," *Latino Leaders Magazine*, 2015 and 2016

---

23 Martínez, *The Story of Latino Protestants in the United States*, 306.

24 "Biography—Rev. Samuel Rodriguez," The Kairos Company, accessed March 2, 2022, https://thekcompany.co/background/biography-rev-sam-rodriguez/.

25 "Rev. Samuel Rodriguez," National Hispanic Christian Leadership Conference (NHCLC), accessed February 12, 2022, https://nhclc.org/rev-samuel-rodriguez/.

26 "Rev. Samuel Rodriguez," National Hispanic Christian Leadership Conference (NHCLC).

- "Top 100 Christian Leaders in America," *Newsmax*, 2015
- "2013 *Time* nomination as 100 most influential people in the world, *Time*, 2013
- "10 White & Brown MLKs of Our Time," *Black Christian News*, 2013

- In January 2013, he became the first Hispanic/Latino to deliver the keynote address at The Martin Luther King Jr. Commemorative Service at Ebenezer Baptist Church in Atlanta, Georgia. It is important to note this was even more special as the fortieth Commemorative Service honoring Dr. King.[27]
- "Pastor Sam worked with and advised President George W. Bush, President Obama, and President Trump. He served on Obama's White House Task Force on Fatherhood and Healthy Families, and he frequently meets and consults with members of both parties in Congress advancing the Lamb's agenda."[28]
- Rodriguez is the recipient of the Martin Luther King Jr. Leadership Award, presented by the Congress of Racial Equality.[29]
- In 2015, he was given the Rosa Parks Courage Award by the Montgomery Improvement Association (MIA).[30]
- In 2016, he received the "Defender of the Dream" award, presented by Alveda King and the King Family as well as Bishop Harry Jackson of The Reconciled Church.[31]
- An award-winning author, Rodriguez contributes to world-renowned publications such as the *Washington Post*, *HuffPost*, *Outreach Magazine*, *Ministry Today*, *Enrichment Journal*, *Vida Cristiana*, *Christianity Today*, *Yale Reflections*, and others. He is also the author of *The Lamb's Agenda*, *Path of Miracles*, *You Are Next*, and *Shake Free*. His book *Be Light* made number one on the *LA Times* Best Seller's list, and *From Survive Thrive* is a number one Amazon best-seller.[32]

---

27 "Biography—Sam Rodriguez."
28 "Biography—Sam Rodriguez."
29 "Biography—Sam Rodriguez."
30 "Biography—Sam Rodriguez."
31 "Biography—Sam Rodriguez."
32 "Biography—Sam Rodriguez."

- Rodriguez has expanded his influence in cinema and television. He is executive producer of two films, *Flamin' Hot* and *Breakthrough*, in partnership with Franklin Entertainment and 20th Century Fox. He also serves as cofounder and lead pastor of TBN Salsa, an international Christian-based broadcast television network.[33]

The Kairos Company, a public relations firm, claims that Samuel Rodriguez is "serving as a representative voice for the more than 100 million Hispanic Evangelicals."[34] He has a large audience, including from mainstream sources such as major television news outlets and magazines, and his influence cannot be overlooked or understated.[35] Espinosa says that Rodriguez has been highly influential in sociopolitical issues and a key voice for action and change in favor of Latinos.[36] One of Rodriguez's most important books is *The Lamb's Agenda*, in which he sends a powerful message centered in God and the Bible as the pendulum that brings balance to all social, cultural, and political matters.[37] He is a prophetic voice and role model for future generations.

Dr. Juan Francisco Martínez

Last but not least, I want to share about Dr. Martínez, who has been a faithful leader and has inspired many Latinos to pursue formal education. His work at Fuller Theological Seminary and the Centro Latino at Fuller has been another jewel in Southern California. Today, I meet with educational and ministry leaders who have been affected by his life and service in higher education. I have not had the honor of meeting him in person, but I have close friends and peers who have shared his character and humble heart as a leader. As he was preparing to leave Fuller in 2019, he received the Weyerhaeuser Award. Here are the words of Marianne Meye Thompson, dean of the School of Theology at Fuller:

---

33 "Biography—Sam Rodriguez."

34 "Biography—Sam Rodriguez."

35 "Biography—Sam Rodriguez."

36 Espinosa, *Latino Pentecostals in America*, 348.

37 Samuel Rodriguez, *The Lamb's Agenda: Why Jesus Is Calling You to a Life of Righteousness and Justice* (Nashville: Thomas Nelson, 2013).

> You have *positively influenced* many with your lived commitment to multiculturalism in your person, your writing, and your teaching and work here at Fuller and elsewhere. You have exercised your gifts as a scholar, teacher, and mentor among our students in multiple programs, modalities, and languages. *You have lifted a prophetic voice on behalf of the underrepresented.* Your pioneering scholarly work on Latino Protestantism in the United States has called attention to a neglected part of the story of the American church. In addressing issues of immigration, migration, and transnational identity, you have called our attention to the need to develop leaders for these changing contexts of ministry.[38]

Thompson's words clearly illustrate how others have noted Dr. Martínez's influence and prophetic voice throughout his life and work. He is also a well-known author, theologian, and scholar with national and international influence.

Some of his accomplishments and renowned work include the following.

- Dr. Martínez is an ordained pastor with the Mennonite Brethren Denomination and an experienced church planter.
- He served as director of Hispanic Ministries for the Pacific District Conference of the Mennonite Brethren Church and of Instituto Bíblico del Pacífico, a Mennonite Brethren Bible Institute.[39]
- He served as rector and provost/dean for nine years at SEMILLA, a Latin American Anabaptist Seminary in Guatemala City, Guatemala that serves adult ministerial students from Latin America and the Caribbean.[40]

---

38 "Fuller Honors Juan Martinez as He Accepts New Leadership Role at Ashland Seminary," Fuller Theological Seminary, May 31, 2019, www.fuller.edu/posts/fuller-honors-juan-martinez-as-he-accepts-new-leadership-role-at-ashland-theological-seminary.

39 Eastern Mennonite University Podcast, "Convocation: Juan Martinez," September 27, 2018, https://emu.edu/now/podcast/2018/09/27/convocation-juan-martinez/.

40 "Mission of SEMILLA," SEMILLA, accessed March 2, 2022, https://semillagt.org/seminary/.

- Dr. Martínez served full-time, and in multiple roles, on the faculty at Fuller Theological Seminary in Pasadena. He held influential positions as faculty of Hispanic Studies, director of Hispanic Programs, vice president for diversity and international ministries, vice provost, and associate provost.[41]
- Dr. Martínez launched El Centro Latino at Fuller Seminary to promote higher education within the Hispanic community.
- He was the 2019 recipient of the C. Davis Weyerhaeuser Award for Excellence. This is Fuller Seminary's highest honor of distinction and is awarded to selected faculty members by their peers.[42]
- He is the author of multiple books, including the most recognized, *The Story of Latino Protestants in the United States*, as well as *Iglesias, Cultura y Liderazgo*; *Los Protestantes: An Introduction to Latino Protestantism in the United States*; and *Caminando entre el pueblo: Ministerio Latino en los Estados Unidos*.[43]
- He was an associate editor for the *Global Dictionary of Theology*.[44]
- Dr. Martínez is coauthor with Mark Branson of *Churches, Cultures, and Leadership: A Practical Theology of Congregations and Ethnicities*.[45]
- He received his PhD in intercultural studies from Fuller Theological Seminary (1996).[46]

41 "Convocation: Juan Martinez."

42 "Fuller Honors Juan Martinez as He Accepts New Leadership Role at Ashland Theological Seminary."

43 "Juan Martínez," Wesley Theological Seminary, accessed February 12, 2022, https://wesleyseminary.edu/jgc-lecture-martinez/.

44 *Global Dictionary of Theology: A Resource for the Worldwide Church*, ed. William A. Dyrness and Veli-Matti Kärkkäinen, and assoc. eds., Juan F. Martínez and Simon Chan (Downers Grove, IL: IVP Academic, 2008).

45 Mark Branson and Juan F. Martínez, *Churches, Cultures and Leadership: A Practical Theology of Congregations and Ethnicities* (Downers Grove, IL: IVP Academic, 2011).

46 "Being Christian and Latino: An Interview with Juan Francisco Martínez," *Grace and Peace*, December 2, 2015, https://www.graceandpeacemagazine.org/articles/170-issue-12-winter-2016/448-being-christian-and-latino-an-interview-with-juan-francisco-martinez.

Another highlight of his influence is his leadership of the Hispanic doctor of ministry program at Fuller, one of the first doctoral programs taught in the native language of first- and second-generation Latinos. This program gave access to accredited doctoral degrees for Latinos who wished to pursue higher educational levels. I know several leaders who received their degrees throughout this program and were blessed to do it. Dr. Martínez is a great leader of leaders who has worked his entire life to educate Hispanic pastors and leaders. He is a leader prophet!

Many other Latinos could have been included in this chapter, but we do not have enough time or pages to complete an exhaustive list of divine influencers. Thus, I limited this to a short number of whom I consider great role models. If you think of another, please recognize them and thank them for their work!

Conclusion and Implications

As a student of leadership theory and practice, I have worked to define what leadership is all about, and after a great deal of research, I came to the simple conclusion (which is agreed upon by many scholars in this discipline) that "leadership is influence."[47] I understand that it is more complex than that, but the reality is that there cannot be leadership without influence. Leaders may have a position, title, resources, or degrees, but if no one listens to what they have to say—if they have no impact, no voice on other people's lives and ways of doing things—that is not leadership. Following this line of thought, consider that prophetic leadership is prophetic influence. Or, as I noted before, divine influence. No, you may not *see* the future, but you can surely speak of a preferred future, as Dr. Martin Luther King Jr. once did. We can too.

The Need for Influential Latino Leaders with Prophetic Voices

There is a lot of well-deserved criticism directed at self-proclaimed prophets. Therefore, as I close this chapter, it is important to remember what we are referring to when we say "leaders with prophetic voices."

47 Daniel Ruarte, *Liderazgo y Eclesia: Principios efectivos para pastores y líderes Latinos* (Montebello, CA: Asociación Teológica Hispana, 2019), 19–20.

I define prophetic leadership theory not as predicting the future, but rather the rise of prophetic voices (prophetic leaders) who have a kind of divine influence over a generation for the good of God, the church, and the people. We have reviewed and reflected on the life, work, and legacy of some extraordinary Hispanic leaders who can be considered Latino leader prophets for this generation. My dream is that we will be inspired by them and moved to take the torch, their message, their influence, and see that future generations continue to have strong voices that will advance the work these leaders have started.

CONTRIBUTORS

Pastor Gretchen L. Avila-Torres, DMin (candidate)

Gretchen L. Avila-Torres is copastor with her husband, Rev. Javier Torres, of Templo Jerusalén Iglesia de Dios Pentecostal MI in Holland, Michigan. She is also student support coordinator at Western Theological Seminary (WTS) as Global Leadership Initiatives, Advance Degree Programs, and administrative assistant to the vice president of Strategic Initiatives "to prepare women and men called by God to lead the church in mission." Previously, she taught and served as an administrator at Instituto Ebenezer in Holland, Michigan. She earned a certificate in pastoral studies and an MA from WTS, where she is currently a student in the DMin program.

Rev. Vinicius Couto, PhD (candidate)

Rev. Vinicius Couto is an ordained minister in the Church of the Nazarene of Brazil. He teaches in the Brazilian Theological Nazarene Seminary. For three years he was coordinator and professor of graduate and undergraduate theology courses at the Brazilian Theological College. He holds a master's degree from Paraná's Baptist College in Brazil where he wrote his thesis on Wesley's theology. Currently, his doctoral research at São Paulo Methodist University focuses on the theology of Jacob Arminius. He is editor of *Bona Conscientia* magazine (a journal specializing in Arminian and/or Wesleyan theology), a founding member of NEW (Wesleyan Studies Center), coordinator of the specialization course in Arminian-Wesleyan theology and social transformation of the Seminary Theological Nazarene of Brazil, coordinator of undergraduate and postgraduate courses in theology of the Nazarene Faculty of Brazil, and translator of several works of Arminian and Wesleyan theology.

Rev. César M. Durán, DMin (candidate)

Rev. César M. Durán is an ordained elder in the Methodist Church in Mexico. At six years of age, he began attending the Methodist Church in Piedras Negras, Mexico. He was one of the founders of the Youth League in the early 1980s. After several years in the youth leadership of the league and the youth district, God called him to the ministry. He entered seminary at seventeen years of age. In 1992, he graduated with a BA in theology from Seminario Metodista Juan Wesley (John Wesley Methodist Seminary) in the city of Monterrey. In 1991, he started his studies in the Methodist Conference and was ordained elder in 1995, and is certified as a chaplain. He has over two decades of experience in pastoral work in northern Mexico and the United States. He has been a conference teacher and trainer of pastors. Rev. Durán enjoys preaching the gospel and leading Latin people in Mexico and the United States to serve God through the gifts and ministries that God has given to his church.

Rev. Dr. Daniel F. Flores, PhD

Dr. Daniel F. Flores is an ordained elder in The United Methodist Church. As university librarian at Texas Lutheran University, he holds the Luther W. and Ruth E. Sappenfield Chair in Library Science. He is a third-generation Mexican American and the son of a migrant agricultural worker and a civil service worker. He has over twenty-five years of experience serving churches and parachurch ministries in Connecticut, Michigan, New Jersey, New Mexico, Texas, Wisconsin, and England. He has taught in colleges and seminaries across the United States, Argentina, the Bahamas, Dominican Republic, England, Mexico, and Perú. Dr. Flores is a former member of the United Methodist Church General Commission on Archives and History, the World Methodist Council Committee on Education, the 2018 Oxford Institute for

Methodist Theological Studies, and the national board of directors of Justice for Our Neighbors. He is an active member of the ATLA Board of Directors and the Wesley Heritage Foundation Board of Directors. He is author of *Respectable Methodism: Nathan Bangs and Respectability in Nineteenth-Century American Methodism* (2022). He holds six earned graduate degrees including a MDiv from Princeton Theological Seminary and a PhD from Drew University. Dr. Flores is married to Rev. Thelma Herrera Flores.

Rev. Thelma Herrera Flores, DMin (candidate)

Rev. Thelma Herrera Flores is an ordained deacon in The United Methodist Church. She is the daughter of Mexican American parents who were migrant farm workers in their youth. She has served as Deacon and copastor in congregations in the United Methodist Church, interim pastor in a PCUSA church, and a chaplain in the Christus Hospital system. She has taught Bible at the United Methodist Regional Course of Study School at Perkins School of Theology, world religions at Tarrant County College, and introduction to theology at Texas Lutheran University. Rev. Flores is a member of the Board of Directors of Texas Methodist Foundation and former board officer of the Scarritt Bennett Center in Nashville. She is founder of Misíon Holland, a faith-based ministry focusing on outreach to migrant agricultural workers. She earned a BA in religious studies with a minor in Jewish studies (summa cum laude) at Drew University as well as an MAR with a concentration in Hebrew Bible at Yale University Divinity School. She is currently a doctor of ministry student at Western Theological Seminary in Holland, Michigan. Rev. Flores is married to Dr. Daniel F. Flores.

Bishop Joel N. Martinez

Bishop Martinez was born in Seguin, Texas. He is the grandson of sharecropper parents who emigrated from Mexico at the turn of the century. He was the second Hispanic/Latino elected bishop in The United Methodist Church. He served as director of planning and development at Newark Houchen Center in El Paso and later as executive secretary, Office of Ethnic and Language Ministries, National Division, GBGM. Bishop Martinez served as district superintendent in the Rio Grande Conference and as president of the Greater Dallas Community of Churches. He was a delegate to the Seventh Assembly of the World Council of Churches in Canberra, Australia, 1991. From early exposure to the plight of farm workers, and in student ministry to migrant workers, Bishop Martinez learned to appreciate the urgent need for poor people to organize in order to participate more equitably in society. He worked with César Chávez during the 1970s, worked to establish the first federally funded health clinic for the poor in El Paso, was a founding member of the National Hispanic Caucus in the UMC in 1970, and supported the organizing of poor fishermen on the island of Vieques, Puerto Rico, in the late 1970s. Bishop Martinez worked on the initial proposals to the 1976 General Conference for a Missional Priority on the Ethnic Minority Local Church. He chaired the National Missional Priority Coordinating Committee from 1984 to 1988, and he chaired the National Plan for Hispanic Ministries National Committee from 1992 to 2000. From 1992 to 2000, Bishop Martinez was assigned to the Nebraska Episcopal Area. In 2000 he was reassigned to the San Antonio area, where he served until his retirement in 2008. He served as president of the General Board of Global Ministries from 2000 to 2008 and as the interim general secretary from 2009 to 2010. Bishop Martinez is currently a national cochair of the Industrial Areas Foundation. He is married to Raquel Mora Martinez, general editor and contributor of *Mil Voces Para Celebrar Himnario Metodista* (1996) and *Fiesta Jubilosa: Recursos bilingües para la Adoración* (2022). The Martinezes collaborated to produce *Fiesta Cristiana: Resources for Worship* (2003).

Rev. Joseph A. Ocasio, EdD (ABD)

Rev. Joseph A. Ocasio is an ordained Assemblies of God minister. He has served in numerous leadership capacities in higher education and cross-cultural initiatives over the past fifteen years. He currently serves as the director of the Center for Hispanic Education at Grace Christian University and as the executive director of the Church Leadership Center based in Holland, Michigan. Past positions include serving as the founding director for Hispanic Ministries Programs at Western Theological Seminary, Holland, Michigan; director of admissions and enrollment for the University of Valley Forge, Phoenixville, Pennsylvania; and director of the Hispanic Leadership Center at Southeastern University, Lakeland, Florida. Rev. Ocasio is a fourth-degree black belt in Karate, former restaurateur, and successful businessman. He has been married to his wife, Myra, for thirty-two years. Myra serves as assistant director for Fiscal Services at Ottawa County, has earned her BA and MBA, and is a CPA. Currently, they live in Holland, Michigan, and enjoy spending time with their four children and four grandchildren.

Rev. Dr. Daniel E. Ruarte, EdD

Dr. Ruarte is an ordained Foursquare Church minister. He is the vice president of academic affairs at Life Pacific University (LPU). Dr. Ruarte holds an MA in pastoral studies from Azusa Pacific Seminary, a second MA in strategic leadership from LPU, and a doctoral degree in education from the University of Southern California. The focus of his doctoral dissertation was to help educational leaders rethink Hispanic attrition by understanding the value of research-based and proven retention models and strategies that could help Latino students succeed in higher education. Dr. Ruarte joined LPU as a full-time faculty member in 2018 to develop, direct, and teach the MA in leadership Spanish-language program. Dr. Ruarte later assumed interim oversight of LPU's new online AA programs along with his service as faculty representative and administrative council member. He came to LPU with extensive experience as an adjunct professor of theology, ministry, leadership, and Bible at Indiana Wesleyan University, Azusa Pacific University, and Facultad de Teología. In addition, Dr. Ruarte has worked as an educational administrator, business owner, and pastor for over fifteen years, and just recently authored his first book, *Liderazgo y Eclesia* (2019).

Rev. Girien Ricardo Salazar, PhD (candidate)

Girien (pronounced "Gideon") Salazar of Dallas is in the ordination process with the Assemblies of God. He is director of development at SAGU, a private Christian university located in Waxahachie, Texas, and a minister at Hope City (Ciudad de Esperanza). Previously, Girien served as executive director of the National Hispanic Christian Leadership Conference (NHCLC) and the Faith and Education Coalition. He volunteers as a board member for the Latin American Heritage Society and previously was president of the City of Houston Super Neighborhood 34, board member for San Antonio Parks and Recreation, and minister at El Tabernaculo Church in Houston. In 2019, Girien was appointed by Texas governor Greg Abbott to serve on the OneStar National Service Commission Board. In 2021, Girien served as the assistant director of mobilization for Promise Keepers and host of the NHCLC's weekly Facebook Live program, "The Lamb's Agenda Hoy." He received a BS in church ministry and an MA in theological studies from Southwestern Assemblies of God University, and he is in the dissertation phase of his PhD in leadership studies from Dallas Baptist University. He was honorably discharged from the United States Navy Reserves. Girien is passionate about the intersection of faith and politics; clergy political engagement; Hispanic education; and issues of mercy, freedom, justice, and peace. He hopes to inspire and cultivate Spirit-filled servant-leaders to engage and lead at all levels of faith and civic institutions.

Rev. Dr. Eliezer Valentín-Castañón, DMin, PhD (candidate)

The Rev. Dr. Eliezer Valentín-Castañón is superintendent of the Frederick District of the Baltimore-Washington Conference of The United Methodist Church. An elder in the UMC since 1993, has served churches in Maryland, New York, and New Jersey. In 1994, he was appointed to the General Board of Church and Society in Washington, DC, where he worked on public policy issues. In 2005, he was appointed to the General Commission on Religion and Race, where he worked with local churches, annual conferences, and jurisdictions to develop a greater appreciation for the Church's diversity. In 2010, Pastor Eliezer served the Monrovia Charge in the Central Maryland District and in 2013 transitioned to an appointment as senior pastor at Trinity UMC. A native of Puerto Rico, where he spent his formative years, Dr. Valentín-Castañón graduated from the University of Puerto Rico with a BA in psychology. In 1990, he earned his MDiv from Drew Theological Seminary and his DMin from Wesley Theological Seminary in 2002. His doctoral studies focused on Wesleyan theology and history. In 2013, he graduated from St. Mary's Seminary and University–The Ecumenical Institute of Theology, with a certificate of advanced studies in theology, focusing on systematic theology. With his wife Magda and two children (Daniel and Eduardo), he lives in Frederick, Maryland.

www.ingramcontent.com/pod-product-compliance
Lightning Source LLC
LaVergne TN
LVHW050620100826
845148LV00011B/1659